Southlake Carroll Dragon Football

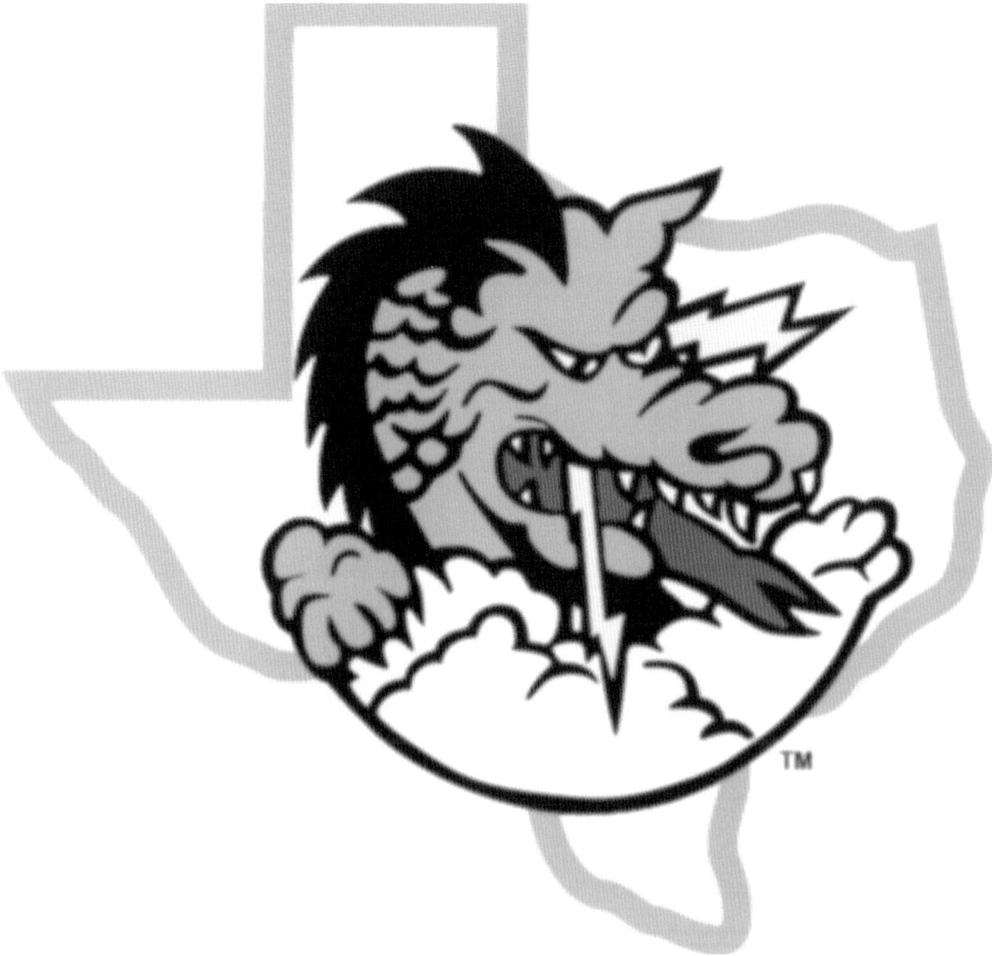

Carroll students voted in the 1950s to make a dragon the school mascot, but those early images (pages 23 and 24) were nothing like this fire-breathing, thunderbolt-throwing dragon many recognize today. It first appeared in 1984 when Carroll head coach Bob Ledbetter adopted a design he had seen on the side of a World War II airplane into a decal for the team football helmets. (Courtesy of the Carroll Independent School District.)

FRONT COVER: Twenty-nine years after the Carroll Independent School District football program began, the Dragons won their first-ever state football title, the 1988 Texas 3A Football Championship. Members from that team gather for a photograph shortly after the win. (Courtesy of the Carroll Independent School District.)

COVER BACKGROUND: Pictured are the 1989 Dragons taking the field. (Courtesy of the Carroll Independent School District.)

BACK COVER: These 1963 Dragon linemen pose for their team picture in socks and loafers. (Courtesy of the Carroll Independent School District.)

Southlake Carroll Dragon Football

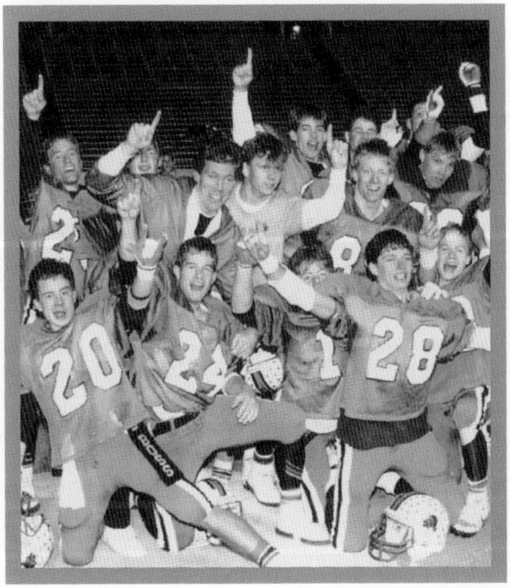

Connie Cooley and the Southlake Historical Society

Foreword by Coach Bob Ledbetter

ARCADIA PUBLISHING

ISBN 978-1-4671-3443-9

Published by Arcadia Publishing
Charleston, South Carolina

Printed in the United States of America

Library of Congress Control Number: 2015937521

For all general information, please contact Arcadia Publishing:
Telephone 843-853-2070
Fax 843-853-0044
E-mail sales@arcadiapublishing.com
For customer service and orders:
Toll-Free 1-888-313-2665

Visit us on the Internet at www.arcadiapublishing.com

This book is dedicated to the memory of Jack D. Johnson,
who laid the foundation for Dragon football.

CONTENTS

FOREWORD

Dear Carroll Dragons,

I hope you enjoy reading this book, as I believe it will give new insights into the rich history and tradition that is Carroll Dragon football. The years I spent as head football coach and athletic director are filled with outstanding moments both on and off the field and shared, no doubt, by players, coaches, and the community. The support shown by parents, booster club members, and football fans has played a big part in the national recognition that follows the Carroll Dragons. And all that community outpouring continues today.

This was a great school system when Sue and I moved here because of a foundation that was already in place. Early administrators, led by Superintendent Jack Johnson, built Carroll Independent School District (CISD) on the principles of allowing students to be the best that they could be and hiring teachers and coaches who believed in kids. The only slogan we ever had on our athletic manuals was very simple: Kids don't care how much you know until they know how much you care.

On a recent evening, I took a drive up to Old Dragon Stadium on Carroll Road and walked onto the field. The sun was setting, and I was reminded of freshly cut grass and the sound of sprinklers coming on. I saw cars lined up turning into the parking lot, and in the bleachers, fans had taped down blankets to save seats. I smelled hotdogs and popcorn coming from the concession stand. And out of the field house came those Carroll Dragons in their bright-green jerseys and white helmets with that great emblem on the side. I recognized faces of all the great kids and great coaches I was fortunate to work with.

As a coach, it is not all about the records and the wins, the championships, trophies, and plaques or even the success our program has had. It is about the kids who come through the program as boys and leave as young men. Our athletes. Ordinary kids with a dream, who realize that as long as they believe in themselves, each other, and the program, they can be anything they want to be.

For Sue and me, it has been a great ride, Carroll Dragons.

Protect the Tradition.

—Coach Bob Ledbetter

ACKNOWLEDGMENTS

The groundwork for this book began with nine scrapbooks kept by Jack Johnson. The collection includes newspaper clippings, photographs, and documents from 1957 to 1986, without which there would be no written record of early Dragon football.

Much appreciation goes to Superintendent Johnson's daughter, Sheila, and her husband, Larry Croy, for sharing family photographs and remembrances; Phil Barber for his deep Dragon knowledge; and Crystal and Bob Steele for their long love affair with the Dragons.

Thanks go to Superintendent David Faltys and staff members Paige Buck, Irene Gonzalez, Rick Herrin, Jayme Rodriguez, Julie Thannum, and Barbara Yelton; Cindy Dumont at Johnson Elementary; and Sarah Chase, Shawn Duhon, Kathy Lochrie, Linda Rose, and Karen Terry at Carroll Senior High School. Special thanks go to Ken Cook, Martha Durham, Dr. Ted Gillum, Sue Ledbetter, Sara McCombs, Eli Melton, Kevin Ozee, Ronnie Tipps, and Chauncey Willingham for their remembrances.

A thank-you is owed to the following people: Dragons John Blackburn Jr., Tim Bock, Sheri Hight Brunson, Linda Cate Carter and other Dragons via Facebook, James Crawford, Tony Eubanks, Keith Fuller, Lance "Booger" Hight, Dane Johnson, John King, Matt Lafavers, Mike Lafavers, and Larry Lee.

I thank also Dragon fans Robin Blackburn, Nelsy Fleps, Jerry Johnson, Wanda and Fred Joyce, Merrill Stacy, Rick Stacy, and the Jeroll Shivers family. A special thank-you goes to Mrs. Eddie Cheatham for sharing her husband's Dragon mementos.

Special recognition goes to the many CISD student yearbook staff members who have photographed and written about Dragon football each year for more than 58 years.

A most important thank-you goes to Carroll head coaches Bill Branum, Bob Ledbetter, Tom Rapp, Todd Dodge, and Hal Wasson for their time and oral histories, without which there would be no book.

I thank my Arcadia editor Ginny Rasmussen for her guidance and patience. A special thank-you goes to Anita Robeson for her keen writing and editing skills and assistance in bringing this book to completion.

A personal note to my husband and our family: thank you for your support while writing this book and for the love and encouragement you give me every day.

Finally, for 23 years, members of the Southlake Historical Society have worked tirelessly to preserve the history and tell the stories of Southlake. Their work continues.

Unless otherwise noted, the images provided in the book are courtesy of the Carroll Independent School District (CISD).

INTRODUCTION

Southlake was once small-town Texas with big-time football. Dragon football is a perennial Texas powerhouse with eight state championships spanning four decades.

The patriarch of Dragon football is Bob Ledbetter, who took the program to new heights. He changed the culture. He turned the Dragons into the bull's-eye on other team's schedules. The Dragons reigned over Class 3A in a decade of dominance that included three state titles (1988, 1992, and 1993) and a state record 72-game regular season win streak.

The streak lasted from 1986 to 1994 as the Dragons scored blowout victories that included 34 shutouts and wins by an average of 37 points. The streak saw an unrivaled reloading of talented, well-trained athletes. Carroll outscored teams 3,136-441. Ledbetter's coaching staff remained stable and included future head coaches. (One of the best was Steve Lineweaver, who served as the offensive coordinator for eight years before winning multiple state titles as head coach with Commerce and Trinity.) The execution of Lineweaver's run-based offense helped the streak shatter the previous state record by 19 victories.

In 1994, Carroll's first year in Class 4A, the streak ended.

Todd Dodge was hired in 2000 to revive the program's past glory, and he quickly proved to be the perfect fit. Embracing the past, Dodge branded the moniker "Protect the Tradition." By his third season, the Dragons were back in the spotlight. In Carroll's first year in Class 5A, the team defied the odds and rolled to a 16-0 finish and its fourth state championship title. Once again, the Dragons were making history—this time as the first-ever team to move up in classification and finish the season winning the state championship.

The Dragons were special again.

Dodge's innovative offense was the cover story to this chapter. In his no-huddle, spread offense, passing became the trend in a state known for wishbone offenses and running back recruits. With the passing came the glory. Carroll became "Quarterback High," producing four 5A offensive players of the year: Chase Wasson, Chase Daniel, Greg McElroy, and Riley Dodge. Kenny Hill joined that group in 2011.

Dodge's teams from 2002 to 2006 were similar to Ledbetter's teams of the late 1980s and early 1990s. The winning formula was the same: committed athletes and disciplined coaching backed up by school district and community support. In 2007, Dodge's former assistant Hal Wasson stepped up as head coach. He returned the Dragons to the top in 2011 with another 16-0 season and an eighth state championship.

Long before the Dragons were playing in 5A and 6A, the program's foundation was established. Building on that foundation is what makes Dragon football so special: The recognizable logo. The unforgettable games. The records. The championships. The history.

—Rick Herrin

1

Before There Were Dragons

In the beginning, there was no football—just miles and miles of dense forests bordered by open prairies in an ecological region called the Cross Timbers. For thousands of years, Native Americans camped and hunted here. In the early 1840s, nearly 125 years before Southlake was founded, Anglo settlers arrived, attracted by the promise of cheap land. They cleared fields, built homes, and planted crops in the sandy soil. After the Civil War, other families—many from the Old South, which had been economically devastated by the war—moved in to purchase farms and start businesses.

Early communities in this poor, rural area west of Grapevine were named Dove, White's Chapel, and Old Union. Many had a church, a general store, a blacksmith shop, and a school.

In 1917, several one-room schools were consolidated into Common School District No. 99 and named Carroll, after B. Carroll, Tarrant County superintendent of public instruction. In 1919, the men of No. 99 voted to increase their taxes to buy land and build a school—a testament to how much they valued education for their children. That school, still standing at 1055 North Carroll Avenue, quickly became the heart of the community.

But it would be decades before the Friday night lights were switched on.

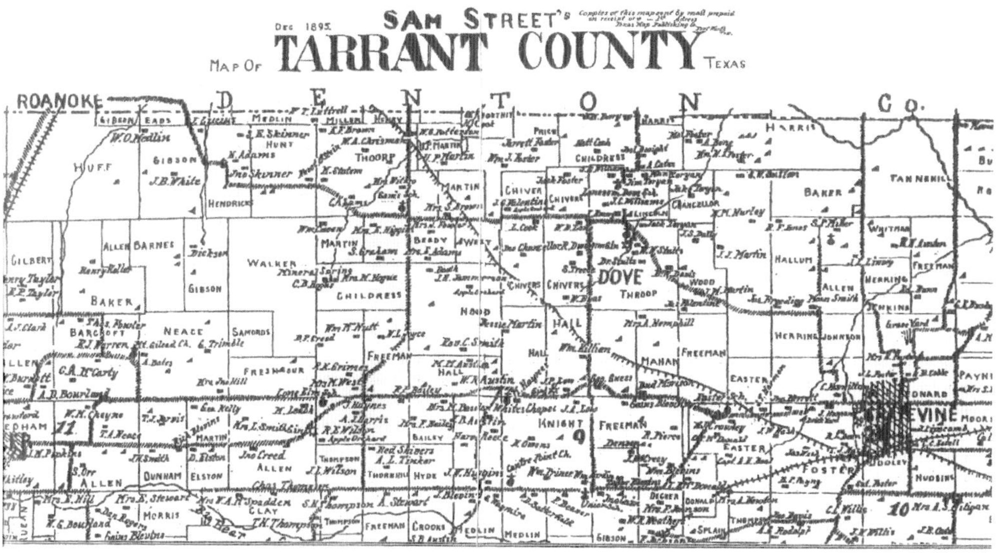

North Tarrant County in 1895 was made up of small communities. Each tract of land on this map has the name of a settler who received a Republic of Texas land grant in the early 1840s. Other names identified the farms and businesses of their descendants for families living here some 50 years later. (Courtesy of the E.I. Wiesman family.)

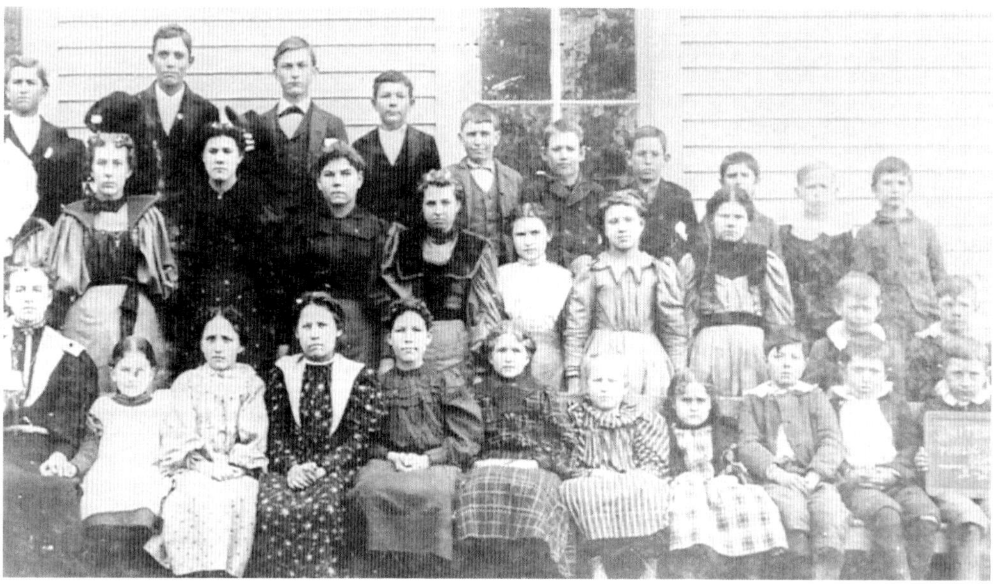
After settlers built their rough log cabins, they wasted no time building a church and a school. Near Lonesome Dove Baptist Church, a log school was started up about 1848. A log school also was built next to White's Chapel Methodist Church, where in the 1890s these students attended class in a wood-frame building that had been added. Other schools opened in the area, but by the turn of the century, the Texas legislature was working to improve rural education. In 1917, the one-room schools were consolidated to form the Common School District No. 99. (Courtesy of the Shivers family.)

In May 1919, men in the district (women could not vote) approved the purchase of $7,500 in bonds to pay for a school—later described as being as plain, sturdy, and practical as the farmers who built it. Constructed on a hill, the school had approximately 23 windows to let in light and breezes. It is the only Common School District schoolhouse still standing in Tarrant County. This sketch drawn in 2009 shows how the original schoolhouse looked. (Sketch commissioned by the Southlake Historical Society.)

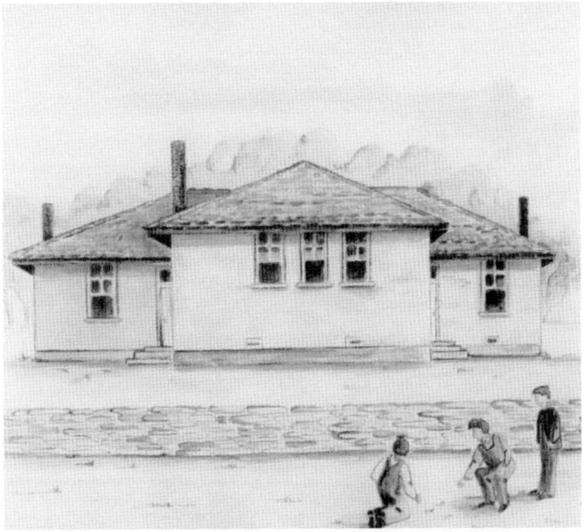

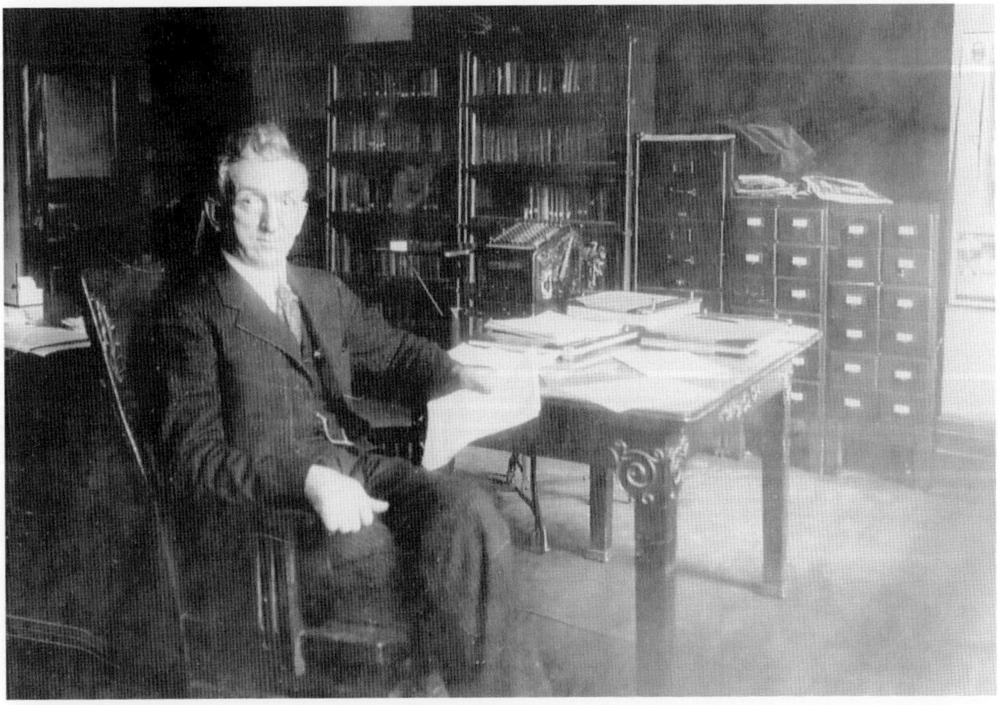

Carroll School and school district were named for Burrell E. Carroll, a longtime teacher and principal in Tarrant County. In 1918, B. Carroll, as he was known, was elected Tarrant County superintendent of public instruction. Until the 1960s, the school named after him would be the only public building in what became Southlake. (Courtesy of the Mary Ann King family.)

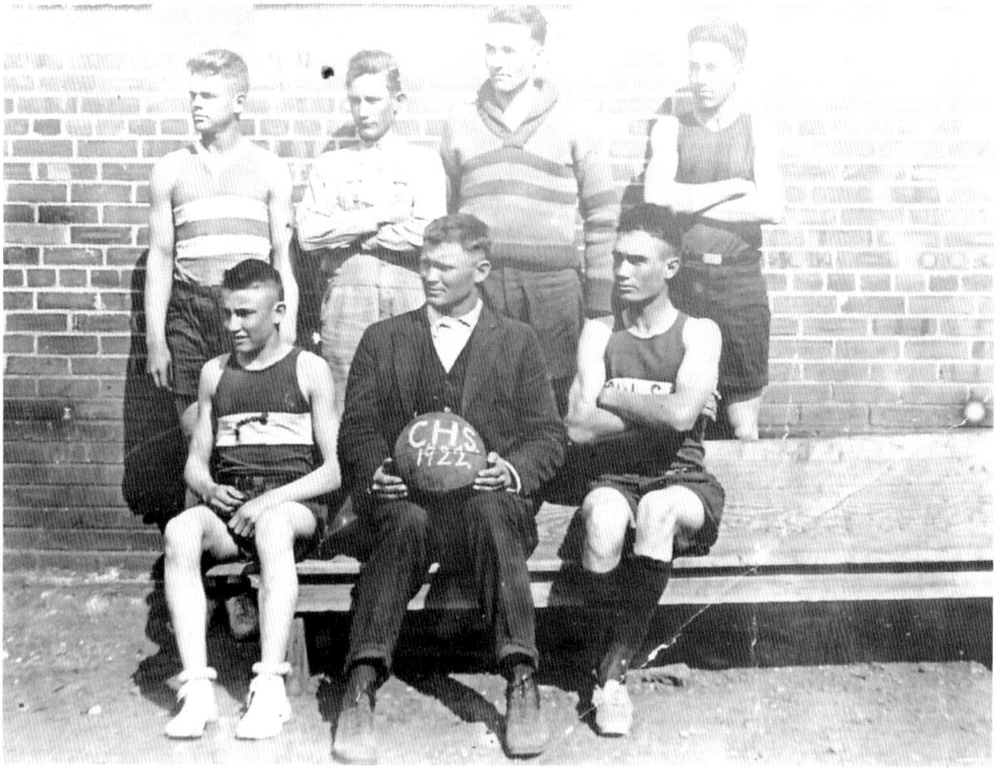

Carroll did not field a football team until 1959, but there was a basketball team practically from the start. In 1922, these six boys were on the team. Letters written on the ball held by teacher Edd Lowe stand for Carroll Hill School, an early nickname for the school built on a hill. During recess, students played softball and other games. (Courtesy of the Shivers family.)

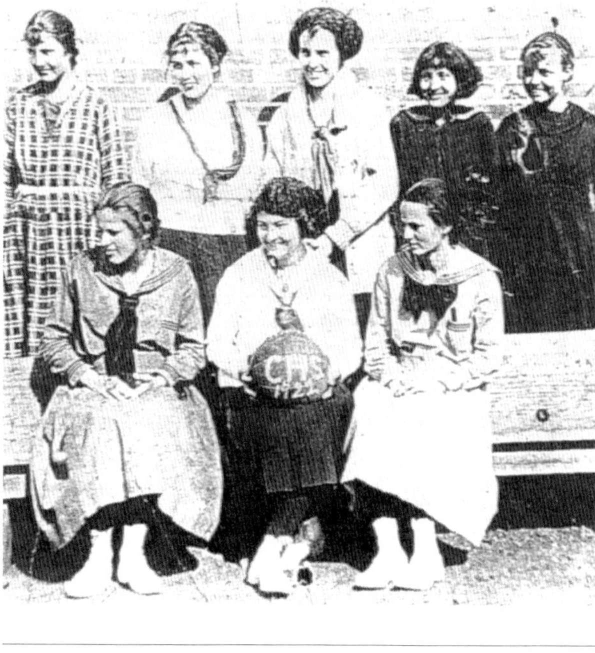

There was a girls' basketball team, too, and it included the Bailey sisters Eunice and Verdie, seated on the left and right. Between them is Hazel McNutt. Standing, from left to right, are Virgie Keegan, Jewel Southern, Valda Livingston, Viola Livingston, and Estha McPherson. (Courtesy of the Shivers family.)

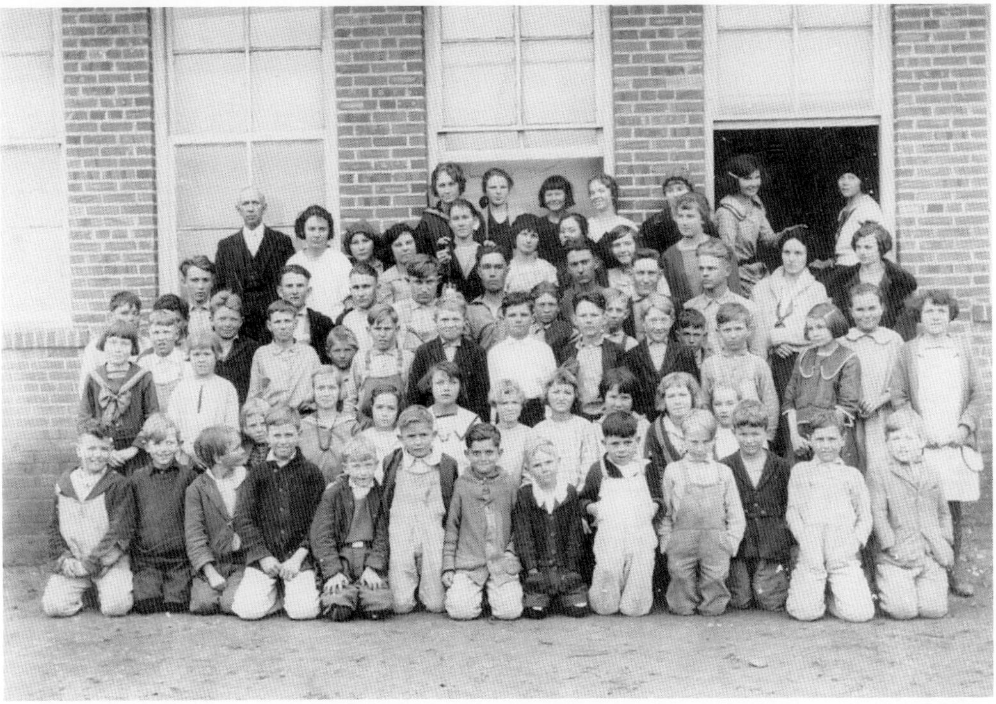

Frank Estill of Grapevine built Carroll School. He also built Pleasant Run School in Colleyville in 1912 (demolished in 2011) and Old Bedford School in Bedford in 1915 (placed in the National Register of Historic Places in 1997). Bricks for Carroll School were brought by mule-drawn wagons from Fort Worth, and the school's wood frame and flooring were first-growth East Texas pine. Some of its many windows were large enough for students to sit in, as seen in this 1923 class picture. (Courtesy of the Shivers family and James Crawford.)

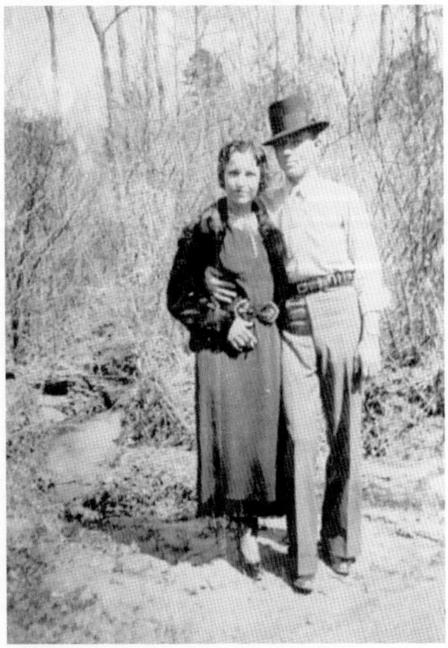

Highway 114, which runs along the roadbed of a bankrupt railroad, was constructed between 1929 and 1932. On Easter Sunday 1934, Bonnie Parker and Clyde Barrow or a member of their gang murdered two motorcycle patrolmen near the intersection with Dove Road. Bonnie and Clyde hung around rural Tarrant County, including present-day Southlake, from time to time, as Bonnie had kin nearby, and Clyde's family is said to have lived for a short time near Kimball Avenue and Highway 114 when he was a boy. He may have attended Carroll School. (Courtesy of the Dallas Public Library.)

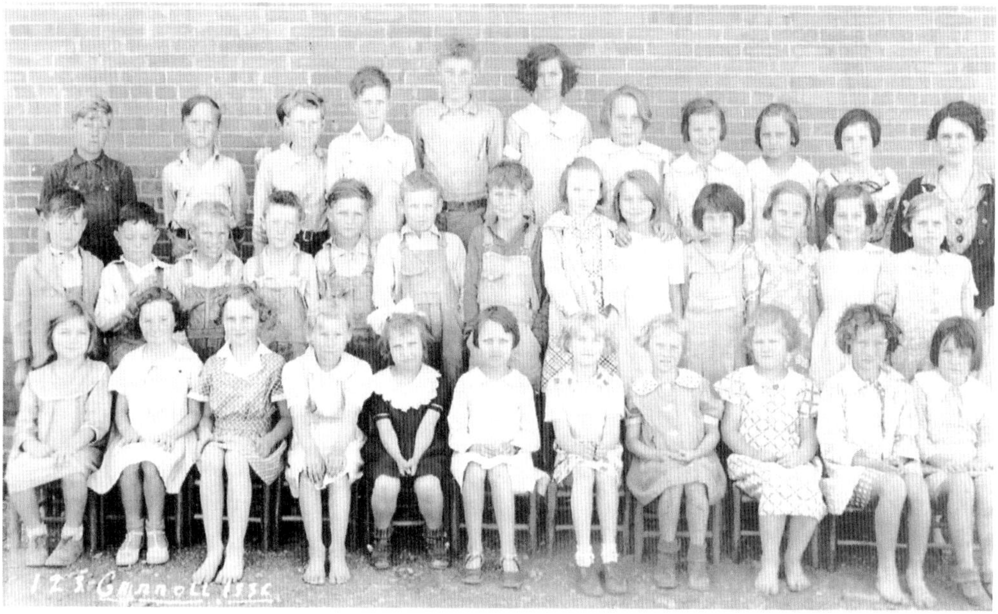

During the Depression, families made do. Into the 20th century, country kids often saved their shoes for Sundays, winter, and special occasions, which for many did not include picture day at Carroll School in 1936. (Courtesy of the Tarrant County Archives.)

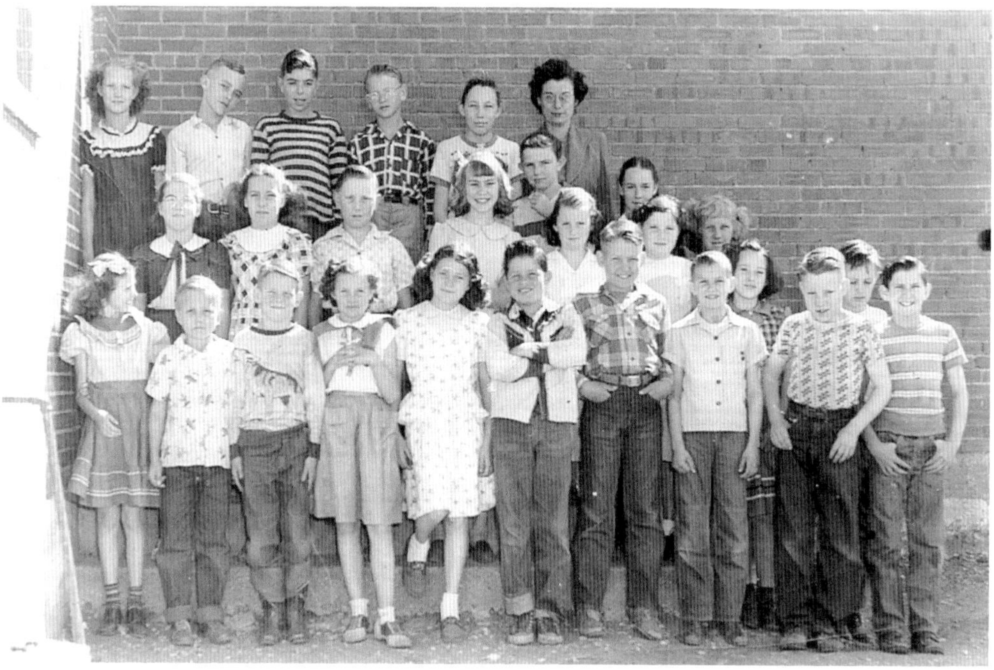

During World War II, troop convoys moved along Highway 114, and the children would stand outside Carroll School and wave. These kids were Carroll students in 1951. The completion of Lake Grapevine in 1952 brought economic change to the area and attracted newcomers. (Courtesy of the Tarrant County College District Archives, Fort Worth, Texas.)

2

MAKING A GAME PLAN

In the fall of 1956, an election was held inside the red-brick Carroll School to decide whether or not to incorporate as a town (the area was an unincorporated part of Tarrant County). The vote was 30-24 in favor. What they named Southlake was truly a one-stoplight town—the stoplight hung at the corner of Highway 114 and Carroll Avenue. Residents could drive Farm to Market Road (FM) 1709 to Keller and back without seeing another car.

Southlake was only a year old when a young educator named Jack Johnson heard about a principal's position at Carroll School. Soon after meeting with the three-member board of trustees, he was hired. In mid-August, Johnson; his wife, Modean; and their two children moved to Southlake.

What he found was a school with six rooms and a frame cafeteria. Carroll was accredited for the first through eighth grades and at the time offered no extracurricular activities or organized sports.

During his interview for the principal's job, Johnson was asked if he could start an athletic program. Carroll students were not getting the opportunity to participate in any school athletics, and many families felt that when their children moved on to Grapevine, Keller, or Northwest high schools to graduate, "they didn't always fit in and couldn't compete," board members complained.

On his first day as principal, Jack Johnson walked into his office—"a cubby hole, really," he said later. In the corner were a softball and a bat. That was it.

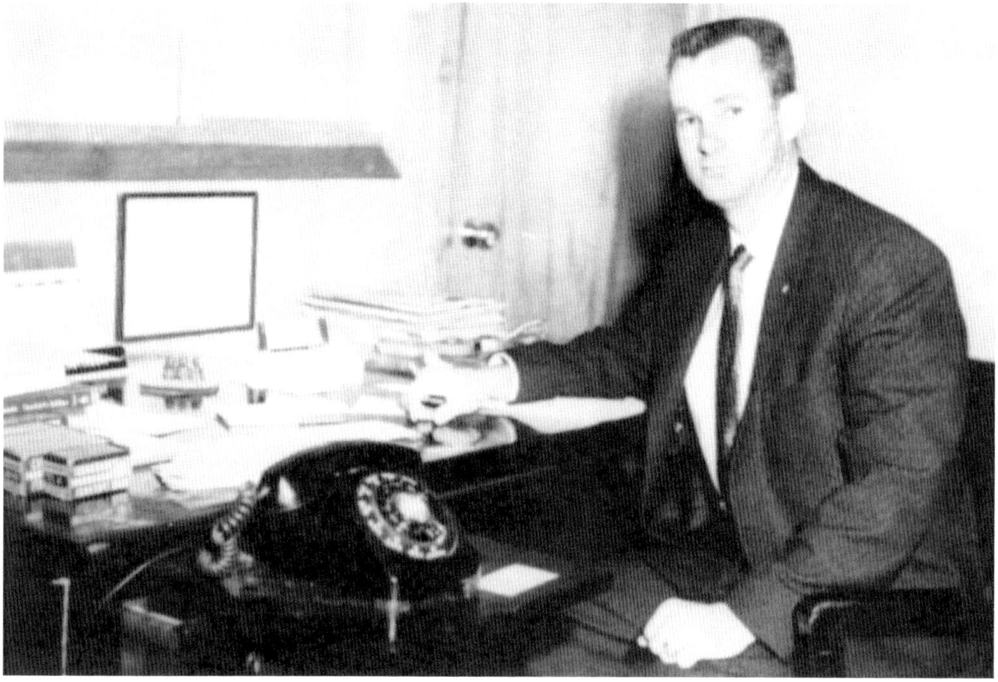

Jack D. Johnson was born in 1927 in Westminster, a farming community north of Dallas. He graduated with a degree in agriculture from East Texas State Teachers College (now Texas A&M Commerce) knowing that he would never use it. "My entire life, my mother and daddy said, 'Jack's going to be a schoolteacher.' And that's what happened. I became a teacher." Principal Johnson is pictured at his desk in 1958. (Courtesy of the Cheatham family.)

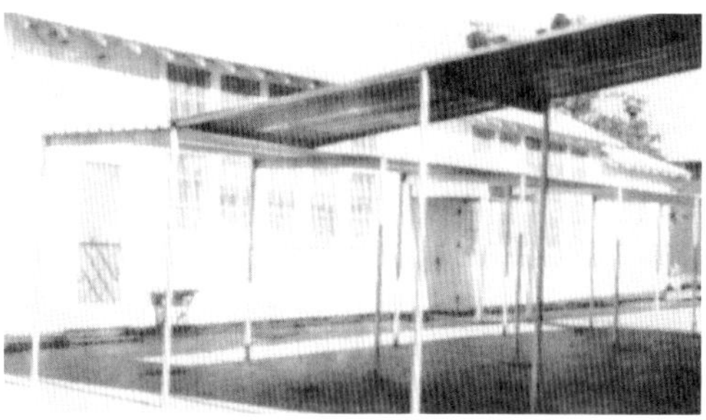

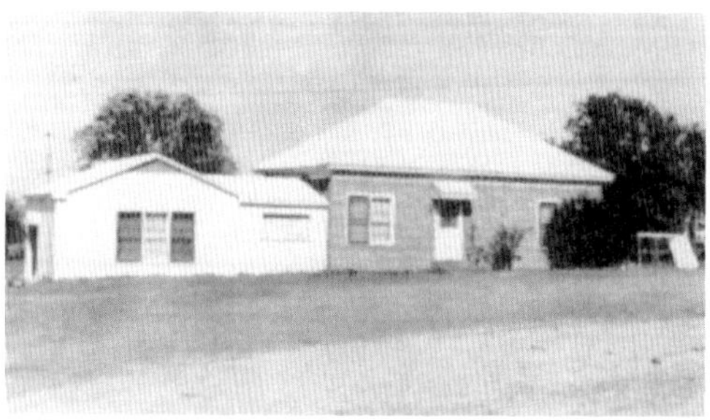

After paying a visit in 1957 to the placement office at North Texas University (now University of North Texas), Johnson received a note: "Principal's position open. Carroll School. House furnished." The little house, pictured on the right in this 1960 photograph, had been built in the 1920s as the teacherage, a place for teachers to live. The frame cafeteria building, pictured on the left, included a kitchen and small stage. (Courtesy of the Cheatham family.)

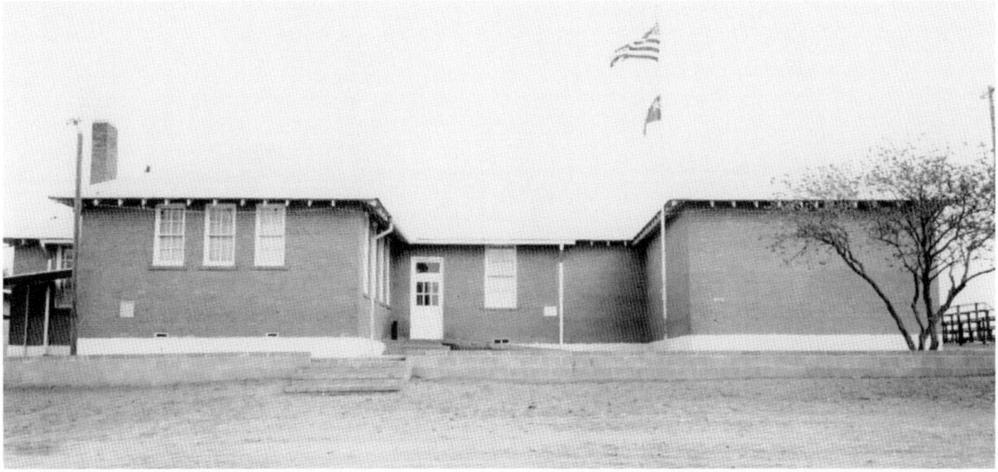

Before he was hired, Johnson met with retiring principal W. Lee Yantis to tour the school and its grounds. "I could tell the grass hadn't been mowed all summer because when we finished, I had grass burrs all over my pants legs," Johnson remembered. "There was a reason. They didn't have a lawn mower." People in neighboring communities sometimes called the school Chigger Hill. The post–World War II addition behind the flagpole had doubled the size of the school.

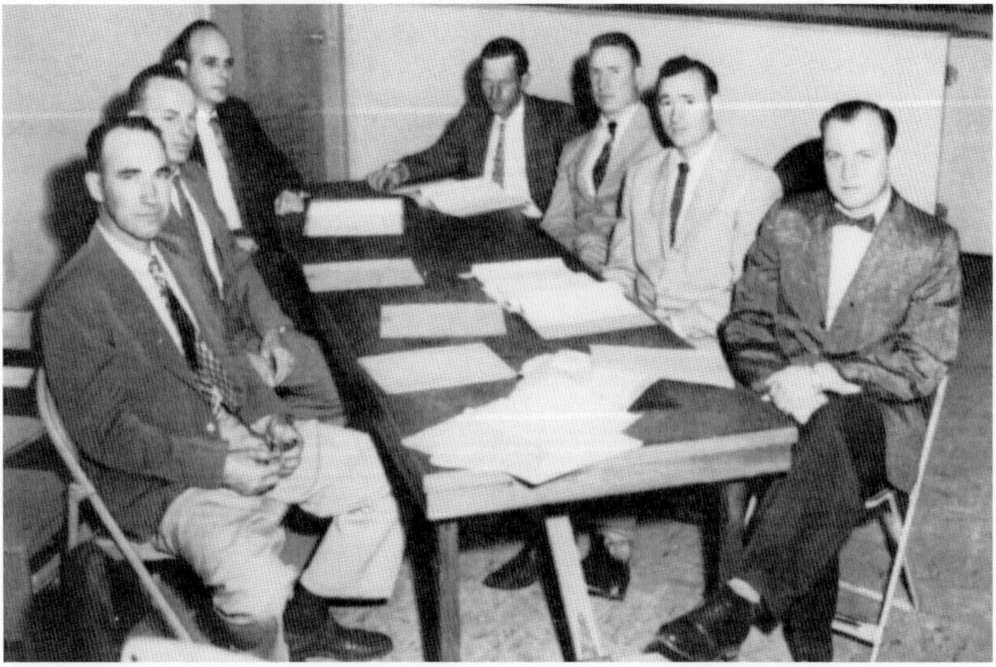

When board members Clyde Cheatham, Colon Sweet, and Cleburne Eubanks had to decide whether to hire Jack Johnson, the men gathered in Cheatham's barn, huddled around him while he milked his cows. The barn still stands on Brumlow Avenue south of Continental Boulevard. Seen here is the following year's board of seven, from left to right, Clyde Cheatham, J. S. "Curly" McPherson, Stan Burney, Buster Lee, Colon Sweet, Wayne Frank, and Harold Knight. (Courtesy of the Johnson family.)

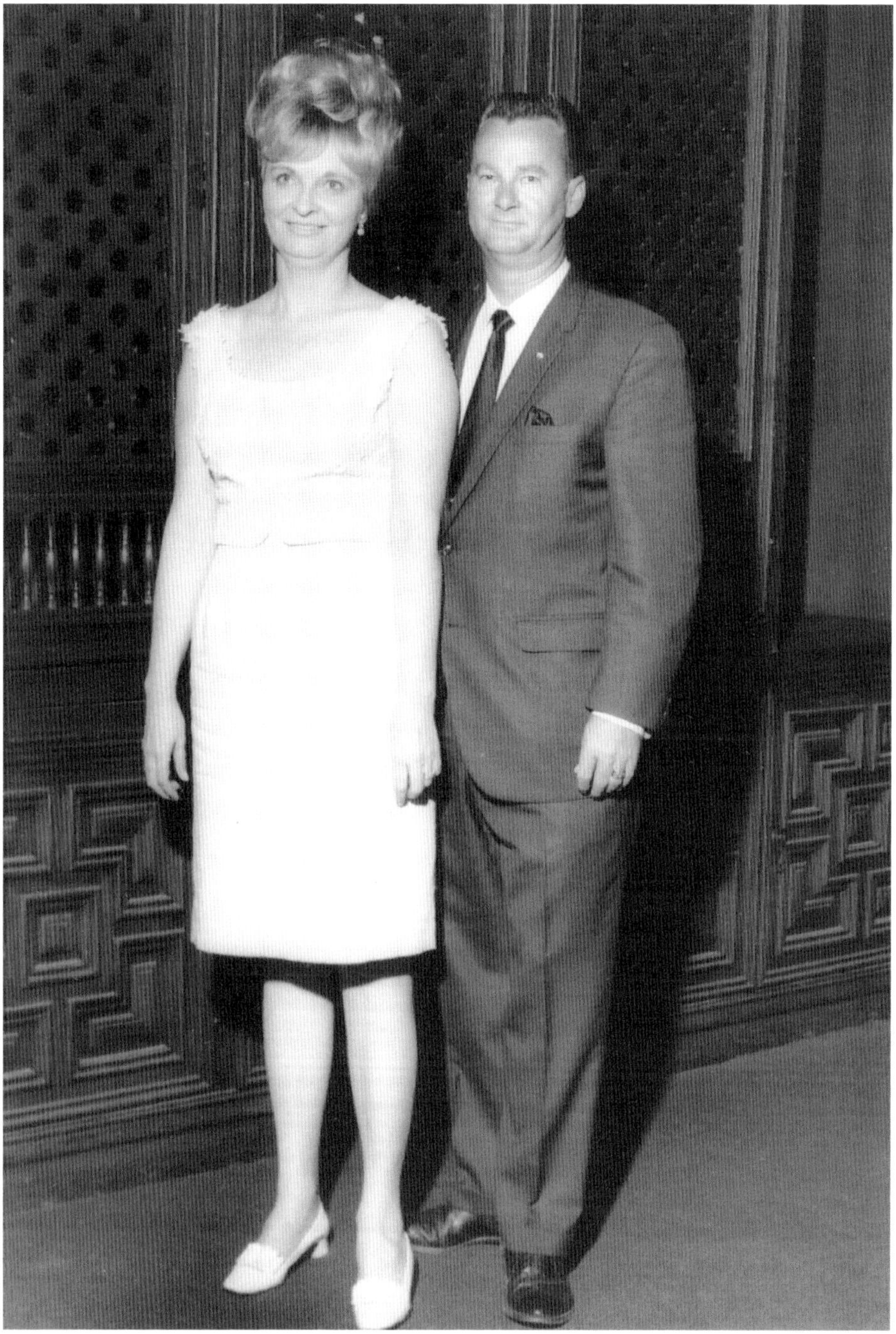

By August 1957, the Johnsons, pictured here in the early 1960s, had moved into their new home. The school year began with 125 students, and it did not take long for the new principal and his wife, Modean, to meet everyone. "Most mornings," she recalled, "mothers would drop their children off at school, and they would drive on around and stop to have a cup of coffee with me." (Courtesy of the Johnson family.)

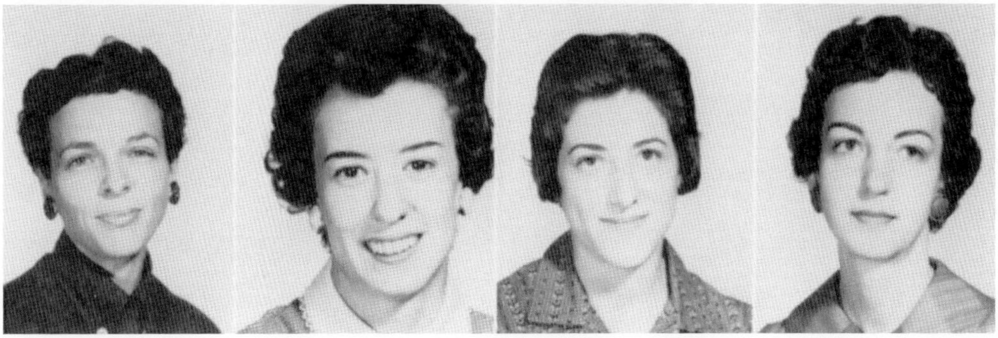

“When I was hired, there were eight grades with six teachers,” Johnson said. “Of course, I was the only man. And I can guarantee you that my wife was almost like a teacher, she worked so hard to assist me in everything that had to be done.” By 1960, the teaching staff included, from left to right, (above) Sue Means, Sue Bell, Maudette Griggs, and Mary Middlebrooks; (below) Novelle Crumbaker, Janelle Pepper, H. G. Griffin Jr., and Johnson. Johnson hired him as a teacher and Carroll’s first football coach. (Both photographs courtesy of the Cheatham family.)

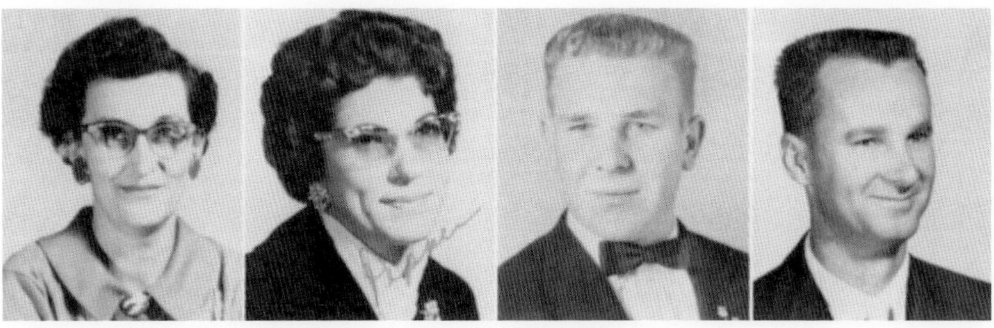

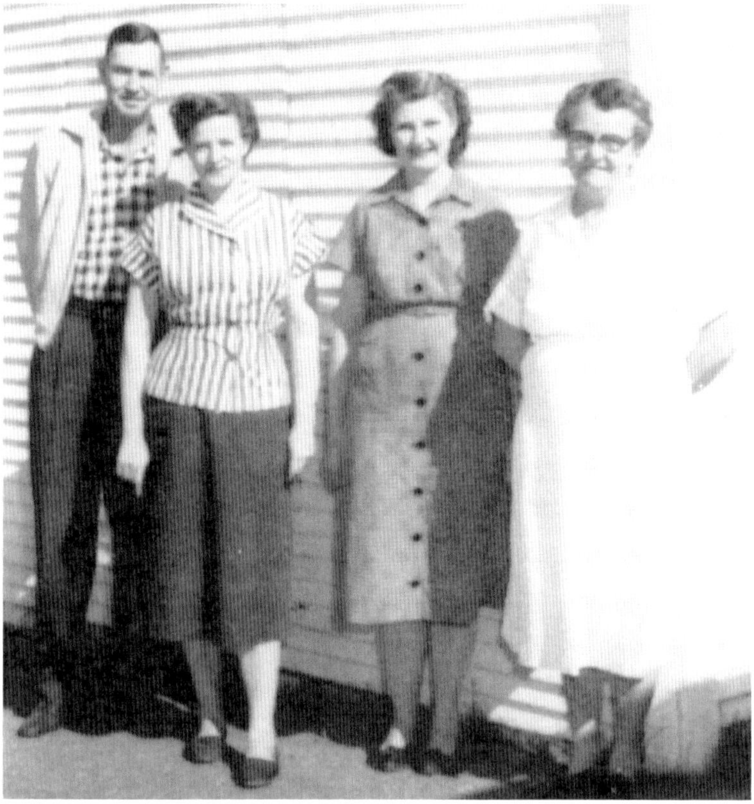

Former board member Cleburne Eubanks took over as head of maintenance, a position he held for 30 years. Standing next to him, from left to right, are cafeteria staff members LaVonne Field, Ruby Hitt, and Estha McPherson Rodgers, who had attended Carroll School and played on the school's 1922 girls' basketball team. (Courtesy of the Cheatham family.)

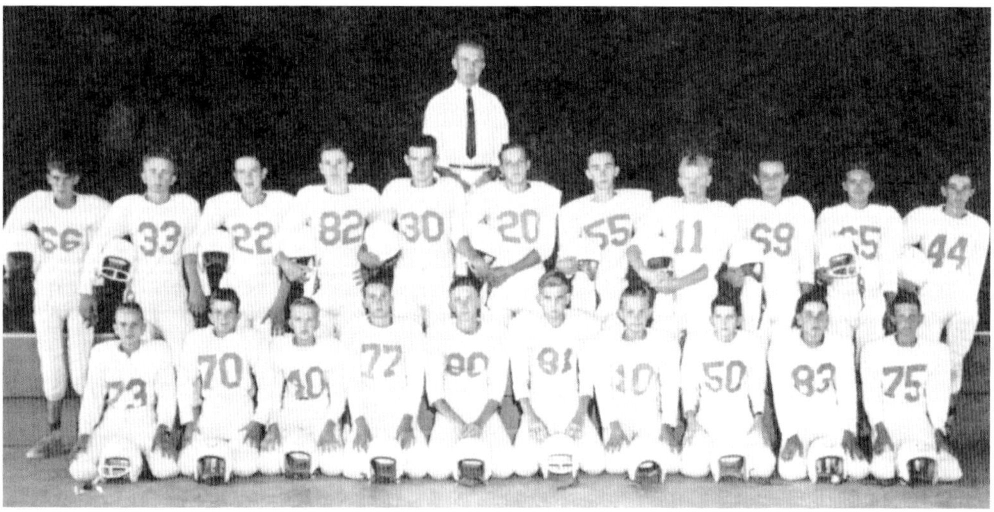

On March 23, 1959, Southlake residents voted 102-9 to become the Carroll Independent School District, and Johnson was appointed superintendent. Longtime Carroll teacher Sara (Bussey) McCombs grew up in Colleyville and remembered her father's disbelief in hearing about the vote. "How do those farmers out there think they could have a decent school system?" Mr. Bussey asked. "How will they ever get enough kids together to play football?" The first team was fielded that fall in 1959. This is the 1960 team picture. (Courtesy of the Cheatham family.)

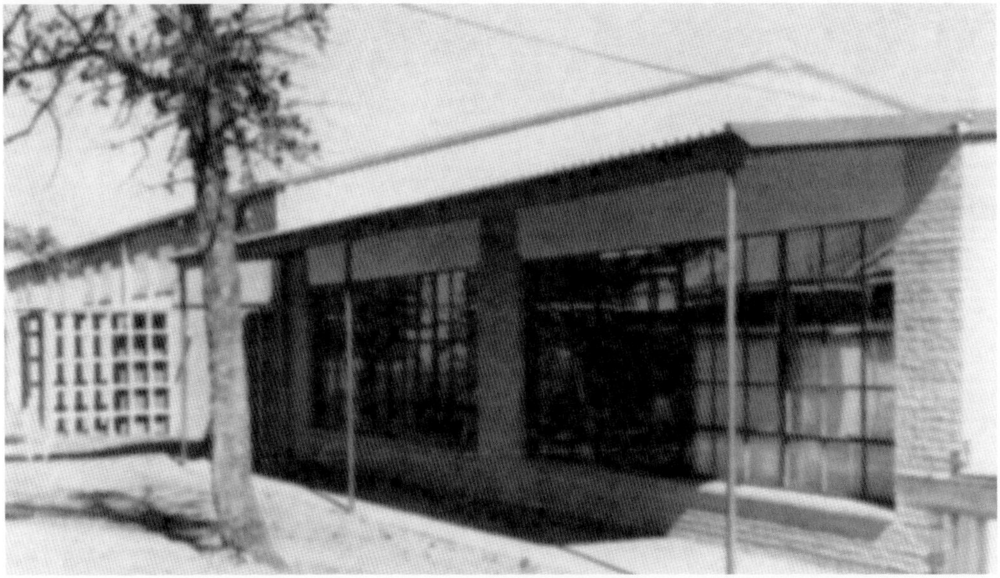

Through the 1960s, Carroll's entire campus was located on 17 acres at the corner of Carroll Avenue and Highland Street, just north of Highway 114. Pictured are the first junior high (above) and the 1919 Carroll School (below). Indoor bathrooms, covered sidewalks connecting the school buildings, and a football field were built soon after Johnson's arrival. A gymnasium added in 1958 provided a place to play basketball games, hold Parent-Teacher Organization (PTO) meetings, and stage student theater productions. The ninth grade was included in the curriculum, and in 1961, a new high school building was approved (the building later became Carroll Intermediate School) to house through grade 12. The elementary school remained on the original campus until Johnson Elementary School opened in 1979. As schools were built in Southlake, the 1919 schoolhouse served as an art studio, warehouse, and transportation office. It was closed in 2001. (Both photographs courtesy of the Cheatham family.)

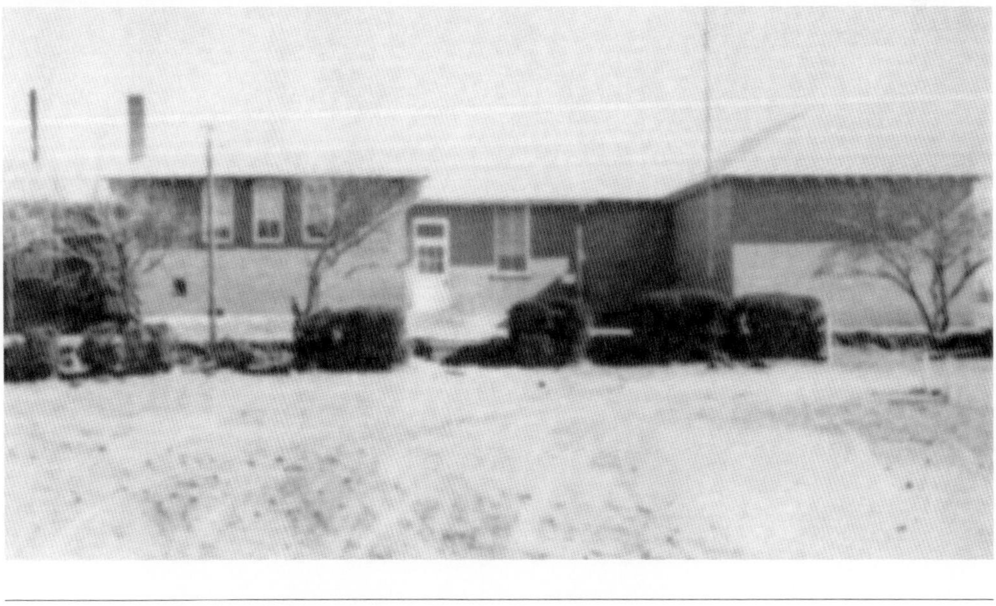

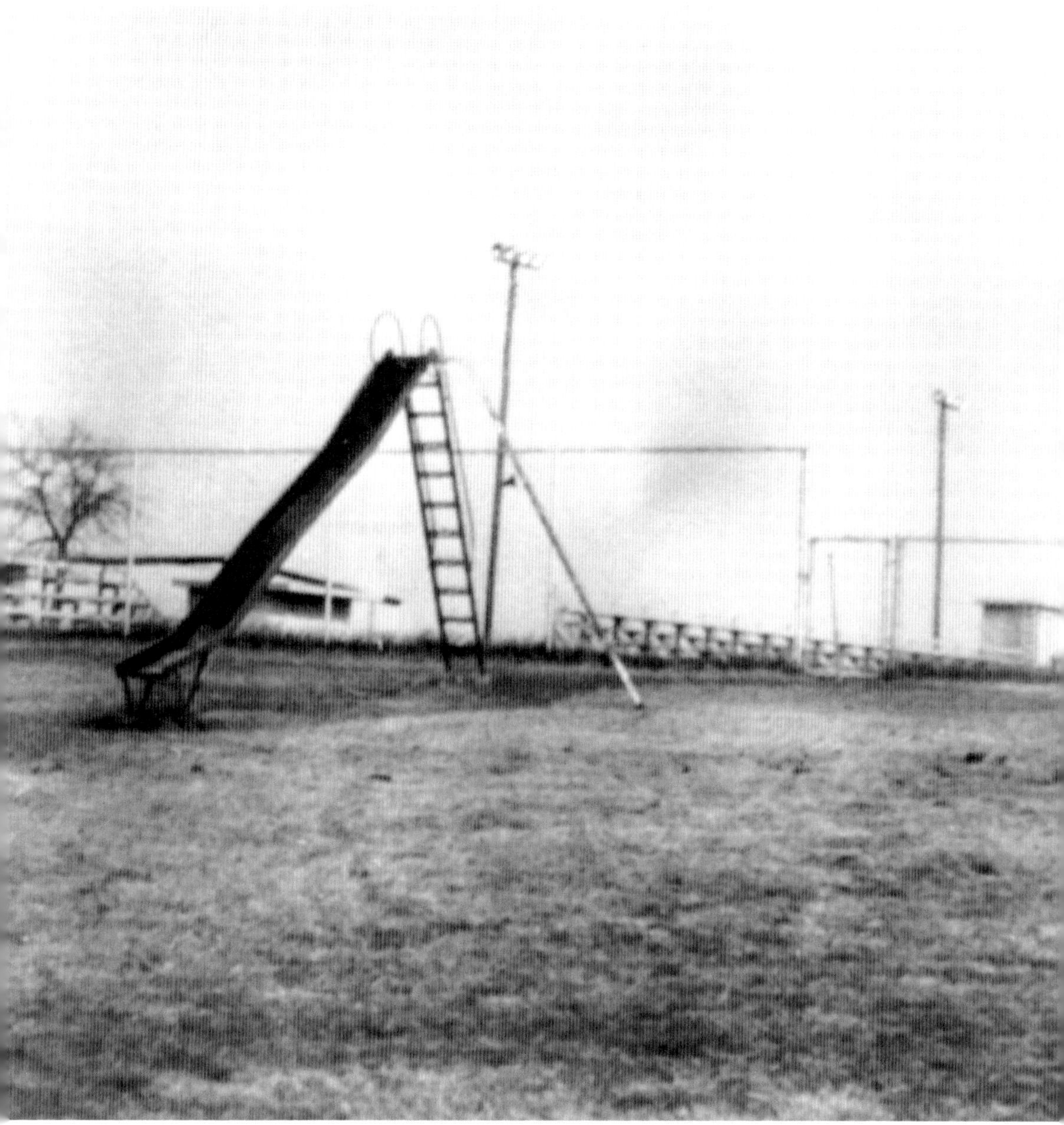

"We needed a place to play [football]. We had a little bit of land on the southeast corner of that campus," Johnson said. "But we didn't have any money." He called the county commissioner, "who sent a man with a grader—Bernie Brown. Bernie worked that ground and the dust flew like flour. By the time he finished, he was covered with dirt, sand, and burrs, but we came up with 80 yards. The first football field was an 80-yard field here at Carroll." Clyde Cheatham and Johnson hand-sprigged the field. As for the nearby practice field, "It ran downhill and was so full of rocks and pebbles that after practice, kids came in almost crying." This 1967 photograph shows the football field on the right beyond the playground equipment, two light poles, and the bleachers in the middle of the image.

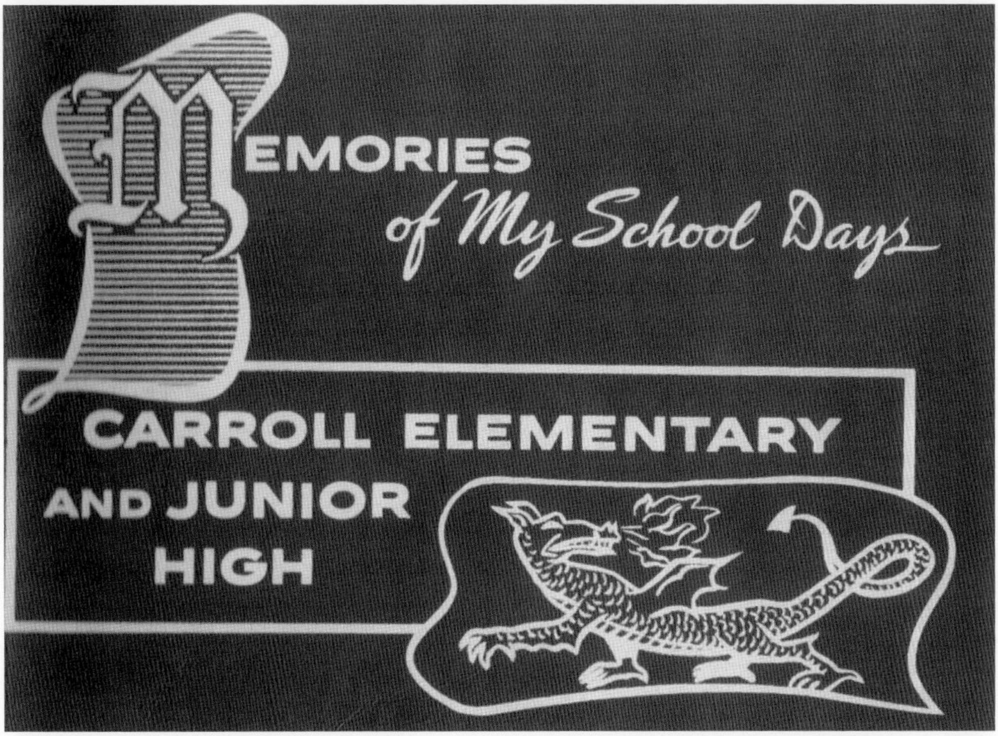

The school mascot can be traced to the early 1950s when student Tony Eubanks (now an internationally acclaimed Western artist) sat in class doodling a dragon. When Eubanks's friend Freddie Cate snatched the drawing off the desk, he showed it to their teacher and declared, "We'll be the Dragons." A few years later, another student, Larry Lee, drew a dragon, seen here. Lee and James Crawford recall their class voting to decide on the mascot. It is said the girls voted against a Dragon mascot because they did not want to be known as the Dragonettes. (Courtesy of Larry Lee.)

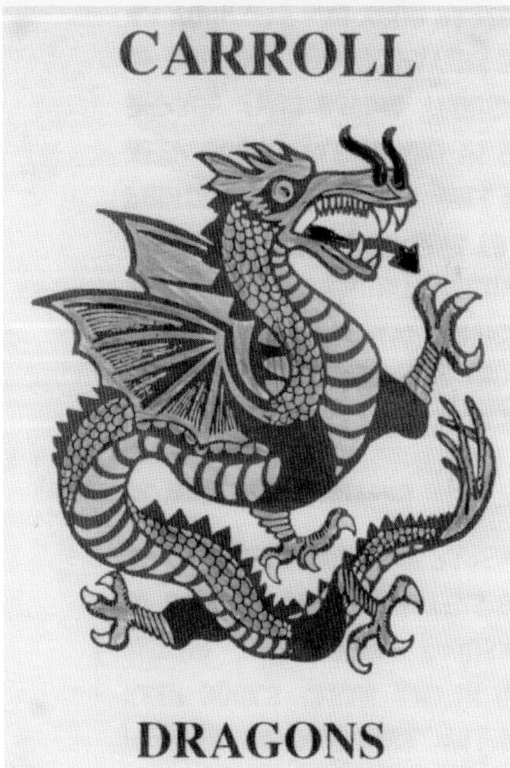

Dragon logos have changed over the years. This one is from the 1960s.

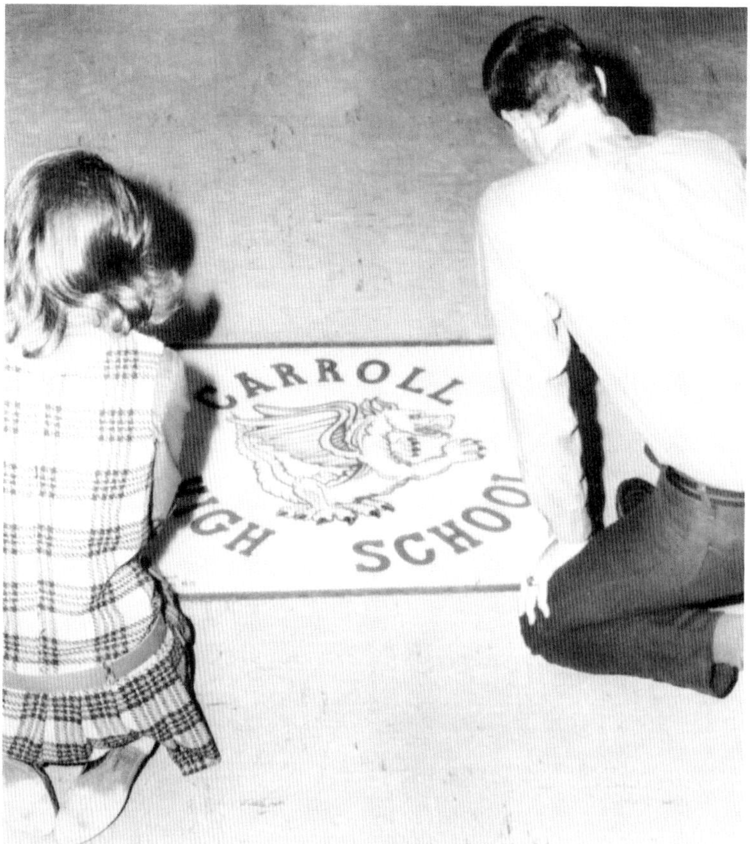

This logo greeted all who entered the original high school. In the lower-left corner are the words "Student Council '65," the year of Carroll's first graduating class. It was understood that no one stood or walked on the Dragon.

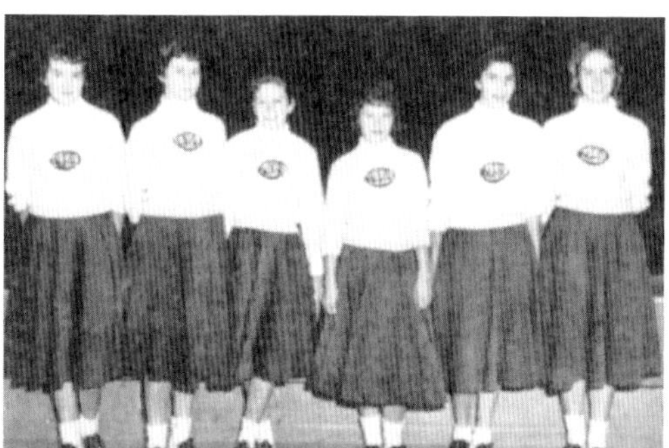

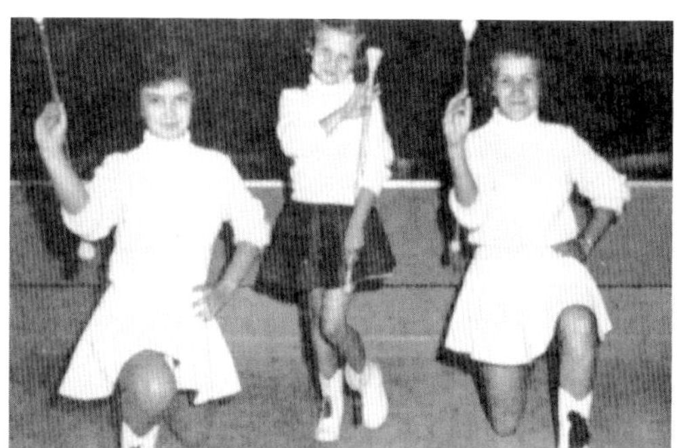

Carroll students were finally participating in their own extracurricular activities, which included football and boys' and girls' basketball, a cheerleading and pep squad, and twirlers. (Courtesy of Cheatham family.)

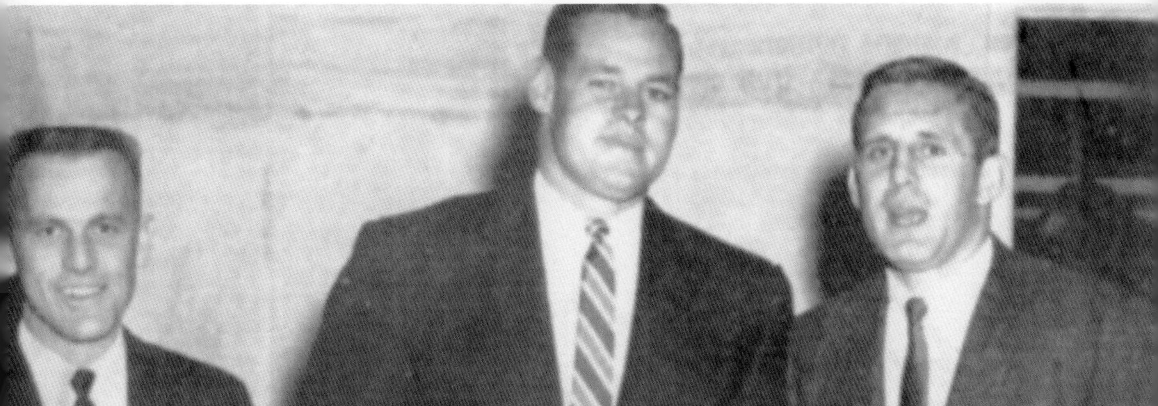

H. G. Griffin coached for one year and was succeeded by Gene Whitsell, George Crawford, and, in 1964, Max Boydston. Boydston grew up in Muskogee, Oklahoma, and was a two-time All-American at Oklahoma University in the 1950s under head coach Bud Wilkinson. He played professionally for the Chicago Cardinals, Dallas Texans, and Oakland Raiders. "Everyone wondered how in the world we got Max Boydston as a coach," Johnson said. Boydston owned land in Southlake. One day he walked into Casey's Grocery, which sat on the northeast corner of Carroll Avenue and Highway 114 next to Carroll School. Bennie Burrus, also an Oklahoma native, was part of the Casey family and was working at the store that day. He recognized Boydston, struck up a conversation, and later, suggested to Johnson that he interview Boydston. "Of course, there was no way we could hire Max," Johnson explained. "But Bennie insisted, brought him to my office, and sure enough, we hired him." At the 1964 football banquet, Boydston's former Oklahoma teammate and then–Dallas Cowboys split end Tommy McDonald, seen here on the right, was the guest speaker. Assistant coach Don Durham is pictured on the left.

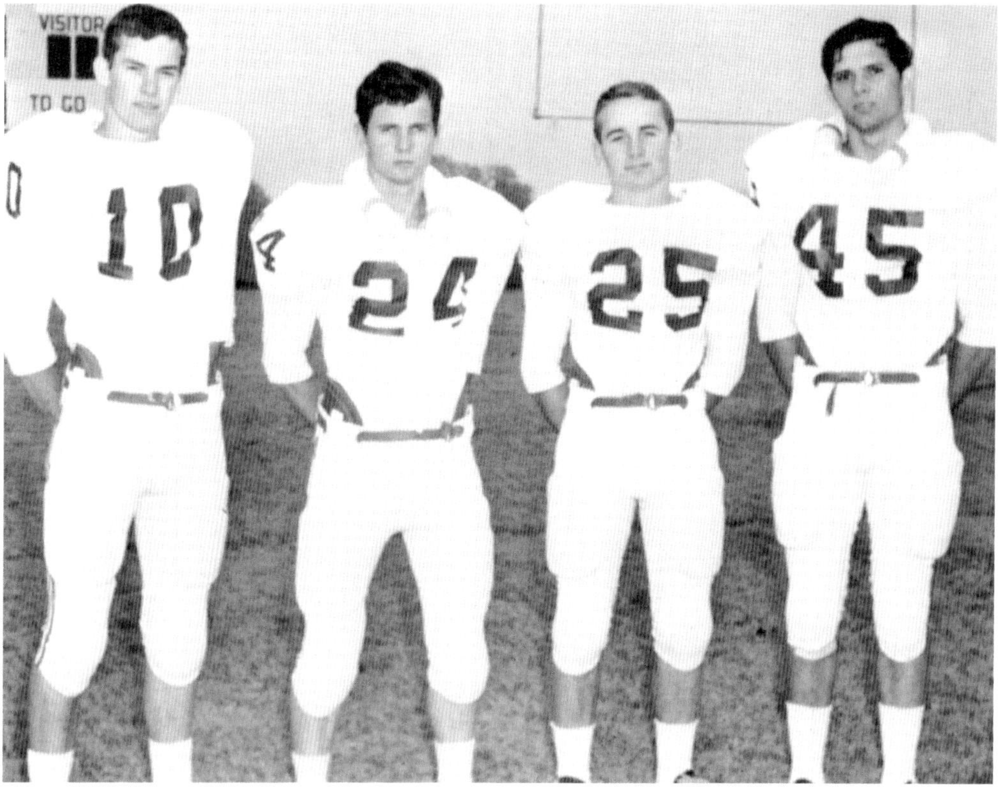

Larry Croy remembered playing for Boydston. "We looked up to him because he showed us his All-American tape," Croy said. "Colleges didn't really look at small schools like Carroll." After Croy graduated, he played for Weatherford Junior College on a full basketball scholarship. "Even Weatherford, coming from here, was a big step up." In 1968, the Dragon co-captains included, from left to right, Jerry Davis, David Carney, Doak Meador, and Wayne Moffat.

CARROLL HIGH SCHOOL DRAGONS

FOOTBALL ROSTER

NO.	NAME	POSITION	CLASSIFICATION	WEIGHT
11	Eddie Cheatham	QB	Sr.	150
12	Larry Croy	B	Soph.	160
12W	Ronnie Anderson	QB	Fresh.	104
20	Jackie Adams	B	Sr.	150
22	Jerry Davis	B	Fresh.	140
22W	Billy Hudson	B	Jr.	122
30	Doug Brumfield	B	Sr.	160
30W	Robert Sands	B	Soph.	120
35	David Harwell	B	Jr.	150
40	Wayne Moffat	B	Fresh.	145
[illegible]	Doak Meador	B	Fresh.	110
44W	Philip Hargis	B	Soph.	117
50	Don Steele	C	Jr.	175
55	Jimmy Strait	C	Fresh.	185
55W	Charlie Murphy	C	Soph.	130
60	Jimmy Hall	G	Jr.	175
62	Jimmy Hays	G	Sr.	185
64	Jimmy Davis	T	Jr.	160
64W	Bobby Thomas	G	Fresh.	186
66	Mike Fielder	T	Soph.	160
66W	David Sparks	G	Soph.	152
70	Terry McPherson	T	Jr.	145
70W	Mike Evans	E	Fresh.	124
72	Richard Willoughby	T	Jr.	165
72W	Tom Sanquinet	G	Jr.	165
75	Bobby Johnson	T	Sr.	195
77	Danny Wiggins	T	Jr.	170
77W	Mike Strange	E	Soph.	125
80	Doug Depew	E	Sr.	165
80W	Robert Henry	B	Fresh.	167
85	Bobby Hitt	E	Sr.	165
82	Bill Jackson	E	Fresh.	140
88	Gerald Spivey	E	Resh.	116

COACH Max Boydston — Manager Steve Strange

Asst. Don Durham — Manager Stan Brown

Don Durham grew up in Slidell, Texas, graduated from Texas A&M University, and returned to his hometown to coach the girls' basketball team. His team won the Class B Girls' State Basketball Championship in 1963. The following year, he came to Carroll. When asked how her husband ended up coaching here, Martha Durham recalled, "I think Jack [Johnson] knew who Don was because of that state championship. I don't know how Jack talked him into coming here, but he did." Pictured is the 1964 football roster.

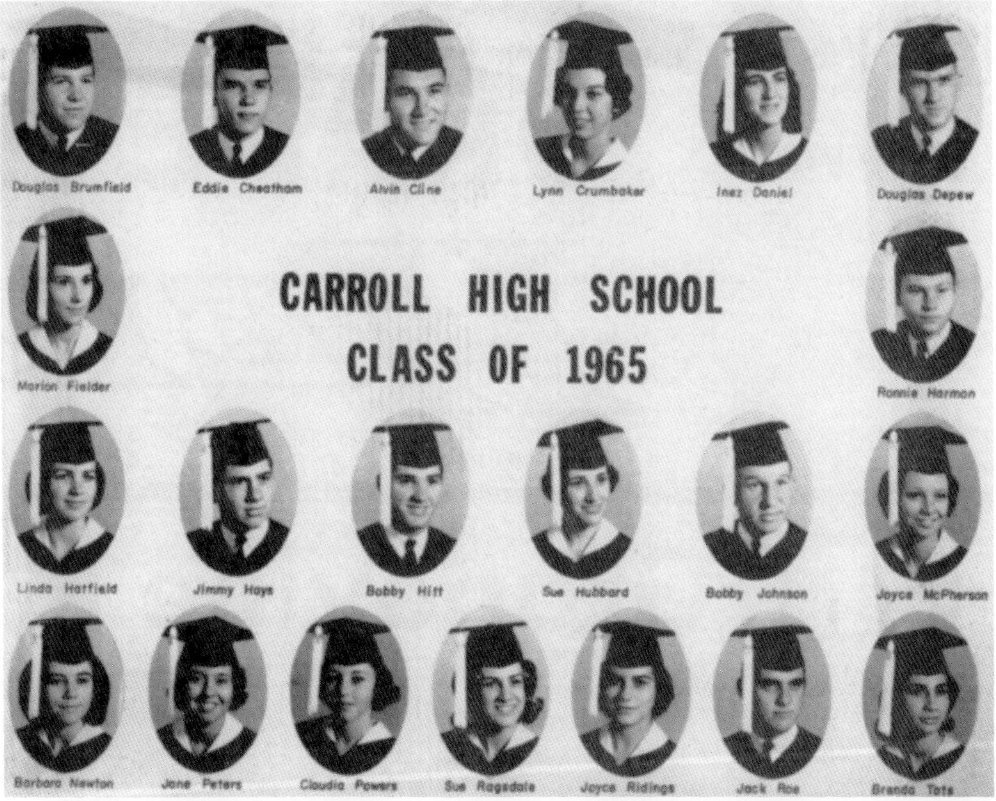

In 1965, the Texas Education Agency granted Carroll ISD full accreditation of grades 1-12, and Carroll graduated its first senior class, 24 students, on May 28, 1965. The district also gained membership into the University Interscholastic League (UIL) that year. Johnson later served on the UIL Legislative Council from 1975 to 1986.

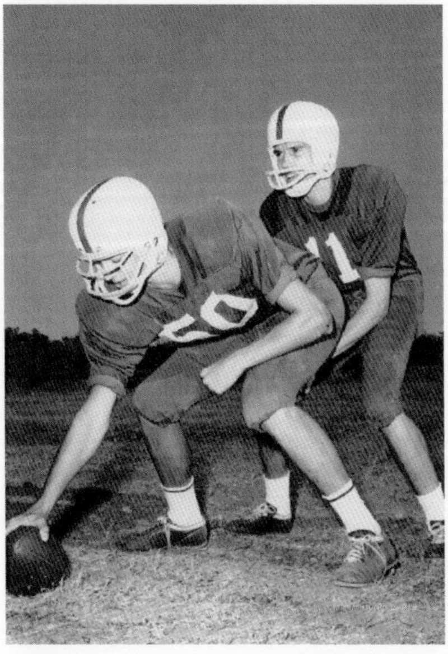

Eddie Cheatham was the son of board member Clyde Cheatham and was in Carroll's first graduating class. He played for the University of Tulsa, and after graduating, he served as Southlake city engineer before forming his own firm. Cheatham worked with Carroll ISD on many projects, including the Dragon Stadium on South Kimball Avenue. Carroll center Don Steele, seen here with Cheatham, was the son of Southlake's longest-serving fire chief, Bob Steele, and his wife, Crystal.

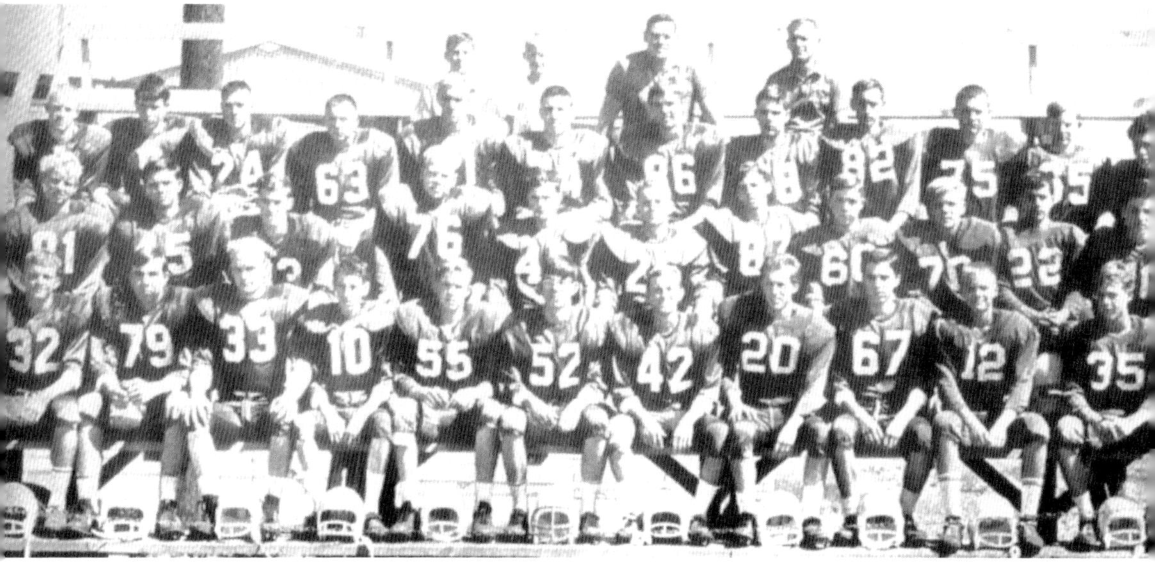

The 1965 season ended 10-2, and the Dragons, seen here, won the Class B District Championship—their first ever. At the end of the year, Boydston left, and A.O. "Buddy" Hinzman stepped up as head coach. John Lowrey, who coached seven years at Sanger, was hired to assist him. Don Durham moved up as the elementary school principal and could only assist with football practice occasionally. Lowrey remembered being short-staffed, and practices were hectic. "Mr. Hinzman would say, 'OK, all you backs go down with Coach Lowrey. Linemen stay here.' Next practice we'd switch roles and I became line coach and he became back coach. Then he'd say, 'And all you AOs, you go down with Coach Durham.' AOs stood for 'all others.' In those days, if you were a male in a small school district, whether you knew anything about sports or not, you coached." Ron Cullum was hired as a teacher in 1968, and within a week, he was an assistant football coach and "No. 1 bus driver," Lowrey said.

The district had two bus routes, and at the end of the school day, "it wasn't uncommon for someone to come running down off the hill shouting, 'We need a bus driver,'" Lowrey remembered. "Mr. Cullum would have to run off to drive the bus." This 1960s photograph of the Carroll campus includes the 1919 Carroll School (with the chimney), the high school, and the elementary school (far left).

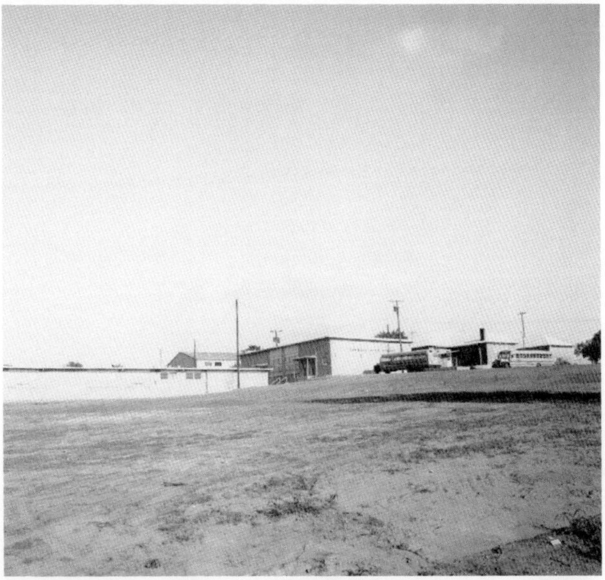

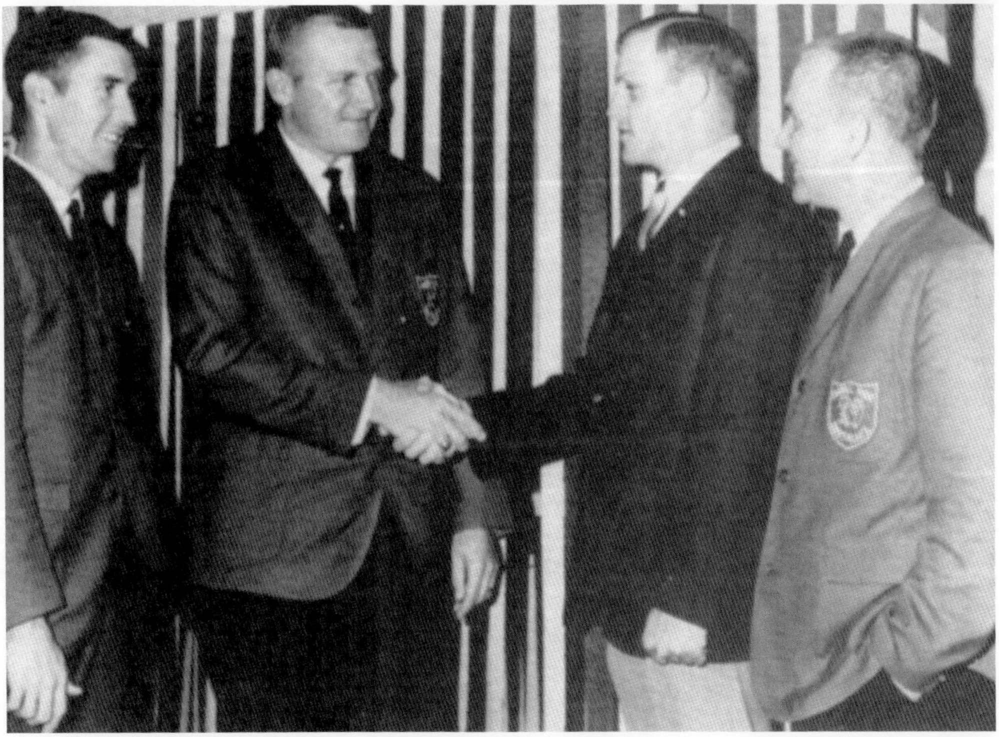

Larry Lee was the eighth-grade quarterback on the first football team in 1959. He attended high school in Grapevine and played football at Ranger Junior College (now Ranger College) for two years before transferring to Texas A&M, where he played for Gene Stallings. In 1967, Lee was invited to speak at the Carroll football banquet and is seen here with Lowrey, Hinzman, and Durham. The Houston Texans picked Lee in the 1967 National Football League draft, and he played professionally for one year.

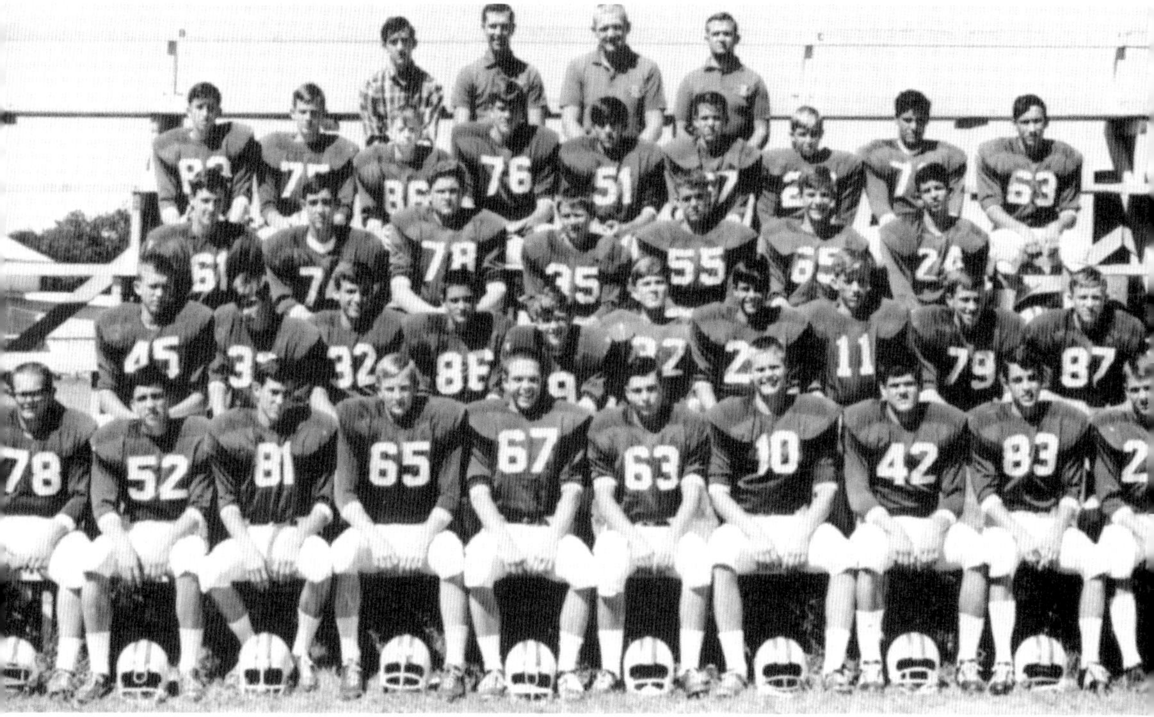

A freshman player on this 1968 team, Elijah "Eli" Melton would return to Carroll years later as a teacher and coach. In his high school days, everyone knew him as "Ligie." "I will never forget Coach Hinzman," Melton remembered. "One day after practice, he and Coach Lowrey called me over. Coach placed his arm around me and said, 'Ligie, you have a lot of football ahead of you. We would like for you to play center for us. Do you think you could learn to snap the ball?' Well, that was all I needed to motivate me as I thought both of those guys hung the moon. I worked like crazy to become the best center I could be. I was named All-District center my junior year. Those two, along with Max Boydston, were the reason I wanted to become a coach myself." Melton is seated second from the right in the fourth row.

Alongside Superintendent Johnson in this 1968 photograph are high school principal Gene Whitsell (left) and elementary school principal Don Durham (middle).

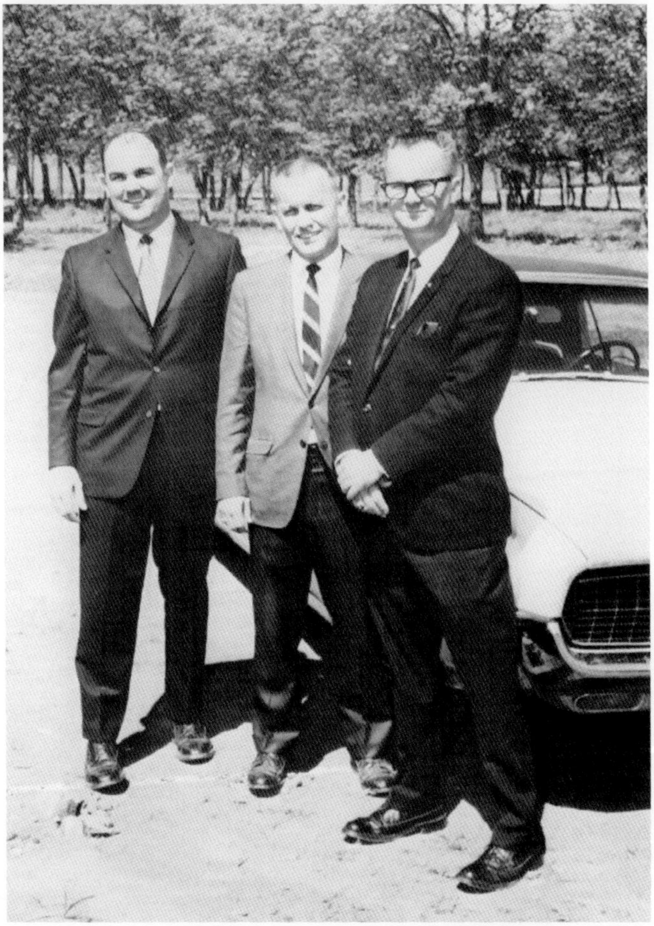

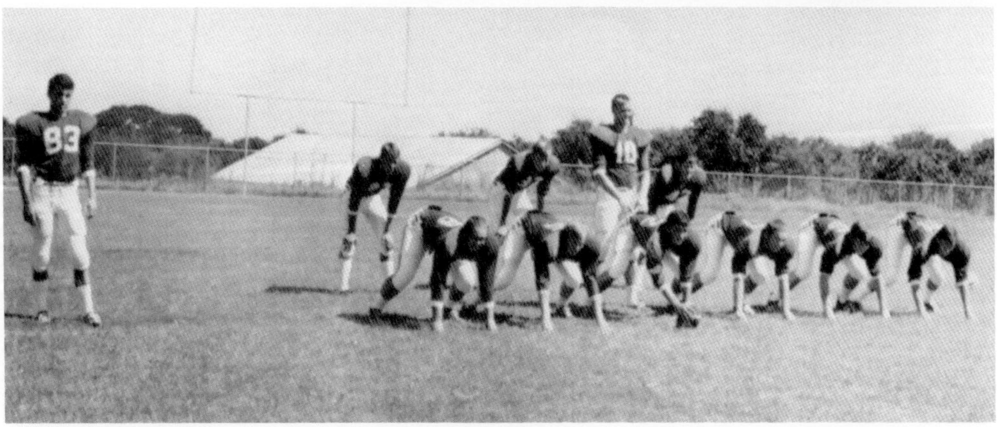

Lowrey became head coach in 1968. "And in my spare time, I drove that bus," he said later. Coaches were team trainers in those days, too. Lowrey remembered one player who would hyperventilate in the excitement of a game. "So, being the knowledgeable trainers that we were," Lowrey said with a laugh, "we always carried a brown paper bag in our first aid kit." Seen here are 1968 players at practice.

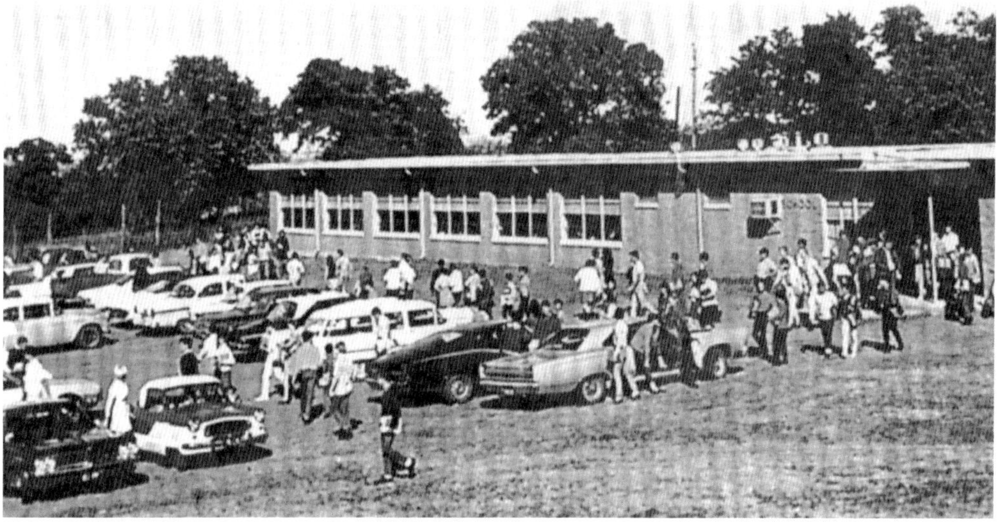

By 1968, the district enrollment had grown to more than 600 students. The high school, pictured in 1969, was a busy place.

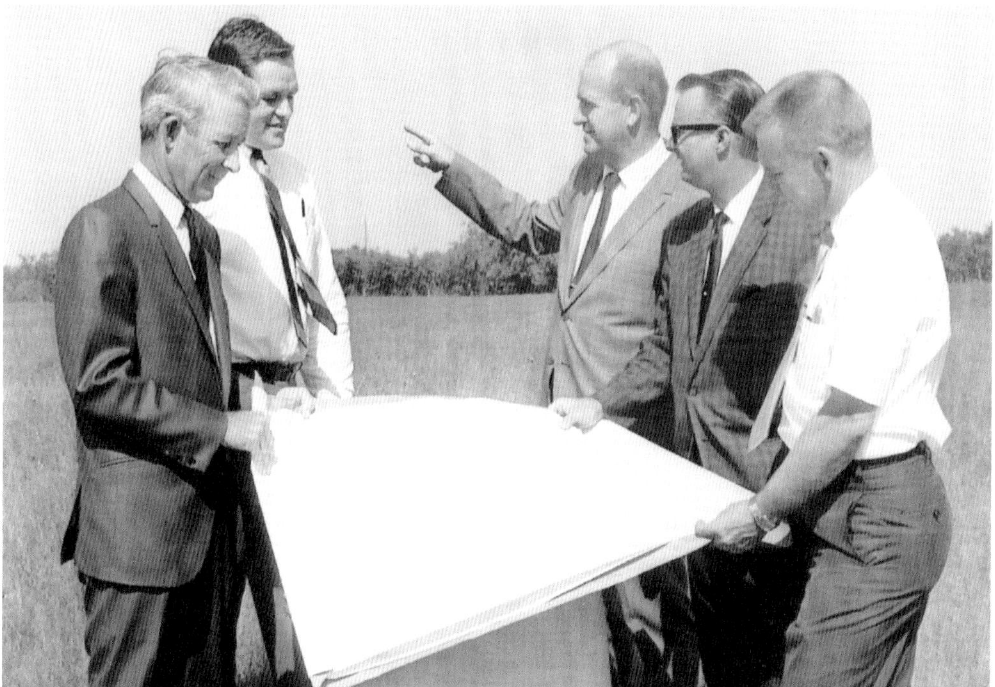

Max Boydston returned in 1969 as the high school principal and found that things had changed. Carroll was fully accredited with more students and a larger staff. Plans were underway to build a new high school at the corner of Carroll Avenue and Dove Road. Pictured surveying the property, from left to right, are school board president Dick Kirkland, high school principal Max Boydston, Dallas architect Joe Pitzinger Jr., Superintendent Johnson, and elementary school principal Don Durham. (Courtesy of the Johnson family.)

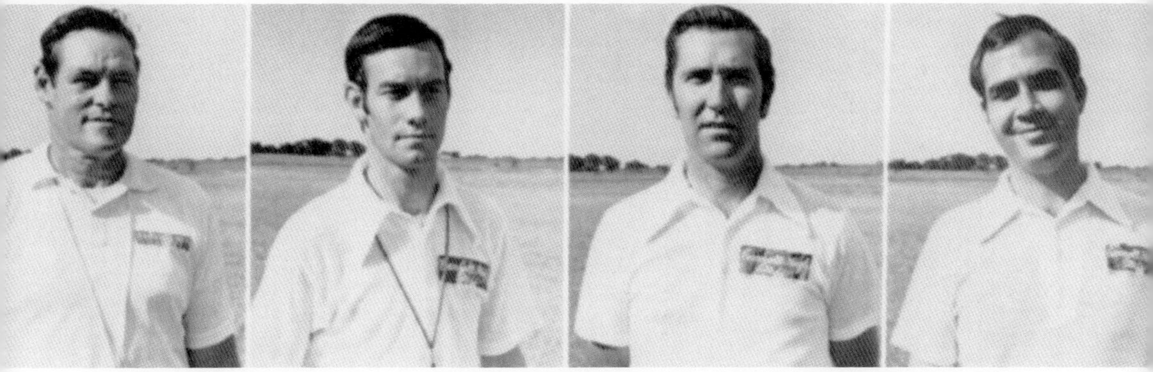

In 1970, Boydston again became head coach. The season ended 4-6. In 1971, the Dragons just missed capturing district honors, and the 1972 season ended 8-2 with Boydston named district Coach of the Year. The 1973 Dragons held on to a winning season, but at the close of school, Boydston joined the Kansas City Chiefs as a full-time scout, leaving behind a six-season overall coaching record of 44-17-1. "Anytime you can join an organization as great as the Chiefs," he said, "you can't be too far off. But the schools, the community, everyone has been just great to me. We've all worked for a well-rounded sports program here. Whenever we did win, it was because everyone functioned as a team." New hire Ken Cook joined the staff, and assistant coach Jim McGuire was tapped to replace Boydston. Shown here are, from left to right, Boydston, Cook, Lowrey, and McGuire.

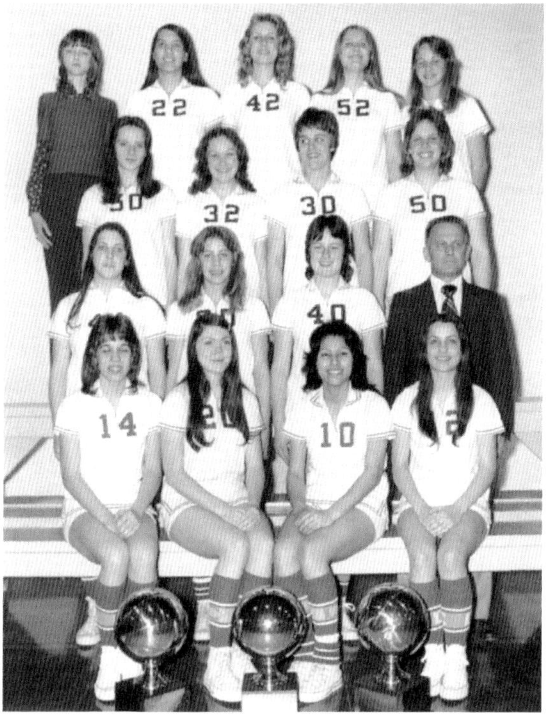

The Dragons' first state title came in 1975, the 1A Girls' Basketball Championship. The players are, from left to right, (first row) Cindy Pennington, Julia Lewis, Mary Casillas, and Sundie Kay Tate; (second row) Karen Harty, Shannon McGowan, Tonya Aslin, and Durham; (third row) Geneva Willis, Mary O'Brien, Kathy Harston, and Sheri Hight; (fourth row) Linda Stowe (manager), Wanda Noack, Sue Green, Becky Elms, and Brenda Anderson. (Courtesy of Martha Durham.)

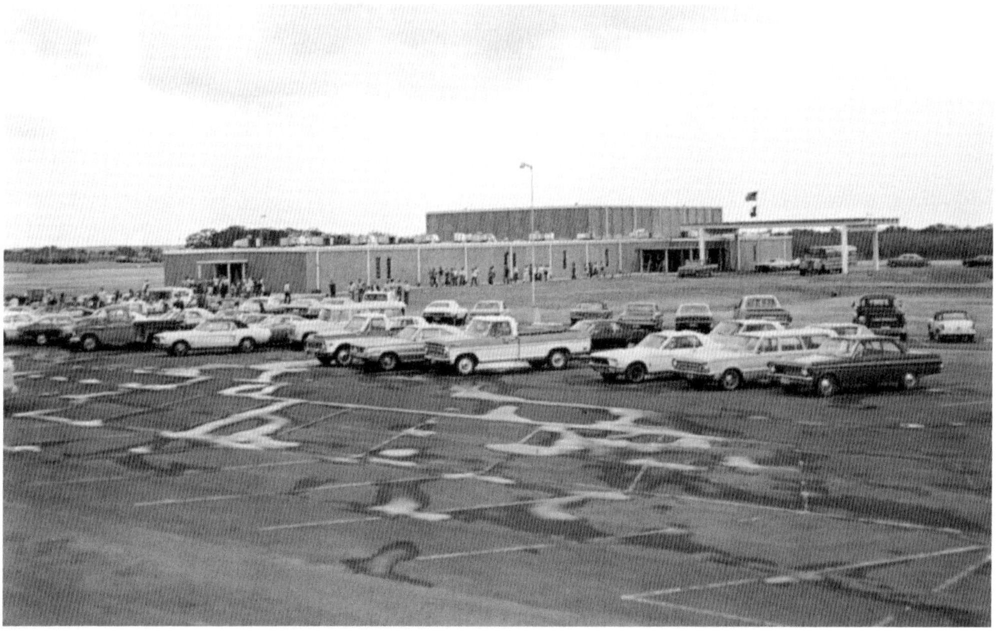

By the time Bill Branum was hired as head coach in 1976, the new Carroll High School at Carroll Avenue and Dove Road, seen here, had been open five years. Branum grew up in Brownwood and played football under legendary coach Gordon Wood. He graduated from the University of North Texas and coached at Lewisville High School and Katy High School (Houston) before applying for the head coach position at Carroll.

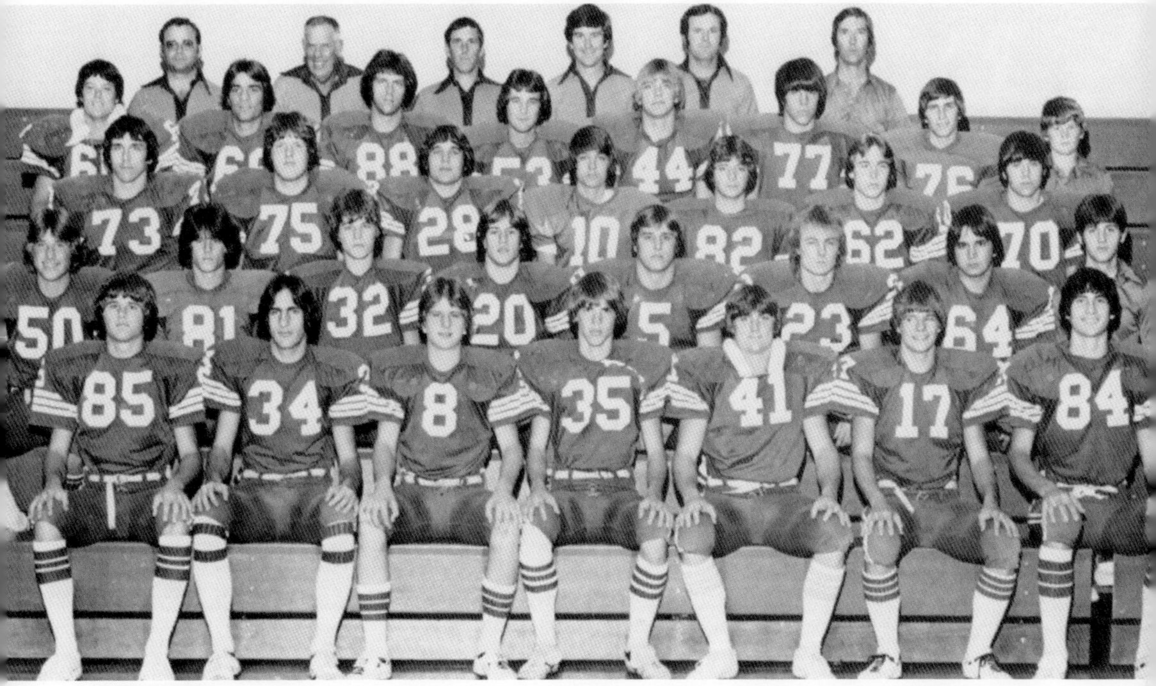

"I met Mr. Johnson and my first impression was that there was pride and tradition in the school," Branum said. The new head coach inherited several coaches who had been at Carroll for 10 years or more. "They knew the kids much better than I did. They knew what our strengths were." Branum recalled that he knew only one way to build the program, which was "roll up your sleeves and go to work." The season ended 4-5-1, and the 1977 season closed at 5-5. In 1978, the Dragons had only one loss when they played No. 1 Farmersville and pulled off an upset win, 32-27. "Our kids just played their hearts out," said Branum. From left to right, those team members are (first row) Steve Strehlow, Kevin Powell, Brian Popkin, Damon Bass, Dan Spradley, Randy Lowrey, and Kenny Lawry; (second row) Chris Rickman, Robie Norman, John Harston, Lester Massey, Chris Kirkham, Brian Smith, Randy Unruh, and Kent Klopper (manager); (third row) Todd Moyer, Brian Hodges, Brent Pennington, Robin Howell, James Jones, Mark Gustafson, and Greg Calhoun; (fourth row) Steve Allen, Craig Reed, Brick Moore, Keith Evans, Jamie Bland, Randy Weeks, Keith Long, and Jeff Miller (manager); (fifth row) coaches Ron Cullum, Rod Venner, Bill Branum, Chauncey Willingham, Jackie Mayfield, and John Lowrey.

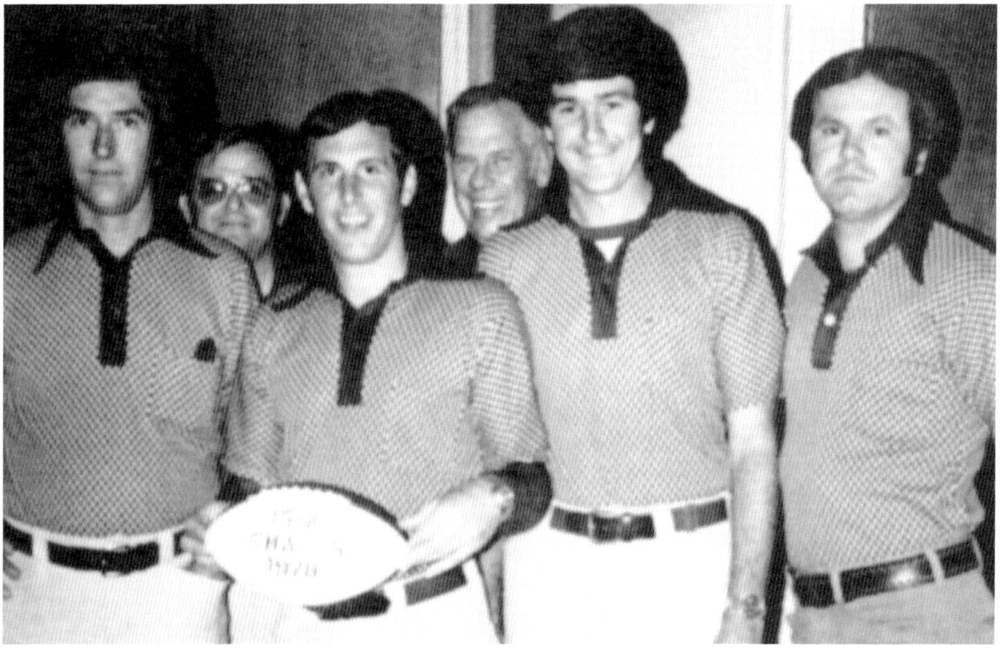

The Dragons won the 1978 District 15A Championship, and for the first time in 13 years, the team was going to the playoffs. Holding the district football is Branum surrounded by, from left to right, Lowrey, Cullum, Venner, Willingham, and Mayfield. The Dragons lost in the first round. Soon after, Branum took a head coaching position at 5A Katy. But leaving his players was hard. "I knew we were going to be really good again," Branum said. (Courtesy of Chauncey Willingham.)

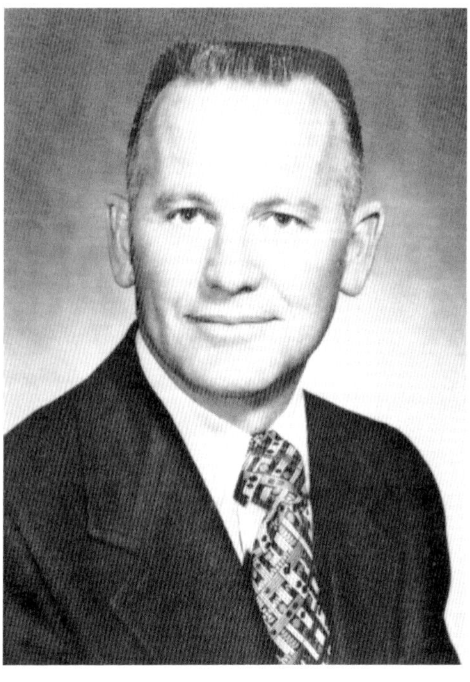

In 1979, Carroll ISD administrators, students, teachers, coaches, and parents suffered a tragic loss. Don Durham was killed in an automobile accident on Highway 114 while making his way home from a school-related event. Durham had been hired in 1964 and, over the next 15 years, successfully served Carroll ISD as an administrator, teacher, and coach.

3

"You Win with Great Kids"

When Bob Ledbetter walked onto 2A Carroll's football field in 1979, Southlake's population was 2,800. Of the 280 high school students, 35 played football. Over the next 23 years, he would build a Dragon football program that no one could then imagine.

Ledbetter was born in Ardmore, Oklahoma, and graduated from Southeastern State University in Durant, where he played football and baseball and ran track. With his wife, Sue, and their two children, he moved to Texas to teach and coach. He worked at MacArthur High School in Irving and Vernon High School before becoming head coach and athletic director at Frisco High School in 1974. The Frisco Raccoons and the Dragons played each other in those days, and Ledbetter was impressed with Carroll: "Their kids were well-disciplined. The administration was at every game, supporting the kids. I can remember thinking to myself—and I'd never even been to Southlake—'This would be a great place to raise our family.'"

In 1979, Superintendent Johnson called Ledbetter to ask if he would be interested in coming to Carroll as head football coach and athletic director.

"I remember sitting in his office," Ledbetter recounted, "and he said to me, 'Coach, we're going to offer you the job here at Carroll. And I want you to understand one thing. You'll never win a state football championship here. We don't have those kinds of athletes. We have great kids. And we have great parents. Our kids are strong academically, but we don't have great athletes.'

And I remember looking at Mr. Johnson and saying, 'You know, Mr. Johnson, you don't win state championships with great athletes. You win with great kids.'"

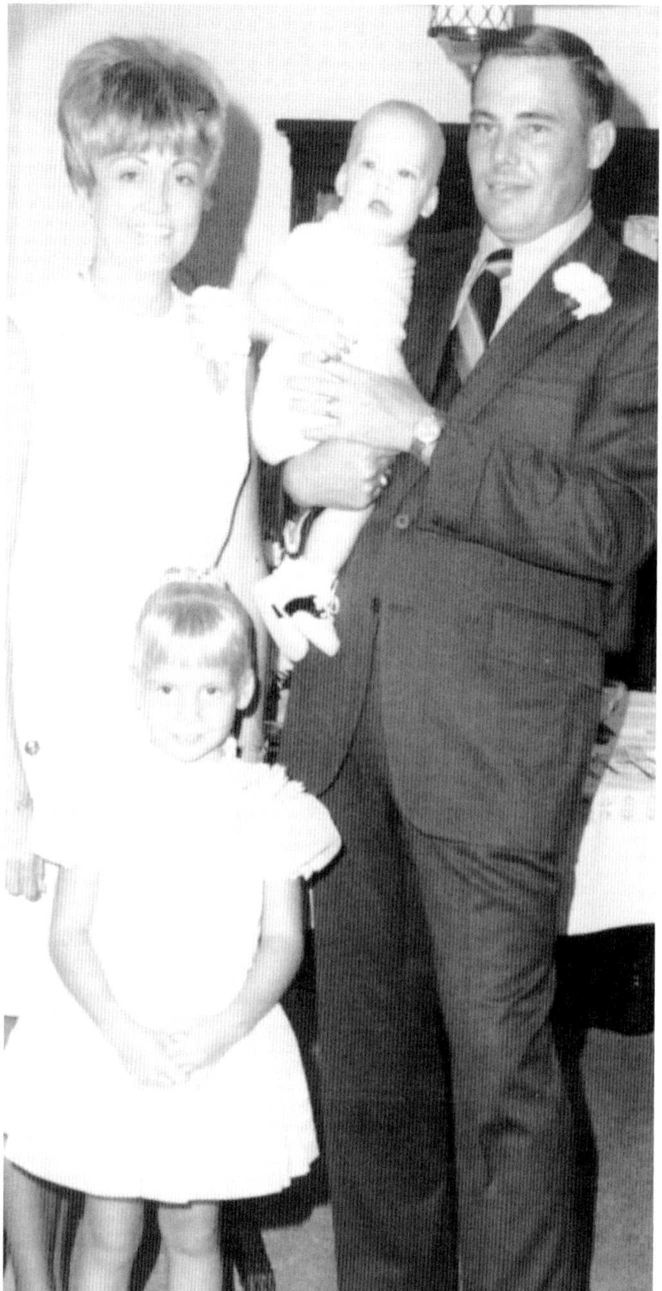

"When Sue and I came here [in 1979]," Bob Ledbetter explained, "it was a whole different world than it is today. Carroll was a 2A school. We had 280 kids in high school. But it was a very strong school district academically, and the reason we came was because I thought it was a great situation for our family," pictured here. As a way to make a little more money, Ledbetter drove the school bus. "I drove the morning bus route. I picked up the elementary kids. They would see me at the grocery store and they'd say, 'Mom, that's my bus driver.'" (Courtesy of Bob Ledbetter.)

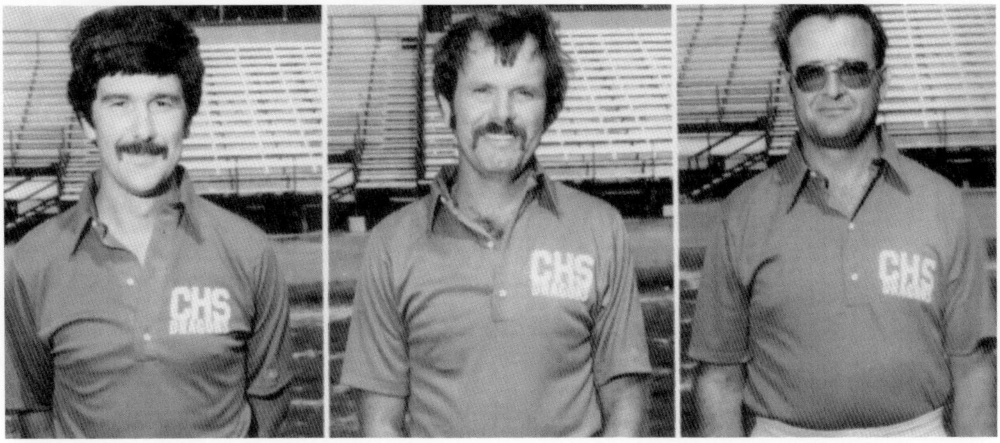

The seasoned coaching staff remained intact except for John Lowrey, who became the high school principal after Don Durham's death. *Dave Campbell's Texas Football* magazine predicted the 1979 Dragons would be No. 1 with returning players positioned "to lead the Dragons to their second straight district crown." The season ended 9-1, the Dragons won district, but lost to Wolfe City in the first round of playoffs. The coaches, from left to right, are (above) Willingham, Mayfield, and Cullum; (below) Ledbetter, Venner, Doug Edwards, and Ken Cook.

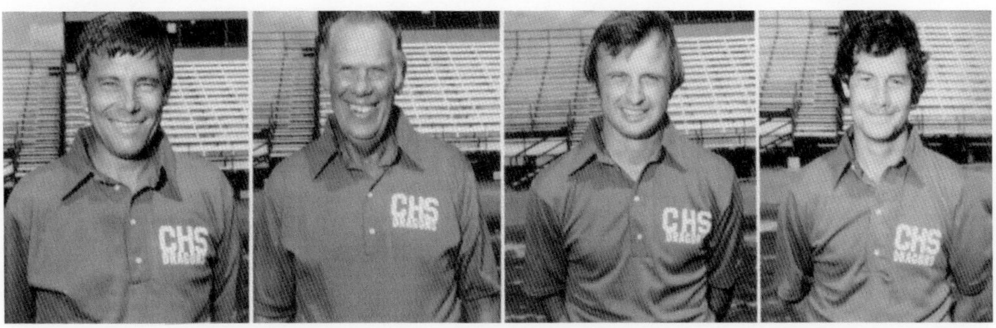

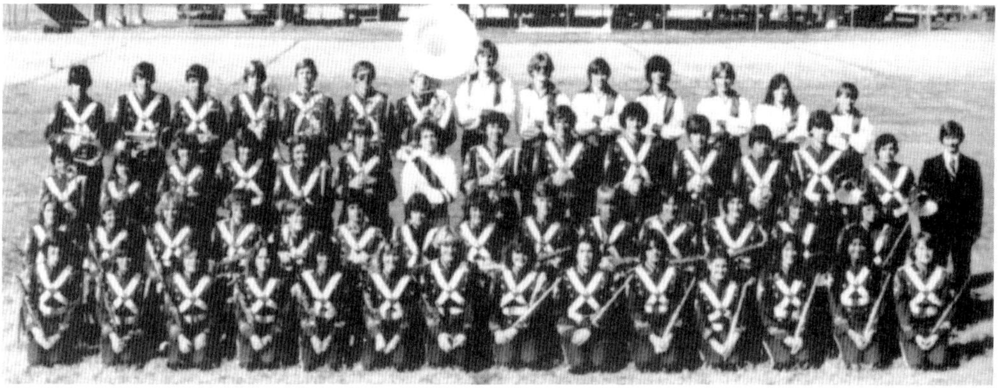

The 58-member Carroll Dragon band, led by second-year director Ron Behrends (in the suit on the right), brought home the Best Class A Band in Texas trophy that year—CISD's second state title. The members are, from left to right, (first row) C. Shera, P. Garrett, C. Pollack, S. Burger, R. Cox, J. Herrington, B. Trietsch, A. Burger, D. Pollack, D. Herron, H. Smith, R. Perry, I. Hernandez, and C. Cotton; (second row) T. Roper, K. Shuping, J. Pekarski, S. Ervin, T. Brittain, D. Howell, B. Hughey, J. Evans, D. Burrows, M. Tucker, J. Harty, R. Wallace, D. Bevill, and C. Arnold; (third row) G. Garcia, S. Miller, T. Campbell, P. Aldred, C. Braun, M. Walsch, drum major S. Andre, B. Strehlow, C. Ramsey, M. Darby, P. South, A. Busbee, K. Pankratz, and M. Stiborek; (fourth row) E. Clement, G. Shuping, R. Ivester, J. Fix, B. Burrows, A. Wayland, S. Wayland, C. Kidwell, M. Dodd, D. Ramsey, C. Ryals, M. Deegan, S. Jacobs, and A. Miller.

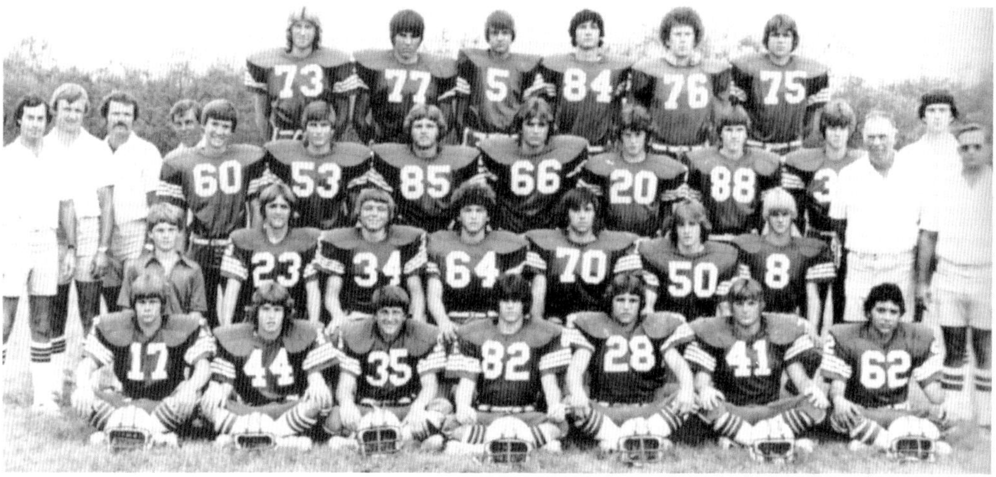

Ledbetter said his first Dragon team was small. "But we've got some quickness that will allow us to do other things," he said. That team included, from left to right, (first row) R. Lowrey, M. Monroe, D. Cullum, R. Norman, B. Pennington, D. Spradley, and unidentified; (second row) J. Miller (manager), B. Johnson, R. Davis, B. Hawk, G. Calhoun, two unidentified, Venner, and Cullum; (third row) Cook, Edwards, Mayfield, Ledbetter, R. Durham, K. Long, S. Strehlow, C. Reed, K. Aslin, R. Lower, J. Harston, and Willingham; (fourth row) C. Rickman, R. Weeks, R. Howell, K. Lawry, T. Bryant, and T. Green.

The 1980 season ended with six wins, three losses, and one tie, garnering second place in the district for the Dragons. 1980 All-District players are, from left to right, (kneeling) Marcus Garza and Doug Unruh; (standing) Roger Lower, Todd Green, and Keith Long.

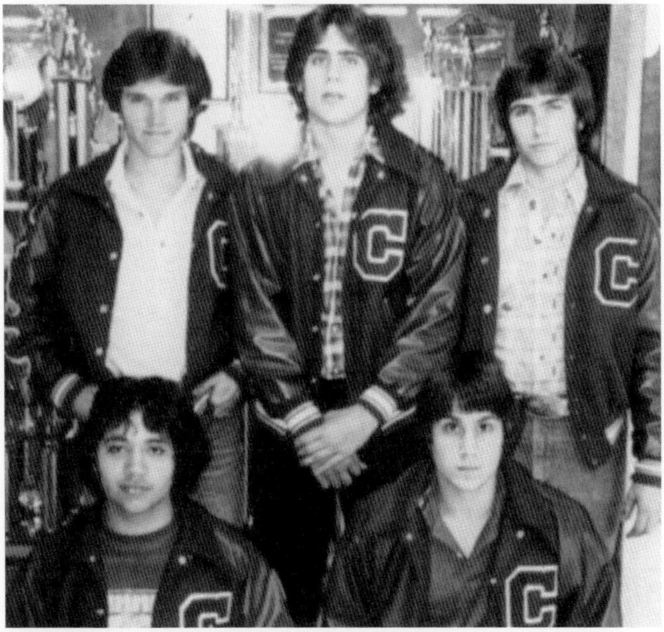

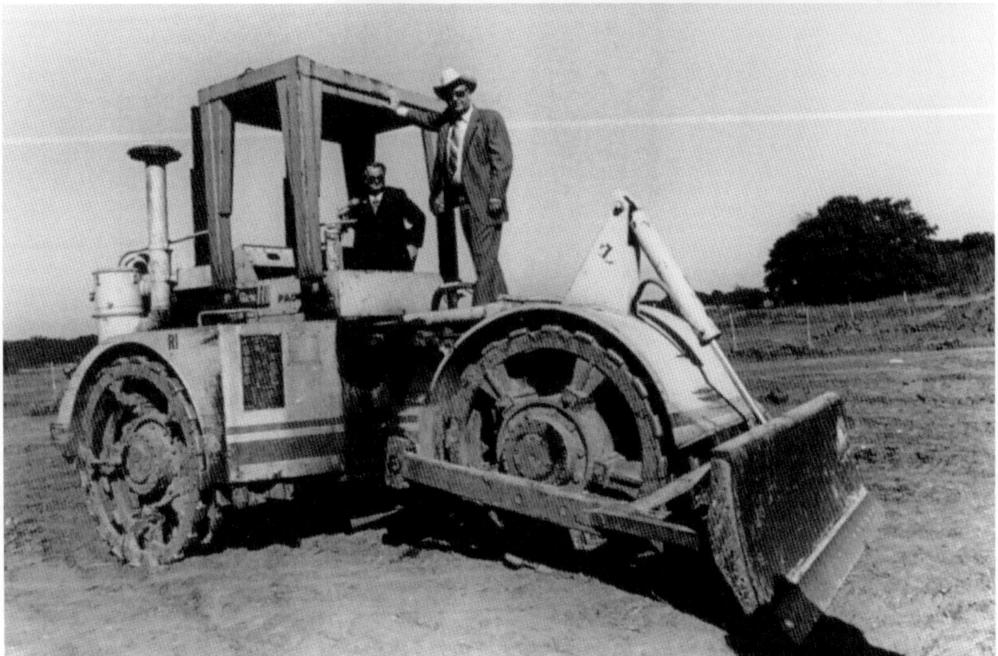

Plans to expand the 10-year-old high school on Carroll Avenue and Dove Road were in the works and included a new stadium behind the school. Construction of a new elementary school, to be named for Jack Johnson, had begun. Seen here at the ground-breaking ceremony are Superintendent Johnson (seated) and Bob Rockenbaugh, who lauded Johnson as "the most dedicated schoolman" he had ever seen in action. "He is thinking about school all the time," he said. (Courtesy of the Johnson family.)

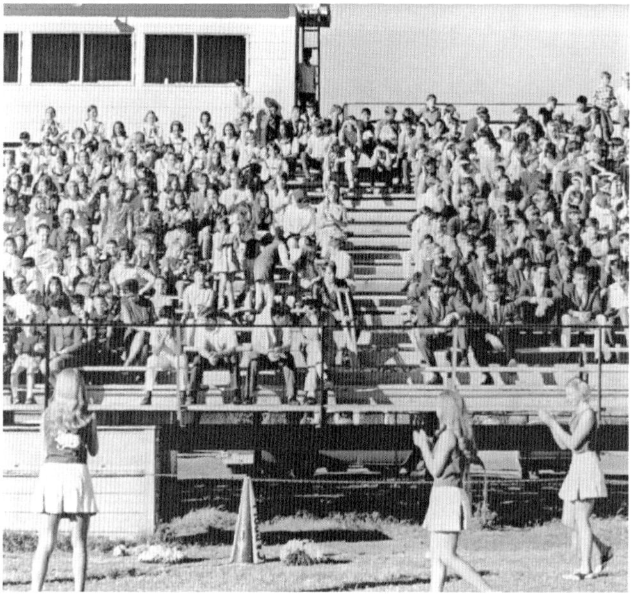

Dragon Stadium, which opened in September 1981, was designed to accommodate 2,970 fans. "We're almost doubling our seating capacity," Johnson said. "We hope we can fill it." The new bleachers are full in this early-1980s photograph. One local sportswriter tapped Dragon Stadium as the area's best playing field. The Dragon hot dogs were his favorite. "They claim they do nothing special in whipping up their dogs, so maybe it's the ultra-clean facility that sways me," he wrote.

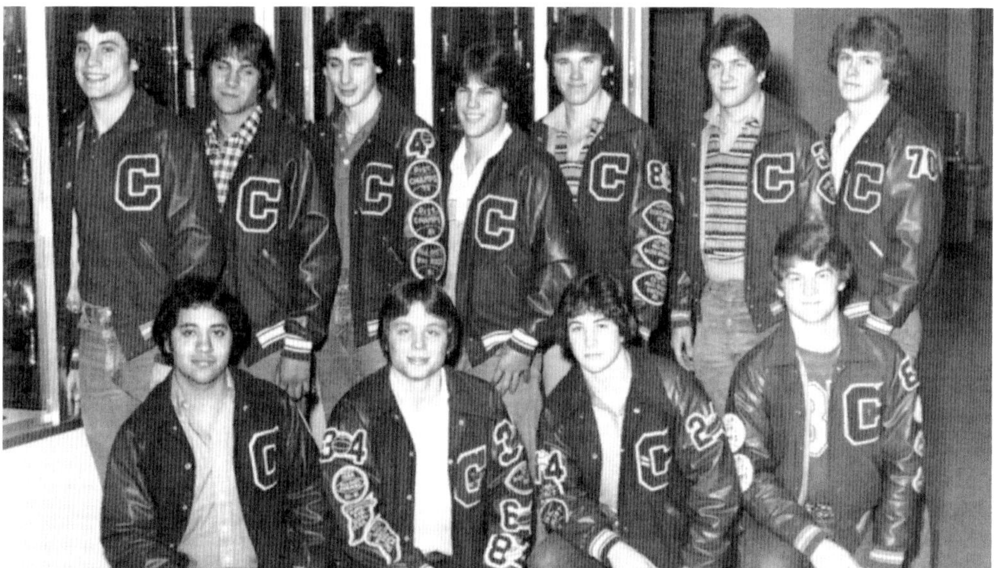

A total of 18 starters returned for the 1981 season. "It will take the offensive line, the backs, the defense, and the people on the sideline for us to win. There won't be anyone just wearing a uniform," Ledbetter said. The team finished the season 9-1 and as district runners-up. All-District players that year included, from left to right, (kneeling) Marcus Garza, Randy Davis, Greg Charlton, and Jeff Miller; (standing) Rod Venner, Doug Unruh, Sam Booker, Tom Ippolito, Roger Lower, Dee Wayne Cullum, and Tim Elms.

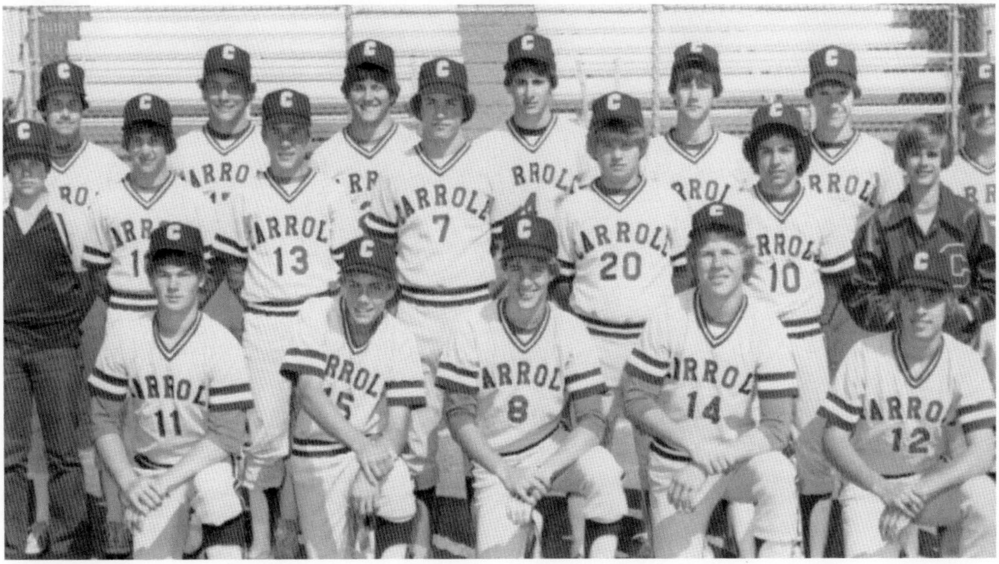

Head baseball coach Ken Cook and his team brought home CISD's third state title, the 1982 2A Boys' State Baseball Championship. Team members included, from left to right, (kneeling) J. Miller, D. Springer, J. Fix, B. Burrows, and M. Deegan; (middle row) J. Edland (manager), G. Charleton, S. Hodges, S. Irving, M. London, T. Franco, and R. Black (manager); (top row) Coach Cook, R. Venner, D. Cullum, S. Booker, E. Sutton, R. Lower and Coach Cullum.

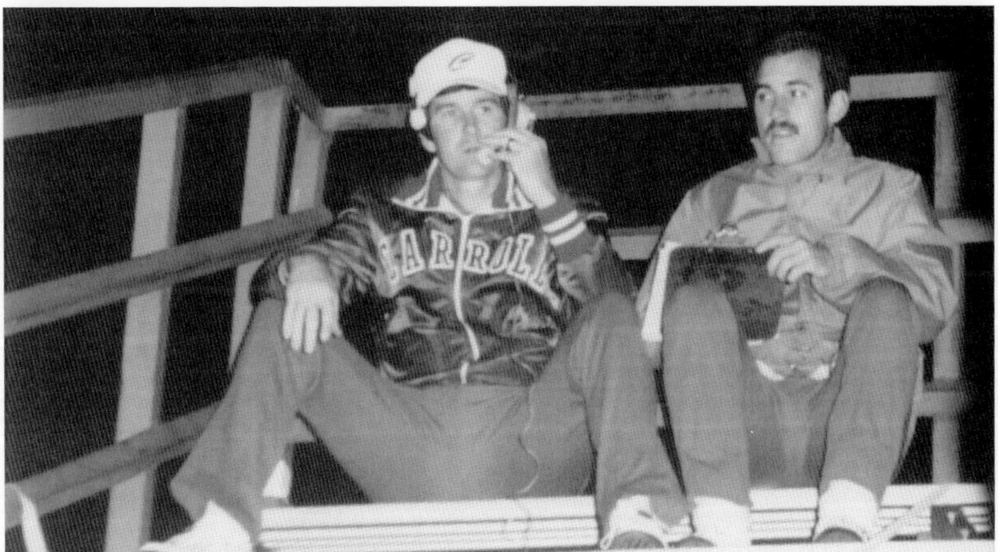

Chauncey Willingham grew up in Boyd, Texas, and remembered playing against Carroll in high school when Max Boydston was head coach. "Max kind of kept up with me," Willingham remembered. "And when he knew I'd graduated from college, he called [then-Carroll head coach] Jim McGuire and told him, 'He's gonna go back to Boyd and you need to hire him.'" This 1982 photograph was taken during a game at Springtown when now-coach Chauncey Willingham (left) and Gary Lejarzar called plays from the stands. (Courtesy of Chauncey Willingham.)

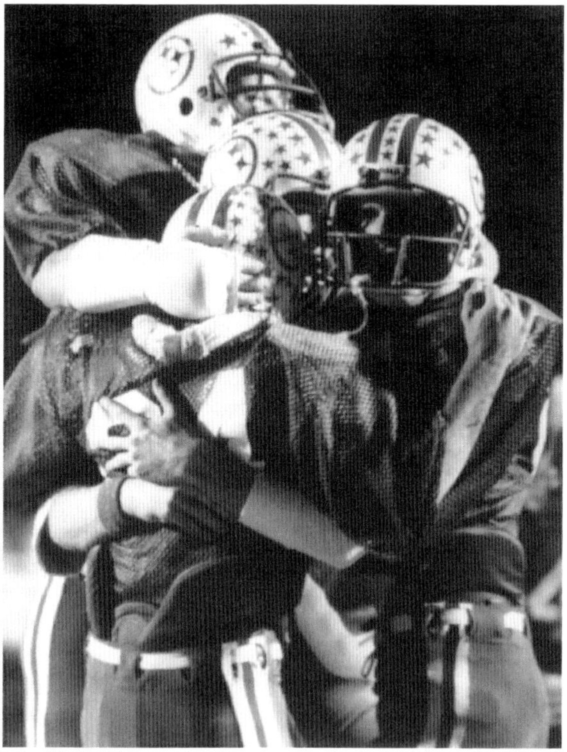

Even with nine returning starters in 1983, Ledbetter acknowledged that his players were still considered small. "I'd rather have them small and quick than big and slow," he said. The first Dragon football helmets went from plain white to white with one or two green stripes running back to front. Coach Bill Branum added a single "C" to the side in the late 1970s, and in 1981, Ledbetter introduced a Pittsburgh Steelers look-alike decal, as seen on these players' helmets.

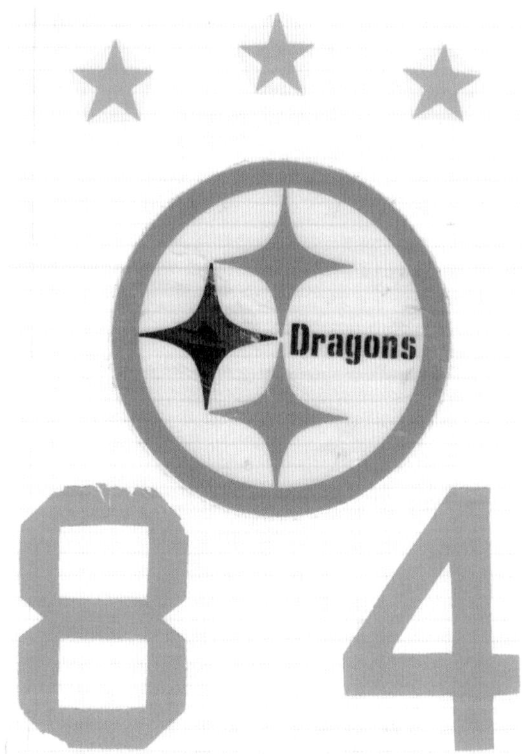

This Steelers-like decal decorated player Keith Fuller's freshman helmet in 1982. (Courtesy of Keith Fuller.)

The fire-breathing Dragon chewing up lightning bolts that Dragon fans are familiar with today first appeared in 1984. Matt Lafavers remembered hearing that Ledbetter got the logo "off a military WWII plane." Willingham remembered that (student) Shawn Lynch sketched the state of Texas around the mascot. The decal pictured here decorated Fuller's 1984 helmet. (Courtesy of Keith Fuller.)

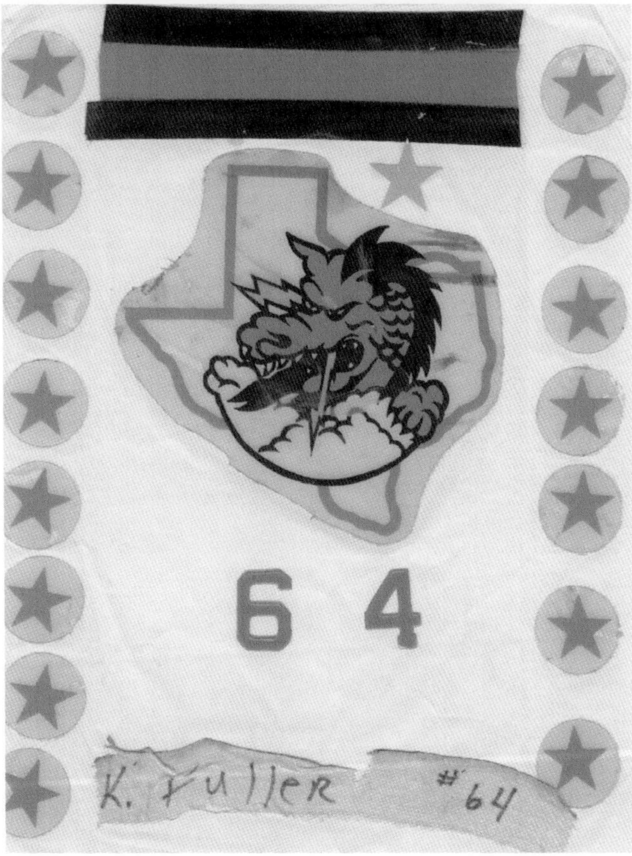

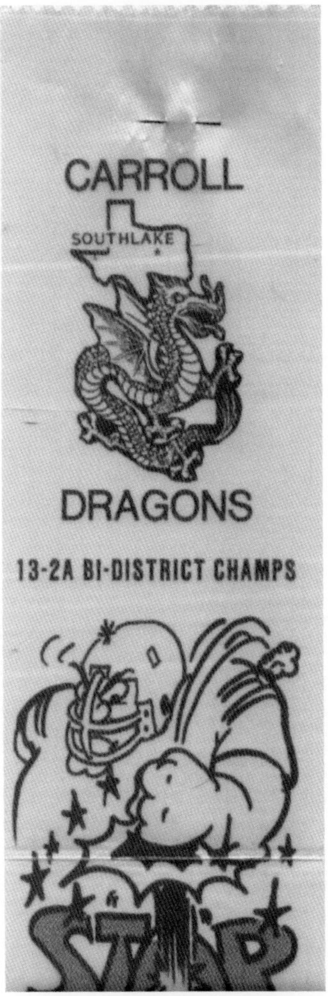

Spirit ribbons were worn by Texas high school students as far back as the 1940s, according to Joe Nick Patoski, author of *Texas High School Football: More Than a Game*. The spirit ribbon shown here is from the Dragons' first-ever playoff season, 1982. (Courtesy of Keith Fuller.)

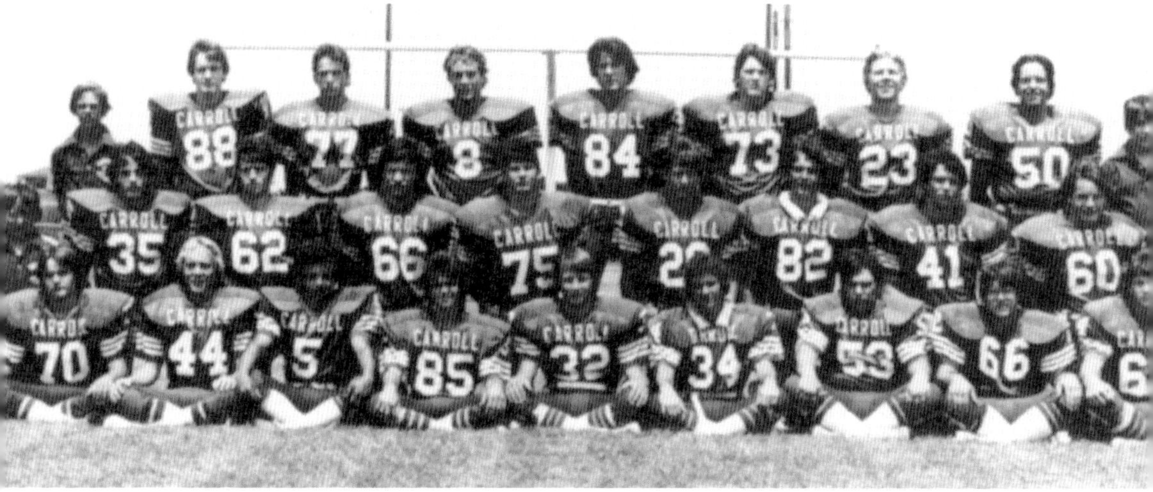

Players Keith Fuller and Lance "Booger" Hight remembered a team practice on TCU's Astroturf field in 1982 in preparation for the playoffs. "It was sub-freezing and the wind was blowing. It was like a wind tunnel," Fuller recalled. Hight continued: "We got new shoes and arm protectors. But Coach Ledbetter forgot all our coats and we froze." With a laugh, Fuller said, "Everybody decided they needed to go to the bathroom because it was in the gym and the heat was on in there." The Dragons made it to the third-round playoffs that year, losing to the Olney Wildcats. Team members are, from left to right, (first row) Lance Hight, Todd Ippolito, Randy Ritter, Jeff Massey, Mike Patterson, Donn Rider, Mike London, Larry Gossett, and Lance Wood; (second row) Randy Simpson, Keith Fuller, Tony Lemieux, Sean Talley, Kyle Vaughn, Tim Burgess, Dusty Rider, Jim Bell, Steve Hodges, and Shawn Massey; (third row) Greg Lewallen, James Stapleton, David Collier, Matt Lafavers, Tom Brittain, Tim Bock, Eddie Sutton, and John Venable.

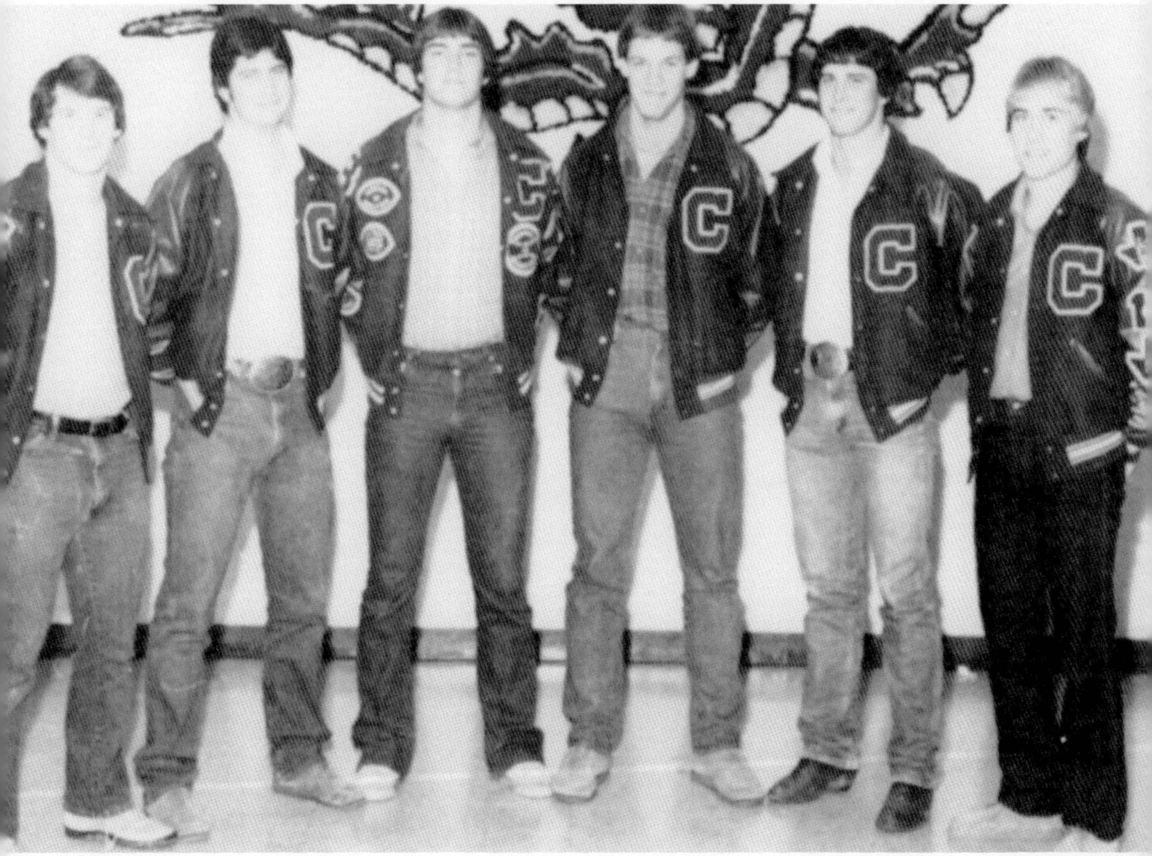

Like other small schools across the state, Carroll's football players were also on the basketball, baseball, and track teams. And some, like Tim Burgess, an All-District player seen here, second from the right, rode bulls. "He was one of the toughest kids in the whole school," John King said. Tim Bock remembered, "He was the first guy I've ever seen come to the sidelines with his helmet completely sideways. His nose was coming out the ear hole. Coach Willingham grabbed the facemask and 'thump,' straightened it back up." The other 1983 All-District players seen here with Burgess include, from left to right, Donn Rider, James Stapleton, Eddie Sutton, Tim Bock, and Steve Hodges. The players are standing in front of a handmade rug created by Carroll home economics teacher Norma Chambers in the late 1970s. Many of the sports photographs over the years were taken in front of this Dragon rug, and it now hangs in Dawson Middle School.

1985 Carroll Dragon Varsity

NO.	NAME	POSITION	CLASS	WEIGHT
5	Jim Noah	QB.DB	JR.	140
8	Frank Blanchard	QB.DE.	JR.	180
10	Matt Lafavers	E.DB.	SR.	185
17	Terry Branum	QB.DB.	JR.	165
20	Mitch Lower	E.DB.	SOPH.	170
23	Lance Wood	RB.DB.	SR.	140
28	Ricky Tambie	RB.DB.	SR.	145
30	Kyle Hendricks	RB.LB.	SOPH.	155
32	Gabe Hagar	RB.DB.	SR.	160
35	Randy Witt	RB.LB.	SR.	205
42	Lance Hight	RB.DB.	SR.	155
50	Chris Nottingham	C.DE.	SR.	175
53	Dusty Rider	T.LB.	SR.	190
54	Don Florence	C.N.	SOPH.	215
62	Aaron Gilmore	G.N.	SOPH.	225
64	Keith Fuller	G.DE.	SR.	185
66	Ryan Smith	G.LB.	JR.	155
68	Greg Tanner	T.T.	SOPH.	220
73	Steve Robinson	T.T.	SOPH.	225
74	Chris Uzzell	G.LB.	JR.	155
75	Dareyl Brunson	T.T.	SR.	280
76	Robbie Burgess	T.T.	SR.	190
78	Kyle Vaughn	T.LB.	SR.	170
82	Robert Dunbar	E.DE.	JR.	160
83	Scott Broadaway	E.DB.	SR.	175
85	Sammy Baker	E.DE.	SR.	175
86	Dirk Stammnitz	K.	SR.	160

Coaches — Bob Ledbetter, Ken Cook, Chauncey Willingham, Doug Edwards, Al Rushing, Steve Lineweaver, Tommy Walling, Mike Brown, Bobby Dudley and Ron Cullum.

Superintendent — Jack D. Johnson

Assistant Superintendent — John R. Lowrey

High School Principal — William R. Branum

Cheerleaders — Leah Patterson, Tracy Tanner, Becky Florence, Dorian Stacy Kim Jaroszewski and Karen Mayes.

Mascot — Kirk Massey

Band Director — Ronnie Behrends and Greg Walker

Cheerleader Sponsor — Lou Jane Cullum

Drill Team Sponsor — Melinda Norman and Sandy Nietenhoefer

Managers — Marcus Foreman and Brian Mikulencak

The 1985 line included four sophomores, each weighing in at 215 pounds or more, and three quarterbacks, Frank Blanchard, Jim Noah, and a new student in the district, Terry Branum. He was the son of former head coach Bill Branum, who had returned in 1982 as the Carroll High School principal. With the quarterbacks, the coaching staff saw the opportunity for more of a passing game. "We've always thought we should throw more at Carroll, but the right situations didn't arise in the past," Ledbetter said. "But we've got a big line this year and quarterbacks who can throw the ball, so we feel we have to pass more than ever." The Dragons finished the season 8-2. In the meantime, CISD continued to upgrade the athletic facilities with a new weight room, lights for the tennis courts, and improvements to the track including an all-weather surface. "We are expanding the potential for all sports at Carroll," Ledbetter said. (Courtesy of Keith Fuller.)

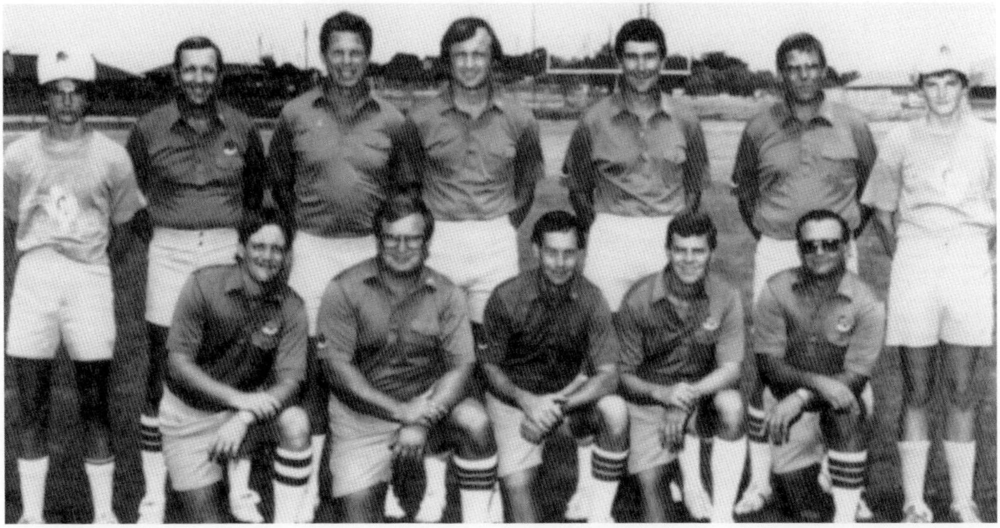

The 1985–1986 Carroll coaching staff included, from left to right, (kneeling) Bobby Dudley, Al Rushing, Ken Cook, Tommy Walling, and Ron Cullum; (standing) Marcus Foreman (manager), Mike Brown, Steve Lineweaver, Doug Edwards, Chauncey Willingham, Bob Ledbetter, and Brian Mikulencak (manager).

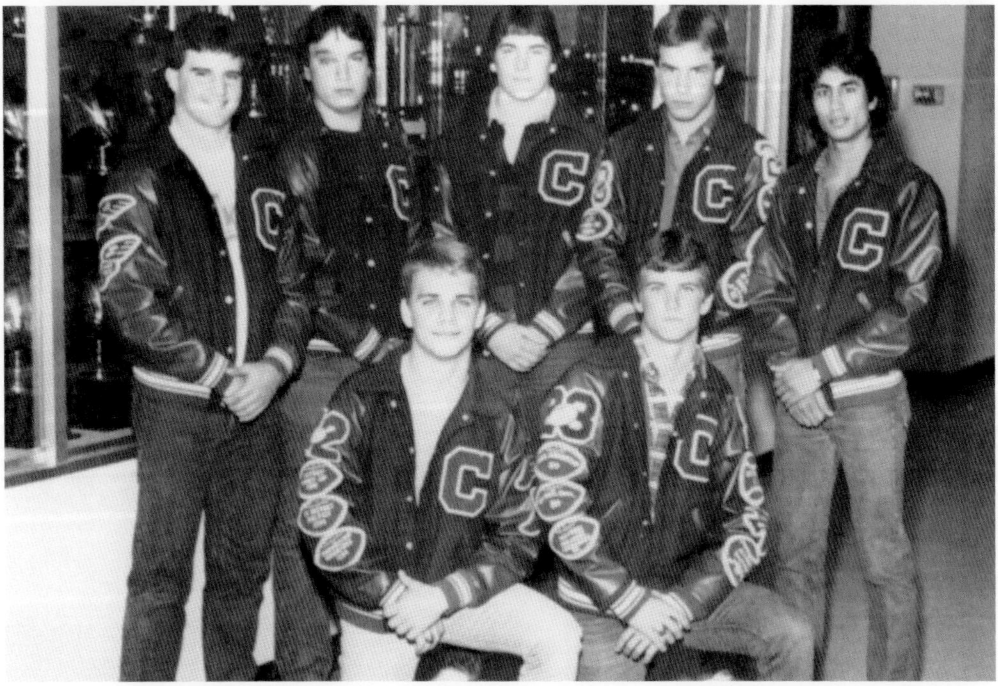

The Dragons moved up to Class 3A in 1986. *Dave Campbell's Texas Football* magazine called them a "contender" in district play. Ledbetter simply said, "We're going into 3A with a 3A program." The season ended 10-1 with a playoff win against Kennedale but a loss to Bonham in round two. Named All-District that year are, from left to right, (kneeling) Lance Hight and Lance Wood; (standing) Keith Fuller, Don Florence, Greg Tanner, Frank Blanchard, and Rickey Tambie.

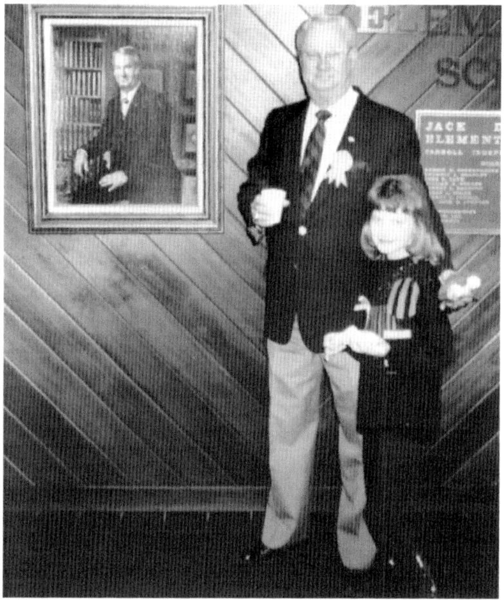

In 1986, CISD was recognized as one of the top-eight school districts in Texas. That same year, Jack Johnson retired after 30 years. "He had a burr haircut then, and now he styles his hair," Bob Rockenbaugh said. "That's the only difference from Jack Johnson then and now." John Lowrey was appointed his successor. Johnson and his granddaughter Mitzi celebrate Johnson Elementary's Grandparents Day in this photograph—she was the first of his grandchildren to attend the school. (Courtesy of the Johnson family.)

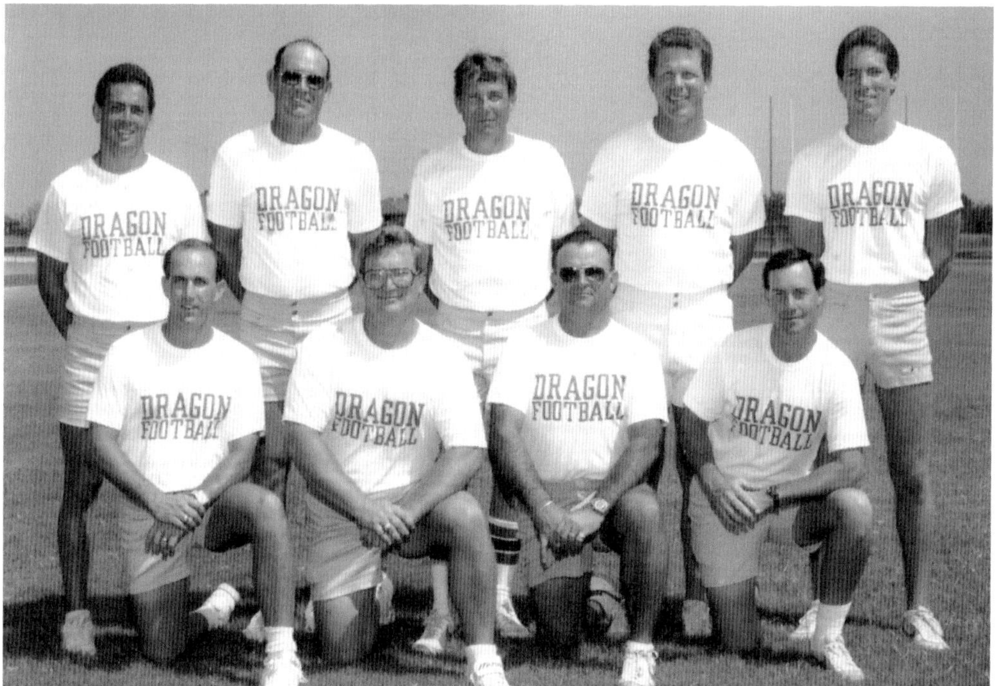

Changes to the coaching staff included new additions Fred Maples, Jim Cain, and Jeff Dixon. The responsibilities for each coach were changing as well. Offensive line coach Al Rushing "is like two coaches, he does so much," said Steve Lineweaver. Joel Berry took over the secondary, while Ken Cook continued as defensive coordinator and boys' head basketball coach. Seen here are, from left to right, (kneeling) Cain, Rushing, Cullum, and Cook; (standing) Dixon, Maples, Ledbetter, Lineweaver, and Berry.

The 1987 Dragons "could be one of the best teams we've ever had," Ledbetter told reporters before the season. Returning players in key positions on both offense and defense averaged 230 pounds. Senior kicker Don Florence put game-winning points on the scoreboard in several district games. Florence is seen here with teammate Phillip Wambsganss.

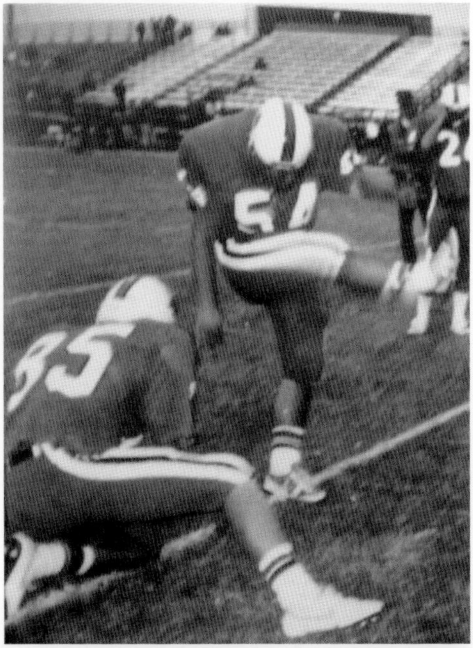

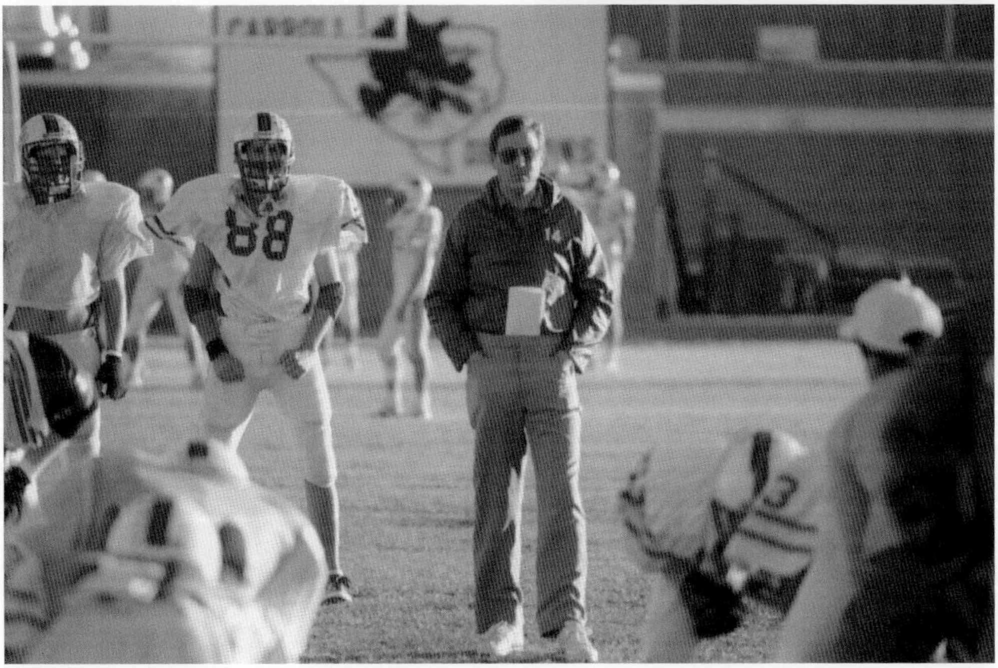

The season ended 10-0, and the No. 4 Dragons made it to the state semifinals for the first time in CISD history and played an unranked McGregor. Here, Ledbetter is running practice at Dragon Stadium in preparation for the game. Several former players recalled his tendency to tuck everything in, including his jacket. "He had the clipboard on one side and the laminated playsheet on the other," Keith Fuller remembered. (Courtesy of the *Fort Worth Star-Telegram* Collection, Special Collections, The University of Texas at Arlington Library, Arlington, Texas.)

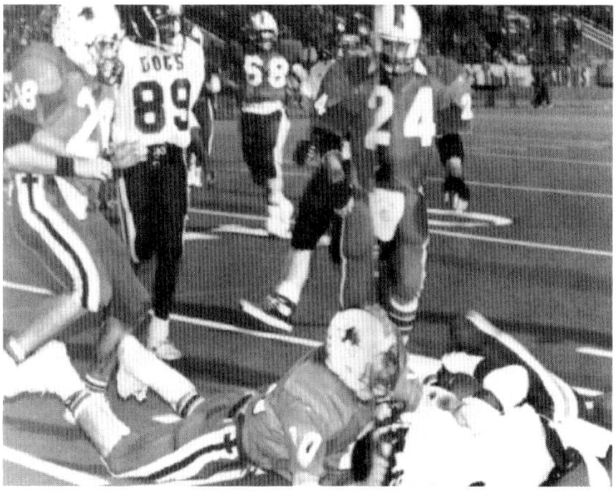

"It was a huge event," Keith Fuller said. "The whole town turned up for the bus rides, lined [Hwy.] 114, convoys of cars, headlights, horns honking." McGregor beat Carroll, 28-14. "We really thought we were going to win that one," Ken Cook said. "But you learn from it." Dragons looking on as Gary Bohnsack (No. 70) tackles a McGregor player are, from left to right, Wayne Walker (No. 28), Greg Tanner (No. 68), and Billy Garraty (No. 24).

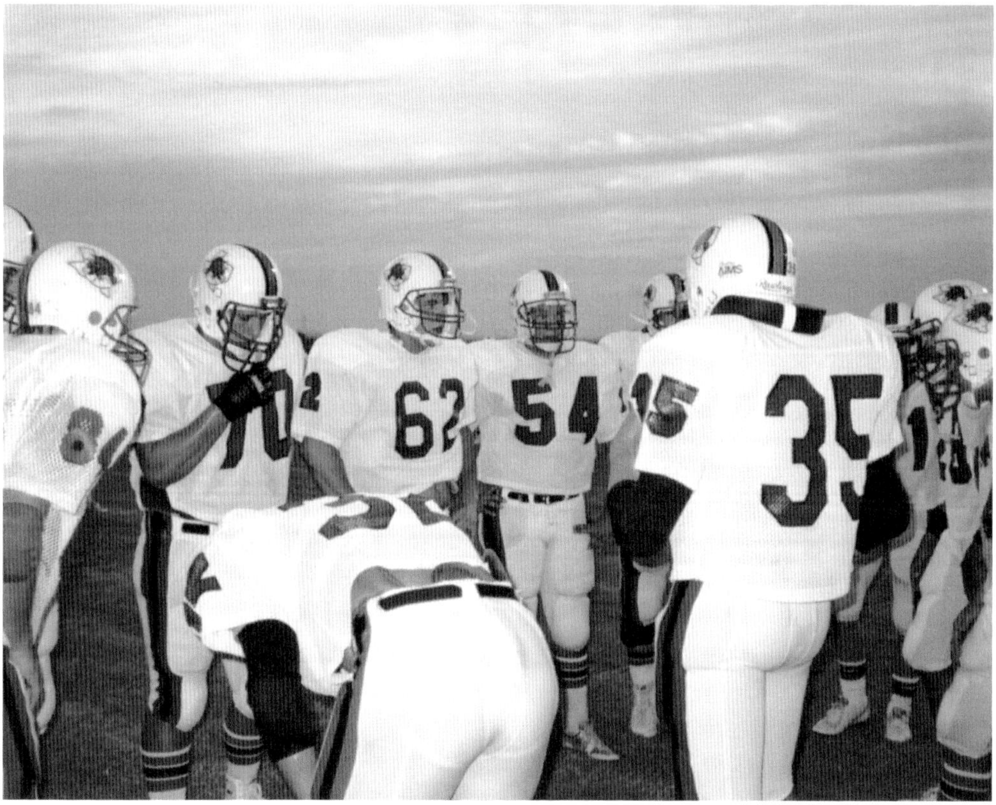

Ledbetter credited his assistants with taking the team further than any Carroll team before. "The coaching staff was very similar to the football team in their cohesiveness and the way they worked together," he said. But coaches and players would remember the loss and carry it forward. These 1987 Dragons are at a late-afternoon practice.

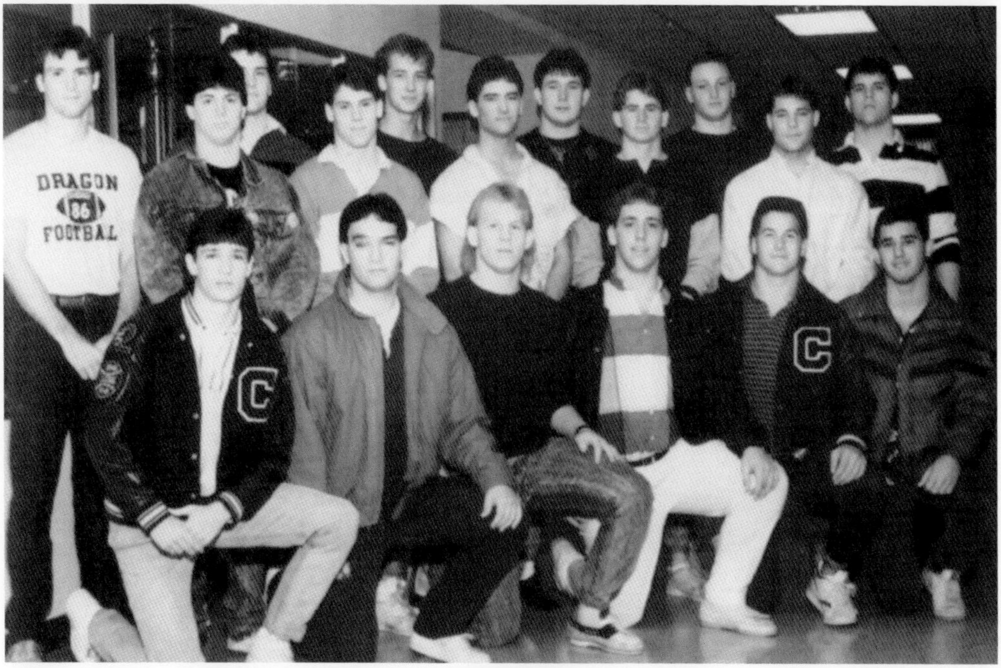

Five seniors received some sort of college scholarship in 1987, "signings which would have been good even for a 5A school," wrote one local sportswriter. The All-District players that year included, from left to right, (first row) Wayne Walker, Don Florence, Mike Riedel, Gary Bohnsack, David Blanchard, and Ronnie Cardwell; (second row) Billy Garraty, Mike Uldrich, Bryan Powell, Thomas Noah, and Ben Foster; (third row) Kyle Burns, Greg Tanner, Brad Bell, Steve Robinson, Marty Dunbar, and Aaron Gilmore.

David Blanchard (No. 32) "was the first big hoss," Booger Hight remembered. Ledbetter told the following story recently about fullback Blanchard, who wanted to be an I-back: "I sat David down and told him, 'David, we're fixing to design an offense around you. You're gonna be the I-back. You're still gonna line up right here, but this is gonna be called the I-back.' To this day, David Blanchard thinks he was the I-back at Carroll. But he rushed for 2,000 yards as a fullback."

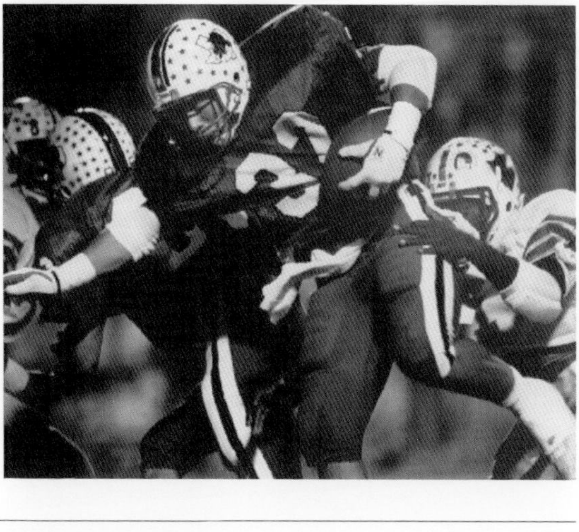

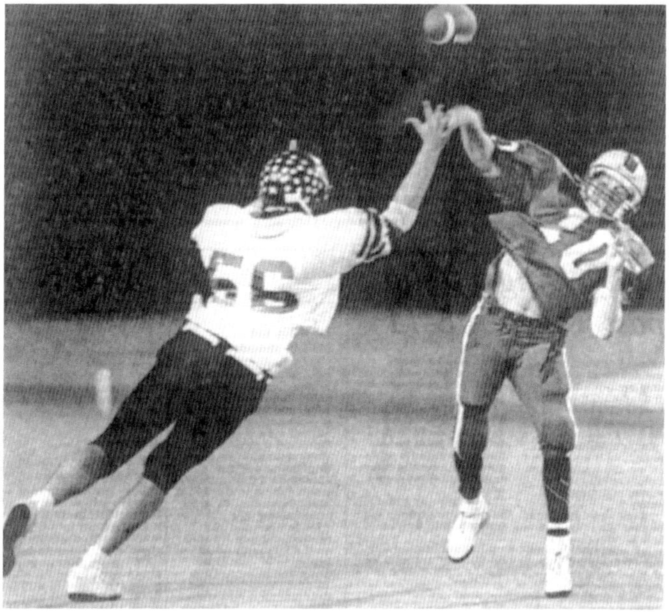

Senior quarterback Mike Uldrich "emerged as a great quarterback," one sportswriter wrote that season. Lineweaver agreed and said, "We knew Mike could pass, so we went out and worked very hard on our passing game." Uldrich was the first Carroll quarterback to break 1,000 yards passing. He is seen here releasing a pass in a win over Commerce. In 1988, for the first time, the Dragons finished with a perfect 16-0 season.

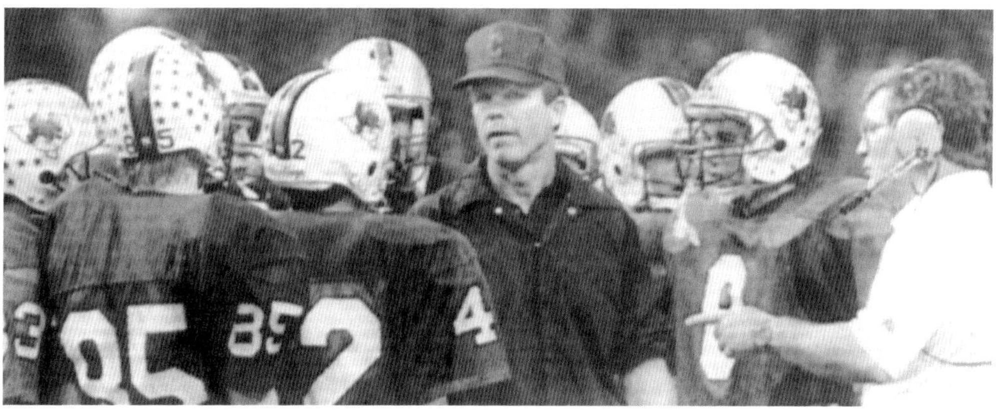

The Dragons blew out their playoff opponents, including handing third-round team Daingerfield their biggest loss in seven years. Steve Lineweaver brought a new style to the Ledbetter wishbone offense that "opened it up. We'd never pitched it inside the 20 or outside the 20, always in the middle of the field. We started getting a little more aggressive," Ken Cook said recently. Here, Lineweaver and Al Rushing gather their special teams players on the sidelines at the state quarterfinal game against Wills Point.

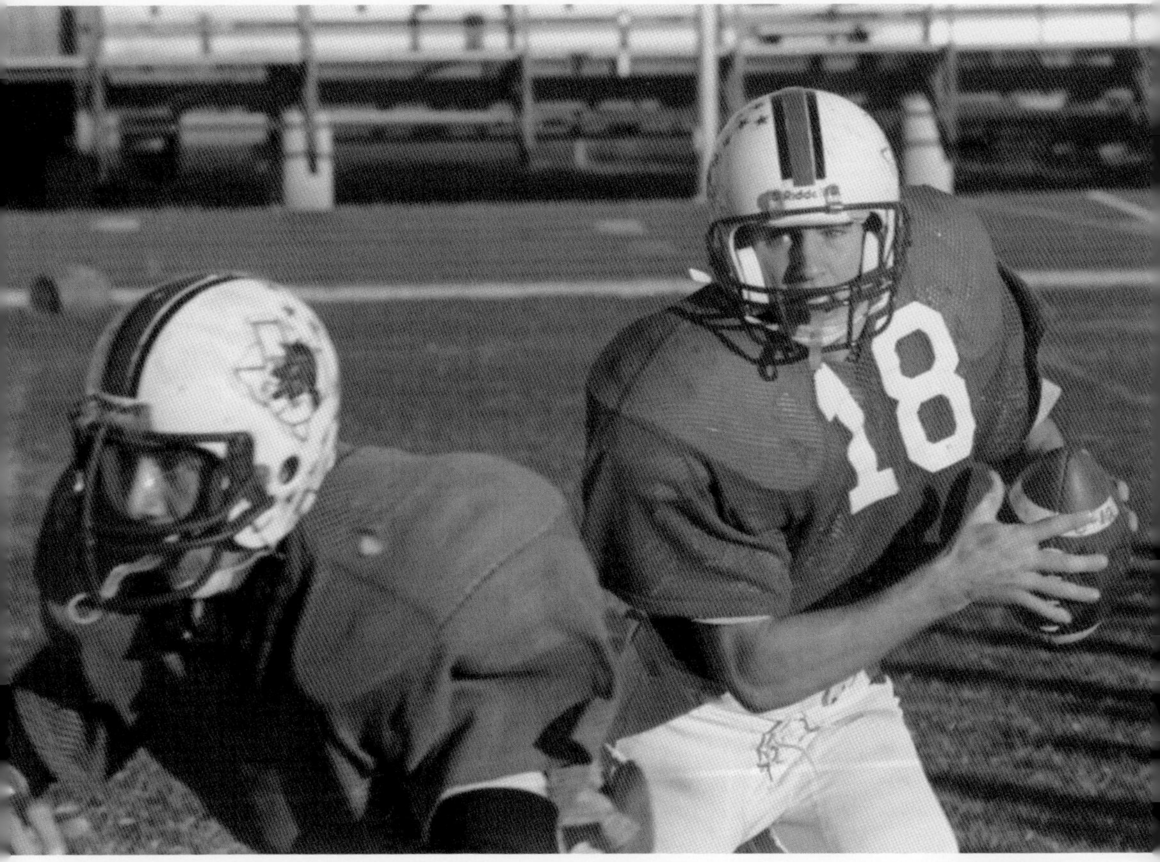

After a Dragon win over Decatur to capture the state semifinals, one local newspaper headline read, "Dragon Nation is State Bound." Carroll fans filled up six 48-passenger buses, arranged by Texas National Bank, for the caravan to the final game with Navasota in Waco's Floyd Casey Stadium. Signs cheering on the Dragons dotted FM 1709, with perhaps the most well known asking, "The last person out of town, please turn out the lights." Quarterback Uldrich is shown in this 1988 photograph taking practice before the state final game. (Courtesy of the *Fort Worth Star-Telegram* Collection, Special Collections, The University of Texas at Arlington Library, Arlington, Texas.)

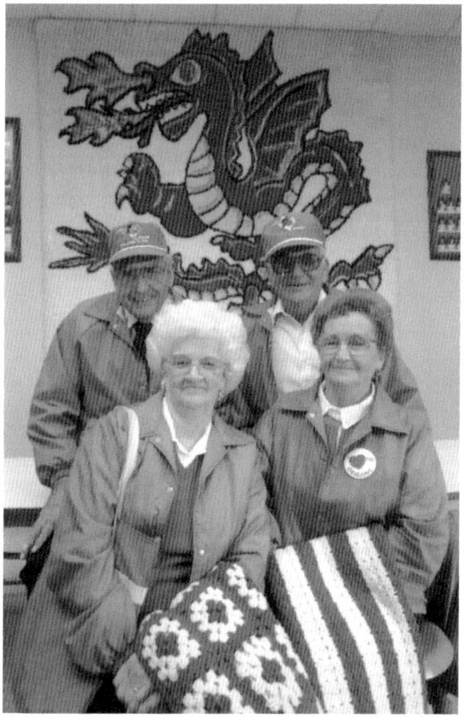

Longtime residents Crystal and Bob Steele (left) and Lou Etta (Joyce) and Chock McPherson were part of the loyal Dragon Nation and seldom missed a Carroll sporting event. Lou Etta and Chock McPherson's families date to the area's settling in the mid-1840s, and the couple began first grade in the original three-room Carroll School. (Courtesy of the *Fort Worth Star-Telegram* Collection, Special Collections, The University of Texas at Arlington Library, Arlington, Texas.)

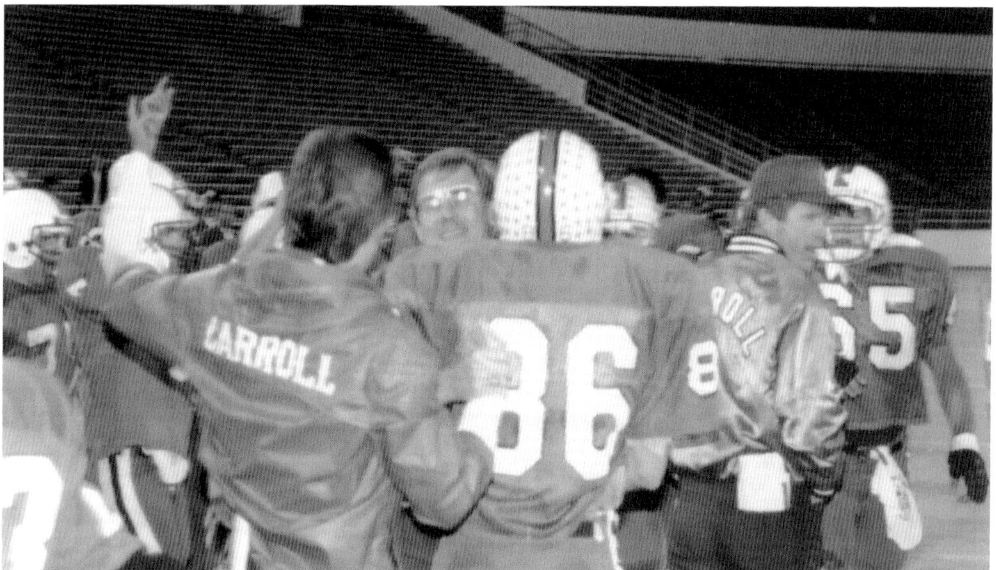

In the 1988 state title game, the Dragons dominated the Navasota Rattlers with "a balanced backfield," wrote *Grapevine Sun* sports editor Mike Heika. Another sportswriter summed it up as follows: "Carroll's success was what amounted to a drastically different offensive plan and a slightly different defensive scheme along with the players' field intelligence. Coaches said this group really grasped the purpose of what a technique or different formation was supposed to achieve." Here, coaches Bob Ledbetter and Steve Lineweaver celebrate the state win with team members.

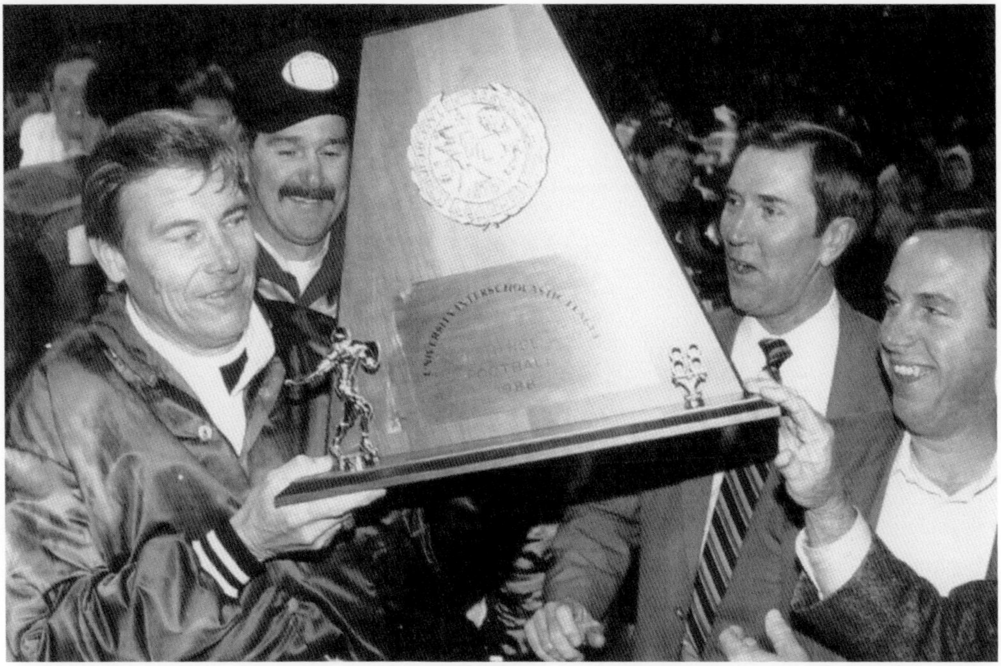

The 1988 season was one for the CISD record books. Sharing the moment with Ledbetter as he holds the 1988 3A Football Championship trophy are, from left to right, Chauncey Willingham, John Lowrey, and Bill Branum.

"What began as a year many figured would be OK, finished as the best football season in Carroll High School history," one sportswriter wrote. "Had you asked at the beginning of the year, there probably weren't many who would have predicted a state championship and a 16-0 record in 1988." No matter the predictions, these Dragons are happy with the outcome.

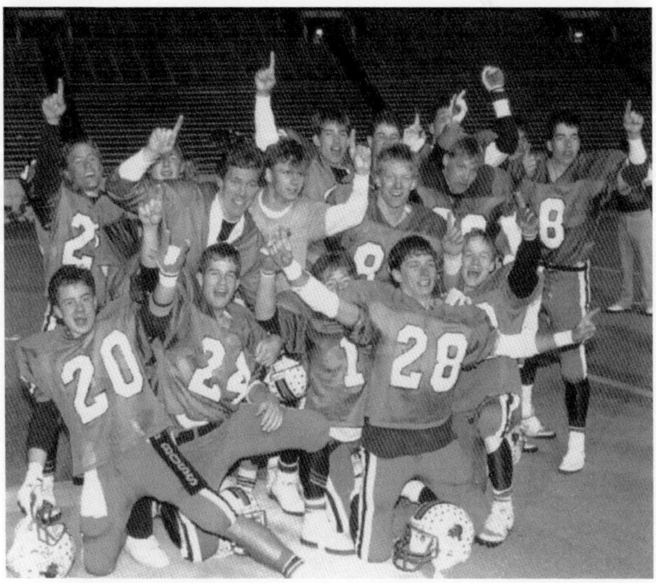

STATE

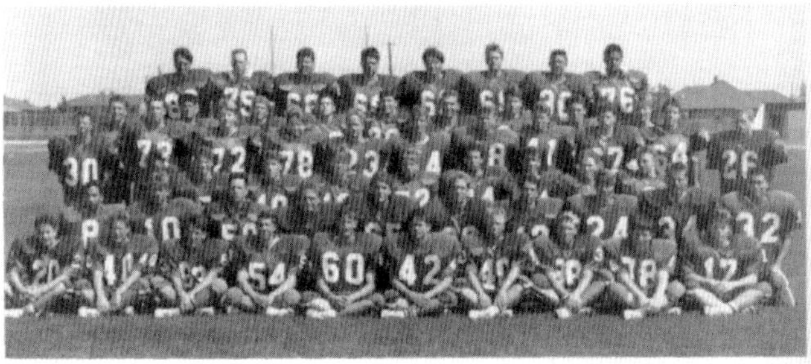

CHAMPS

Other 1988–1989 Carroll athletic teams went on to win or tie for district championships in every sport that year. A parade was planned to honor the team. "However," said longtime Dragon fan and Councilman Rick Stacy, "we don't have a place to hold it, and everyone is involved, so we wouldn't have anyone to watch it."

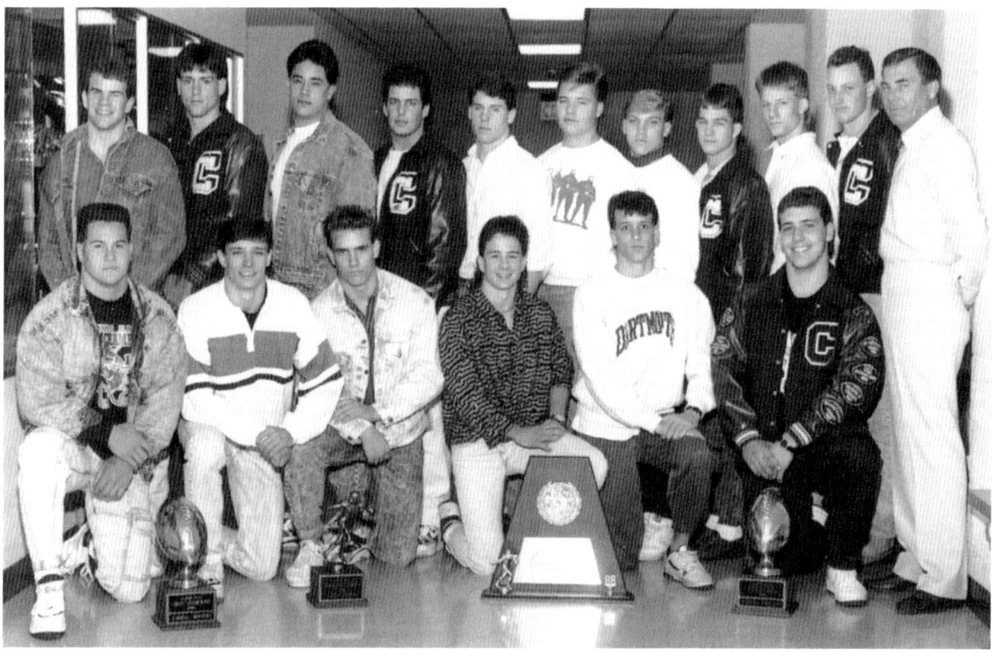

The 1988 All-District players included, from left to right, (kneeling) David Blanchard, Wayne Walker, Bret Maloney, Jason Skinner, David Hackett, and Gary Bohnsack; (standing) Colby Hoefar, Kyle Burns, Brent Reneau, James Martin, Mike Uldrich, Ellis Howard, Donnnie Thaden, J. Myatt, Brad Jacobs, Marty Dunbar, and Ledbetter.

The 1989 coaching staff included, from left to right, (kneeling) Tom Rapp, Jeff Dixon, Ron Cullum, and Al Rushing; (standing) Bob Ledbetter, Steve Lineweaver, Fred Maples, Joel Berry, and Ken Cook.

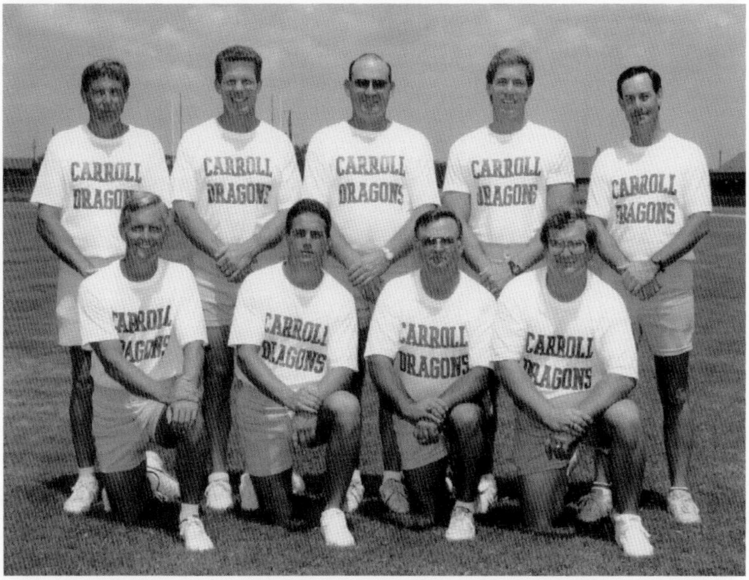

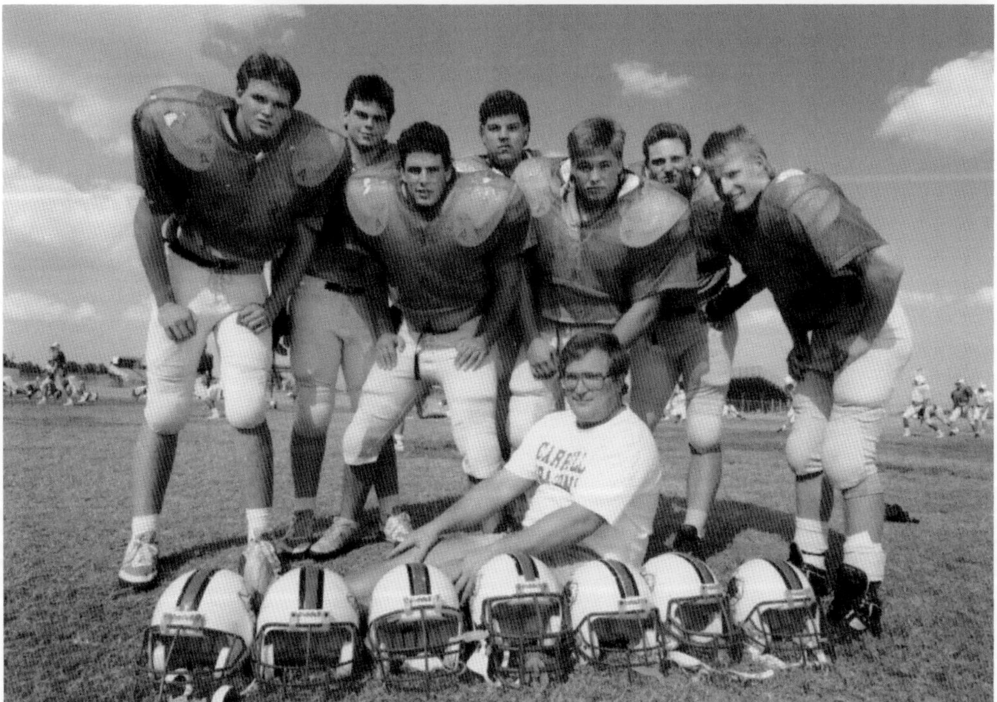

Al Rushing, according to Ledbetter, had a gift. "He took such a great interest in those kids. He would get to the field house at 5 in the morning and was the last one to leave." Rushing is surrounded by his 1989 Dragon line, from left to right, John Kothman, Kevin Holmes, James Martin, Brandon Murdoch, Ellis Howard, Marty Dunbar, and Brad Jacobs. (Courtesy of the *Fort Worth Star-Telegram* Collection, Special Collections, The University of Texas at Arlington Library, Arlington, Texas.)

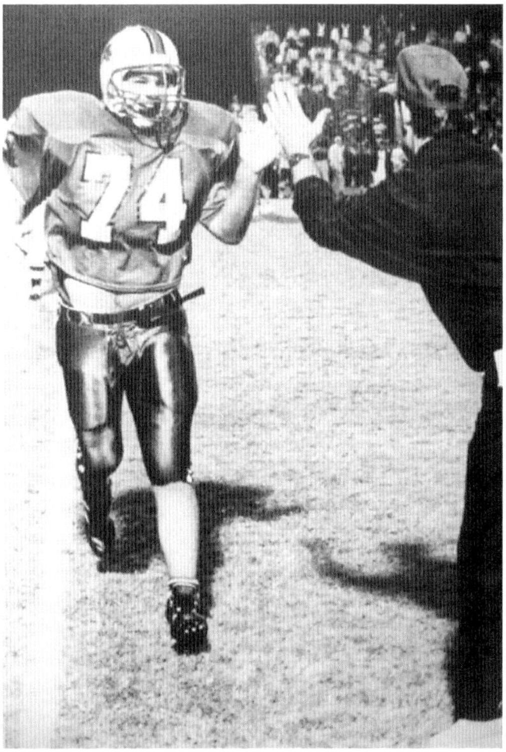

The 1989 season ended 10-0, and the Dragons beat Alvarado in first-round playoffs. But a loss to Daingerfield ended further playoff hopes. Coming off the field during a game that season, sophomore Eddie Pinson gets an "attaboy" from Coach Cook.

The 1989 Dragons made it all the way to the state semifinals but lost to Vernon. Pictured here are defensemen Ellis Howard (No. 78) and, behind him, Brian Summers (No. 5) during the Vernon game.

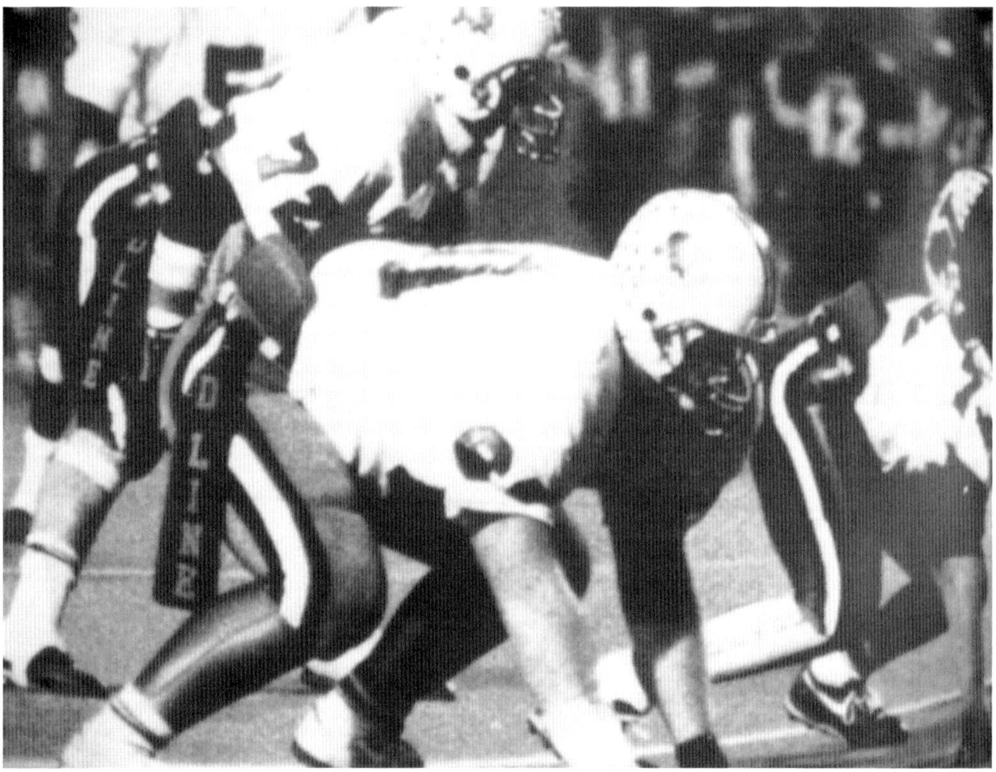

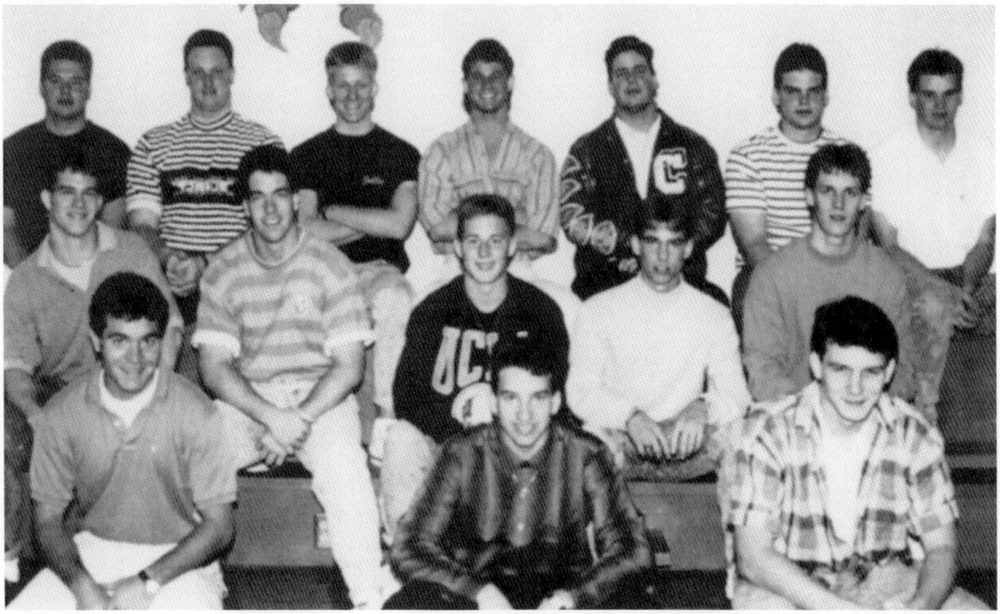

All-District players that year included, from left to right, (first row) Jason Fernandez, Scott Adams, and Bo Renshaw; (second row) Jeff Myatt, Jason Myatt, Shane Rodgers, Todd Strickland, and Brandon Sisco; (third row) Ellis Howard, Marty Dunbar, Brad Jacobs, Craig Nimphius, James Martin, Kevin Holmes, and John Kothmann.

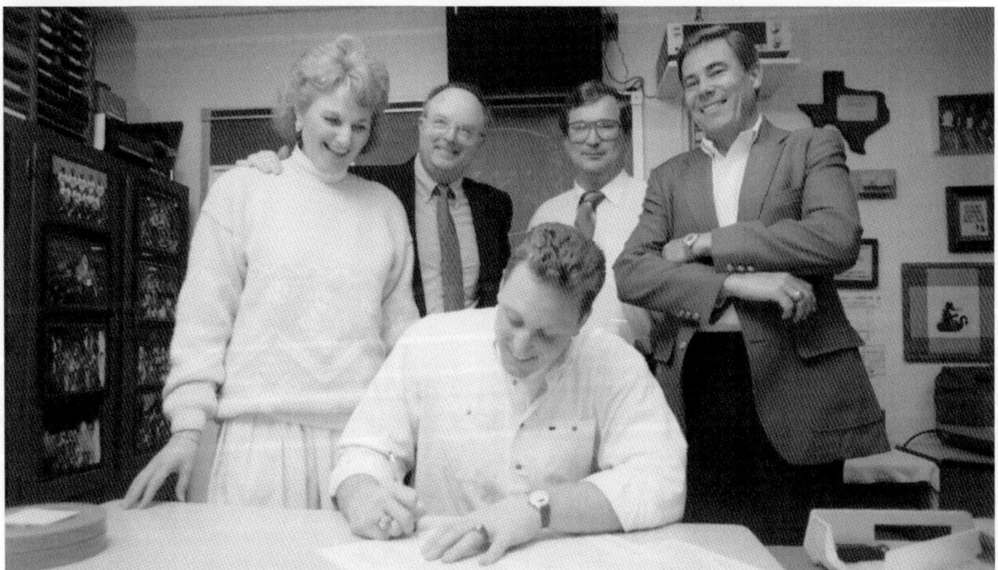

Senior Marty Dunbar was Carroll's first Division I college football recruit. "I take pride in that, and I'm sure there are going to be more after me," said the 250-pound lineman, who signed with Baylor. Looking on as their son makes it official are Bobbi and Martin Dunbar, accompanied by Coach Rushing and Coach Ledbetter. (Courtesy of the *Fort Worth Star-Telegram* Collection, Special Collections, The University of Texas at Arlington Library, Arlington, Texas.)

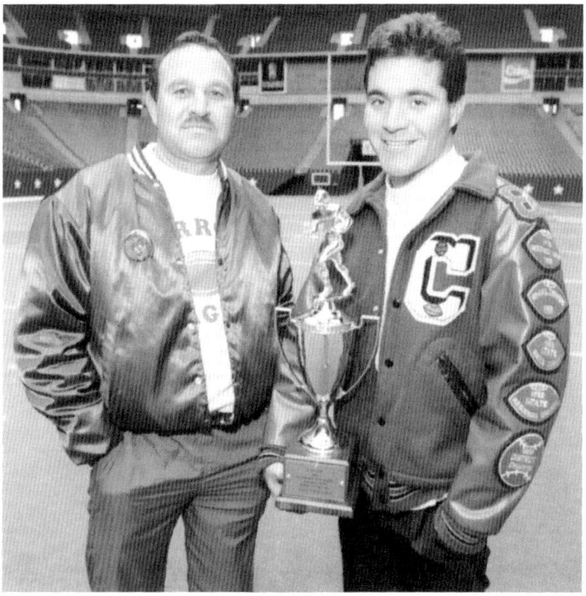

The first national media attention given to Dragon football may have been in 1990 when senior kicker Jason Fernandez was named Co-Player of the Year on *Parade* magazine's All-America High School Football Team. The kicker set a national high school career kicking record and went on to play for Northwestern State University in Louisiana. He and his father are seen here in 1990 in Texas Stadium. (Courtesy of the *Fort Worth Star-Telegram* Collection, Special Collections, The University of Texas at Arlington Library, Arlington, Texas.)

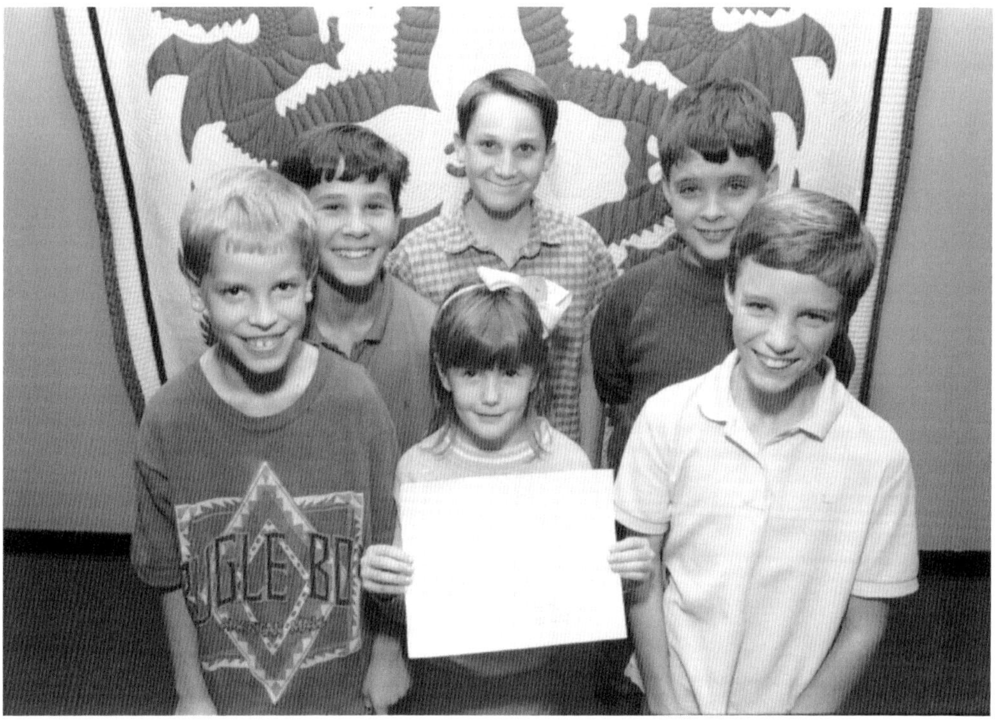

These young Dragons were highlighted in a 1990 *Fort Worth Star-Telegram* article titled, "Dragon Fever Infects Hallways at Johnson." Fifth-graders, from left to right, Shaun Neely, Kyle Blanco, Tyson Olivo, Brien Cardinal, and Andy Kopp encircle a younger Katie Willingham, the daughter of Patty and Chauncey Willingham. Katie is holding a poem the boys wrote that celebrated the Dragon football team. (Courtesy of the *Fort Worth Star-Telegram* Collection, Special Collections, The University of Texas at Arlington Library, Arlington, Texas.)

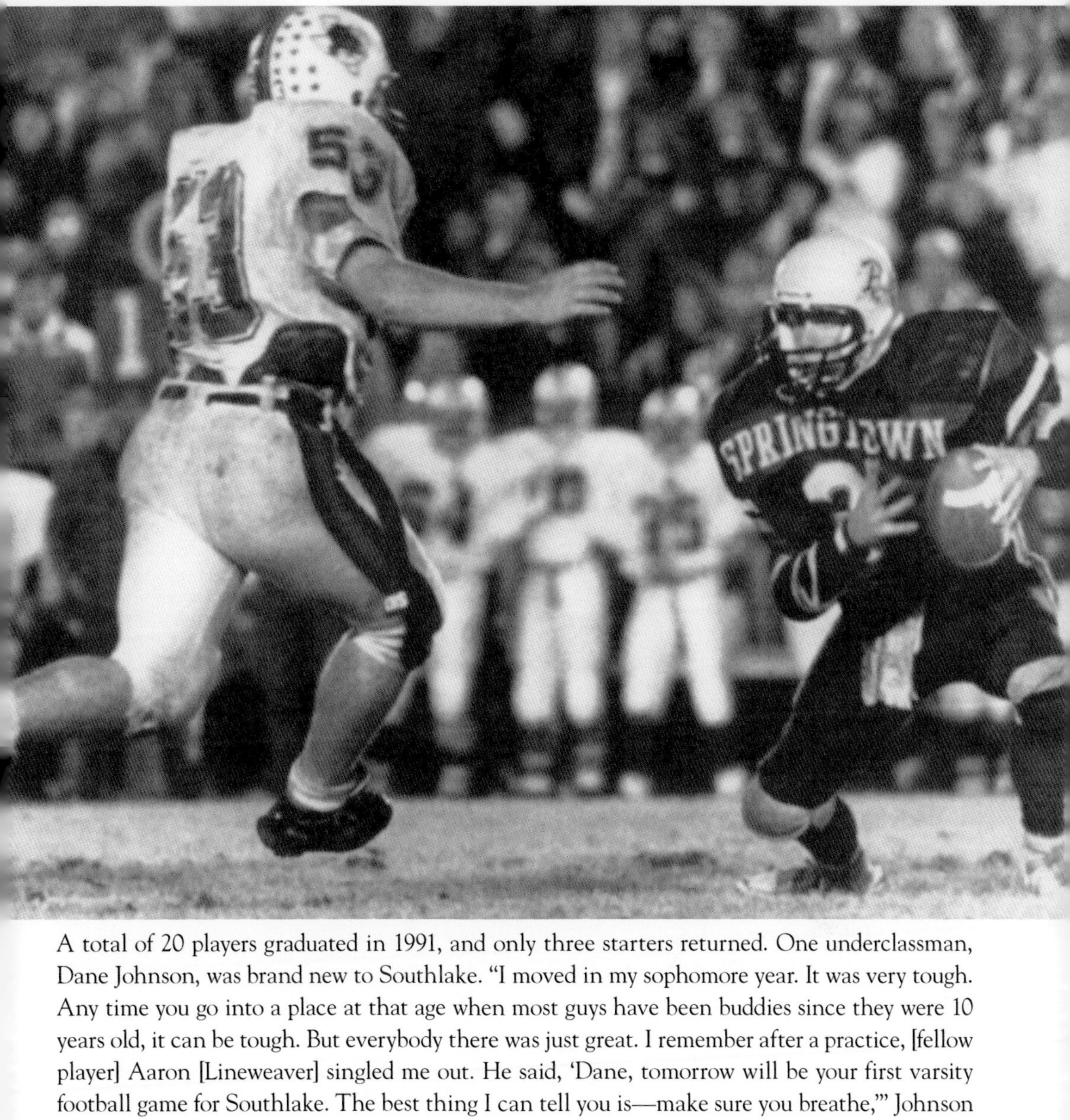

A total of 20 players graduated in 1991, and only three starters returned. One underclassman, Dane Johnson, was brand new to Southlake. "I moved in my sophomore year. It was very tough. Any time you go into a place at that age when most guys have been buddies since they were 10 years old, it can be tough. But everybody there was just great. I remember after a practice, [fellow player] Aaron [Lineweaver] singled me out. He said, 'Dane, tomorrow will be your first varsity football game for Southlake. The best thing I can tell you is—make sure you breathe,'" Johnson said with a laugh. "I remember how hard it was to breathe that first year." One of the returning starters, Todd Story, is seen here barreling toward a Springtown player.

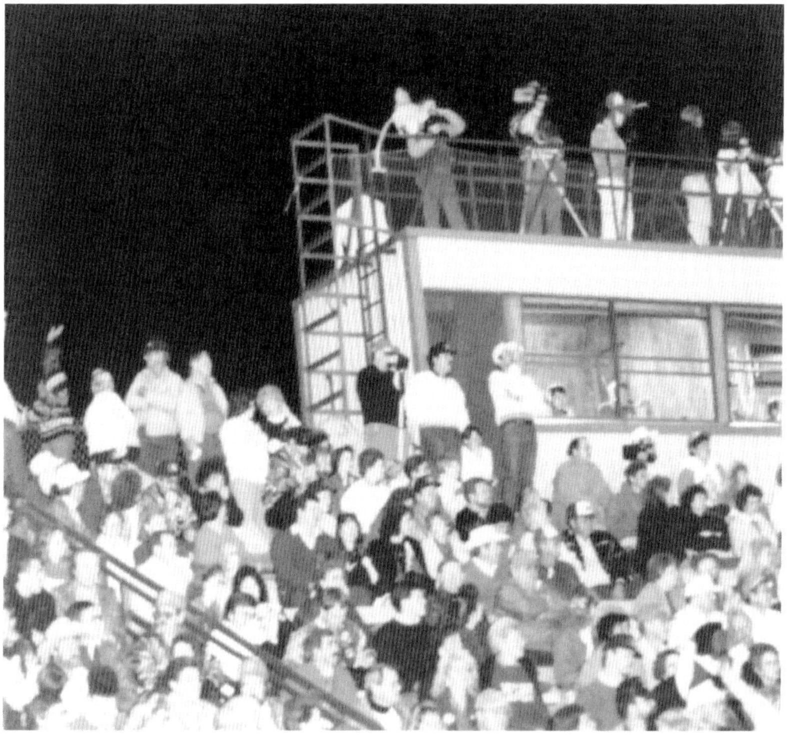

Longtime fans remember the overflow crowds in Dragon Stadium, built in 1981 to accommodate 2,970 fans. End zone bleachers were added, but with regular sellout attendance now at 4,500, the state-champion Dragons were outgrowing their home field.

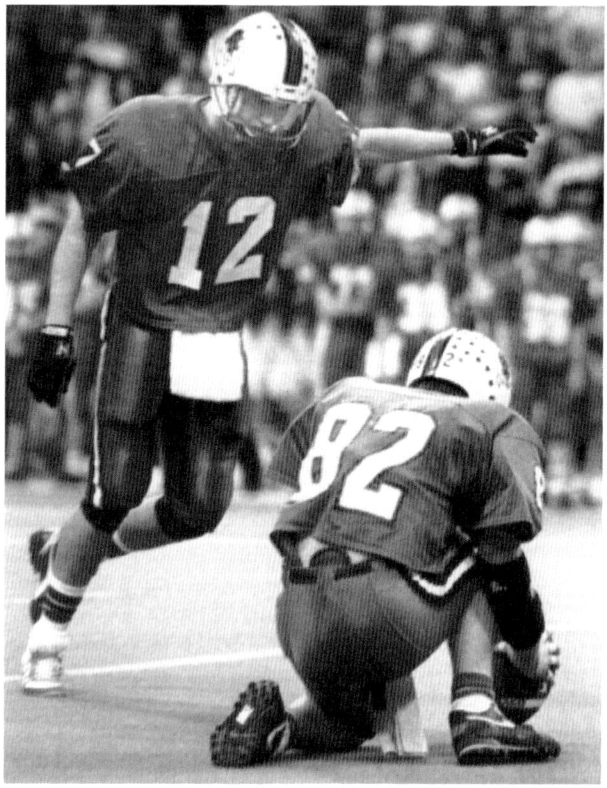

At the half in the last game of the 1991 season, the Dragons led Diamond Hill-Jarvis, 40-0. The coaches agreed to let the clock run out uninterrupted. By the end of the game, the Dragons had scored seven touchdowns, one safety, and a 40-yard field goal by kicker Jeff Graham. The final score of 54-0 secured a 10-0 season, the Dragons' fifth consecutive district title, and the sixth consecutive year to go to state playoffs. Graham prepares to kick while Aaron Lineweaver holds the ball.

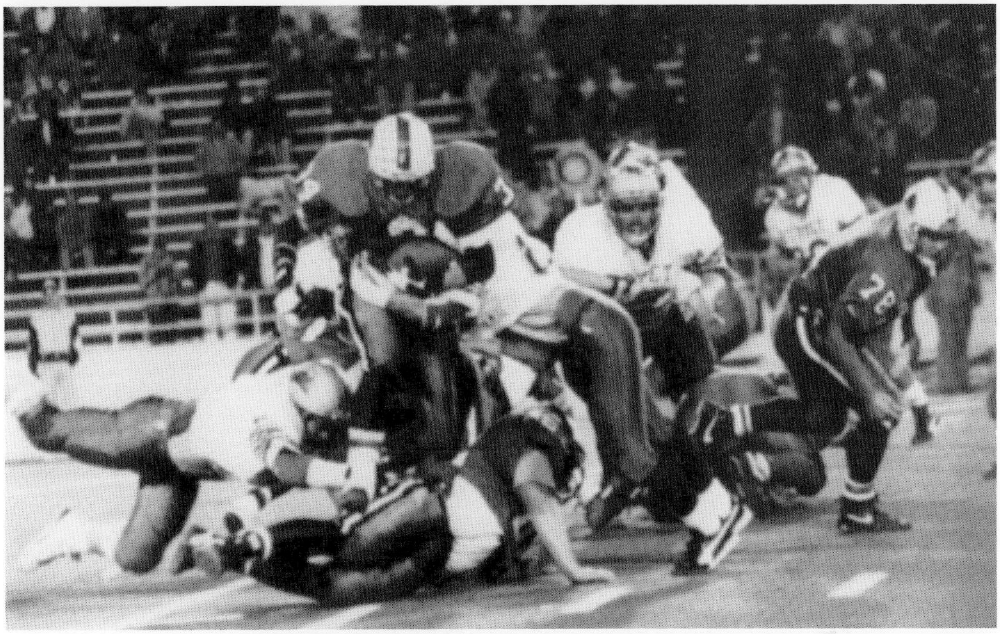

The 1991 Dragons "are seemingly headed toward a state championship," one sportswriter wrote. The semifinal game against the Burnet Bulldogs ended in a 7-7 tie, and Burnet advanced to the finals on penetrations. "We just couldn't believe it," Steve Lineweaver said later. "As soon as that game was over, we started breaking down the film to see how we could only score seven points. And we started working on not letting it happen again." Here, running back Phil Taylor pushes past Burnet defenders.

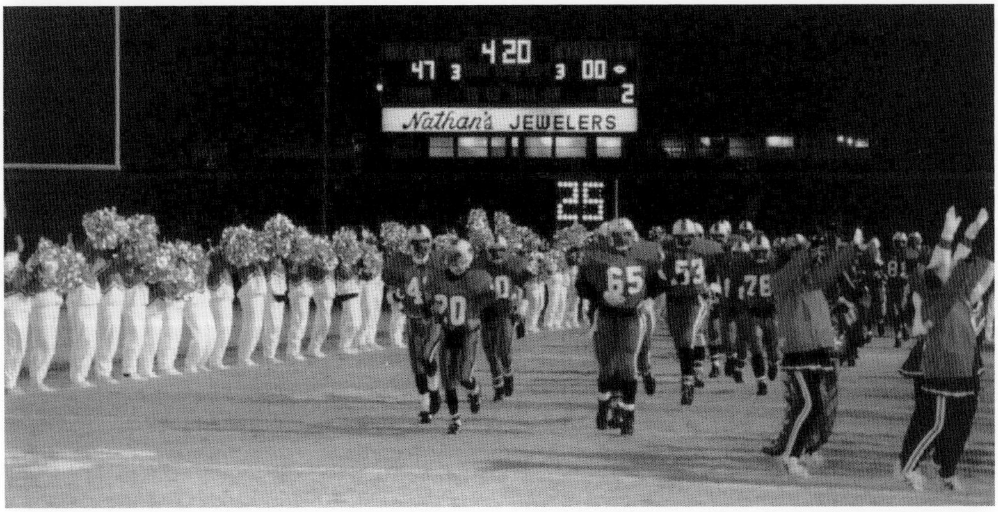

Expectations were high for the 1992 Dragons, seen here. The team won their 54th-consecutive regular season game, breaking a record set in the 1970s. The regular season ended a perfect 10-0, and it was off to the playoffs for the seventh year in a row. In the third-round playoff game that year, No. 1-ranked Carroll played No. 2-ranked Vernon at Pennington Field in Bedford. The event was electric and, many say, one of the most memorable of Texas high school football games.

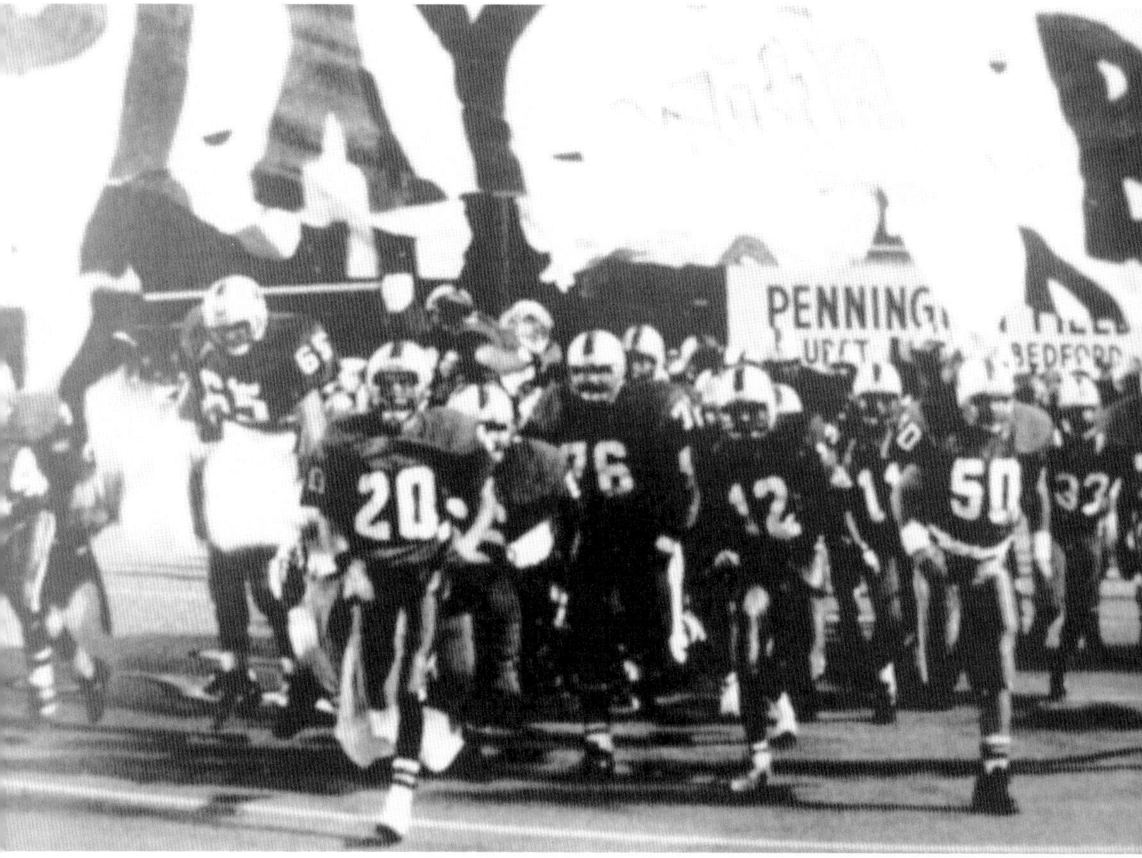

"I remember the game very well," said Dane Johnson. "My junior year. We had a lot of really good players. So did they. It was one of those games that just lived up to its billing. It was No. 1 versus No. 2. Everybody wanted to see it. It was packed. I had buddies that were paid hundreds of dollars to throw people over the wall so they could get into the game. The sideline was full, the end zone was full, they were all around. [Estimates put the crowd at 14,500.] First row would be sitting on their butts, second row would be on their knees, and the rest of them would be standing up." In this photograph from the game, the Dragons bust through their banner. (Photograph by Shawn Nance.)

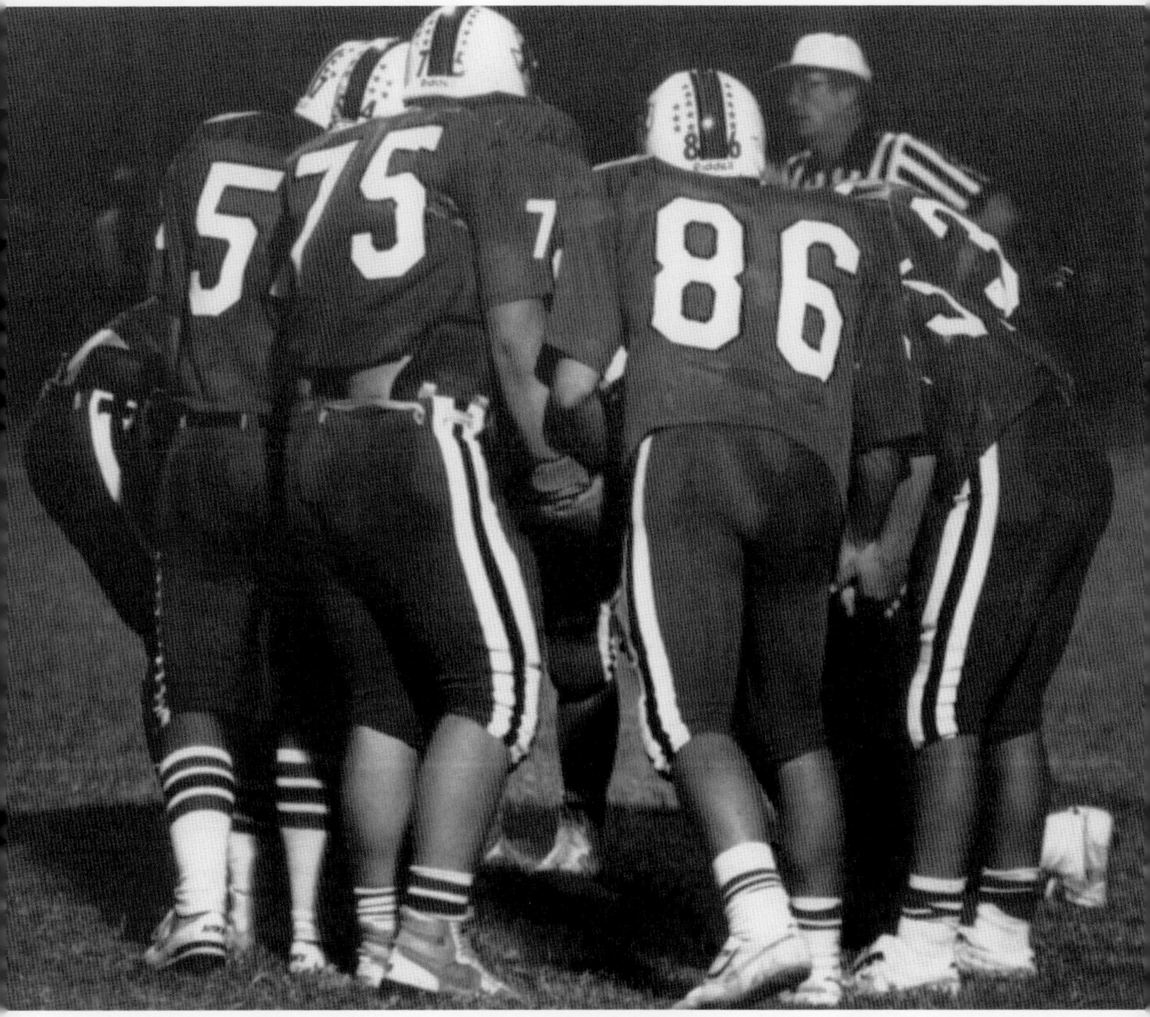

"Coach [Leo] Brittain [the Vernon coach] and I have talked about this [game] many times," Ledbetter said in 2004. "It was a very volatile situation. Vernon was a football team that taunted a lot. They did a lot of things that we didn't allow. As we came out of the dressing room that night, we couldn't get to the field because of people sitting all around. Finally, we got the police escorts to get us on the field. [After the game] as I walked over to Leo, I said, 'You know, Leo, we just witnessed one heck of a game.' We knew it was almost a state championship game because two years before we lost in Vernon [1990 semifinals] and they went on to win it [the state title]. The thing I remember the most was when that game started, there was not any taunting [but] there was some hitting—there was a lot of that. It was a tough physical football game [between] two teams, two schools with kids that respected each other." The Dragons, seen here in a huddle, prevailed 39-35.

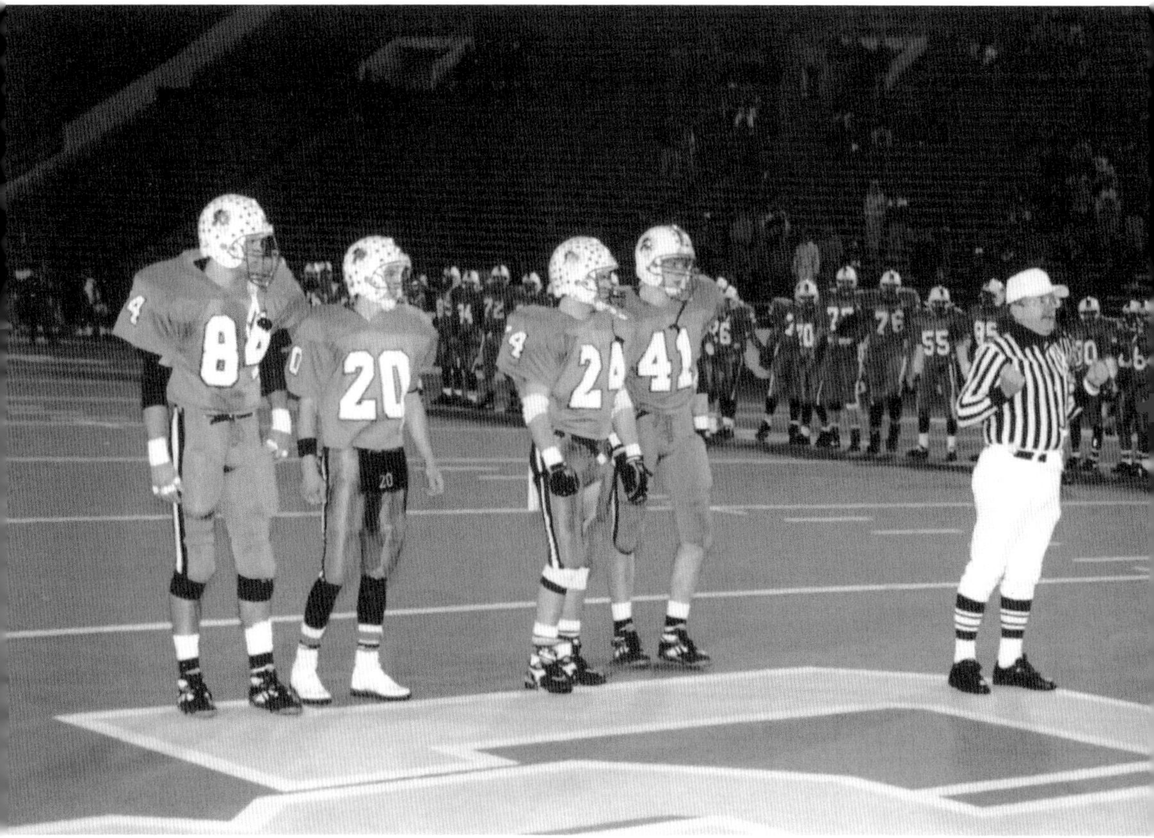

"We've had some great players who have gone on and played in college," Ledbetter recalled of the 1992 team. "But then there was Will Mantooth." When Mantooth, who competed in rodeos riding bulls, made the team as a sophomore two years earlier, Ledbetter called him into the field house and sat him down. "Will, you've got a chance to play as a wide receiver," said the coach. "So I'm going to move you to wide receiver and maybe by your junior year you'll have a chance to start. Will said, 'But, Coach, I want to play quarterback.'" Ledbetter told Mantooth that his chances of ever playing quarterback were "slim to none." "But we could see he had ability. He was the smallest kid on that football team. And during 2-a-days, Will began to pick it up," Ledbetter said. Mantooth made quarterback his junior year. The 1992 co-captains, seen here before the state final game, from left to right, are Mark Herron, Mantooth, Stephen Moreland, and Jeff Croy.

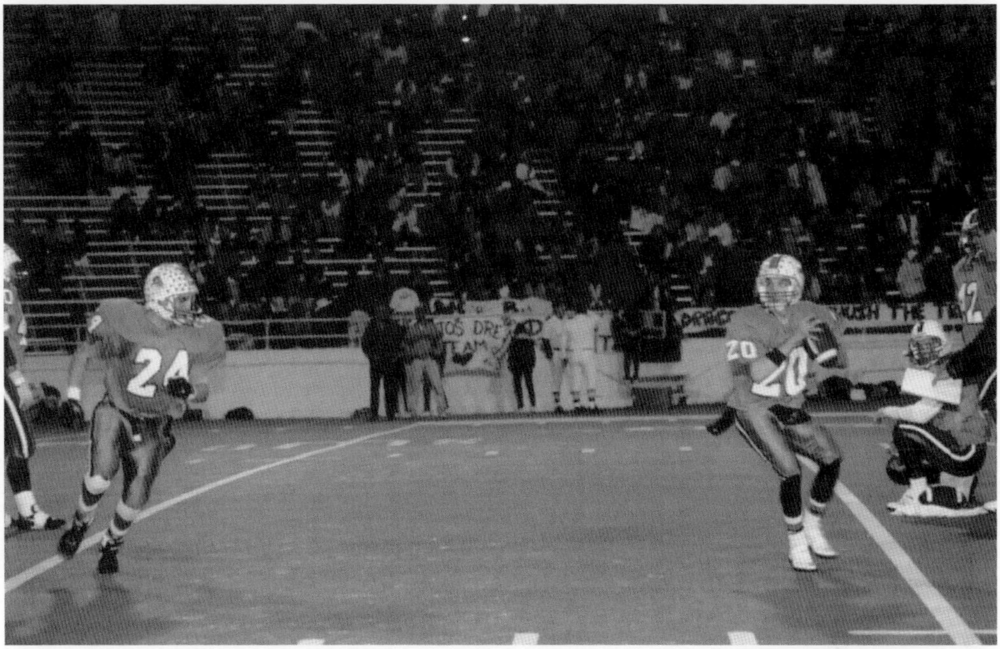

"The point of that story," continued Ledbetter, "is that nobody—not even us—believed in Will, other than Will believing in himself. At the end of the year, I met with Will and we talked. When he got up and started out of the office, he turned around and said, 'Coach, slim to none, huh?'" Here, Mantooth (No. 20) prepares to make a pass in the 1992 state final game against Coldspring.

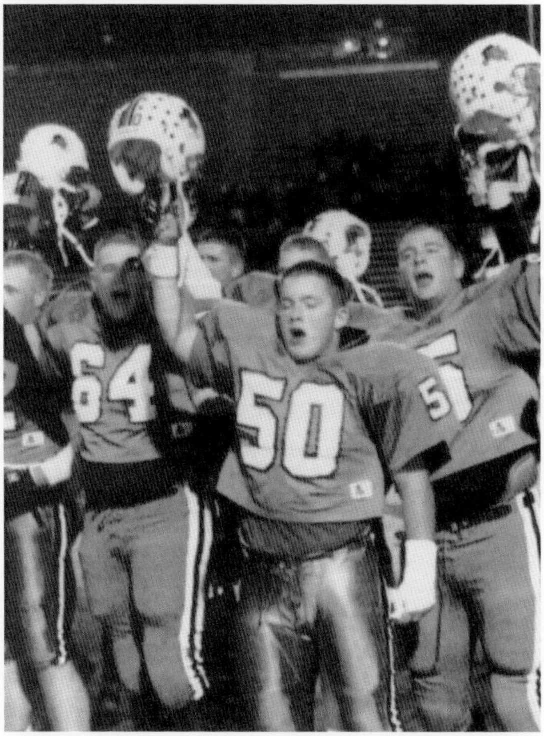

"That '92 team," Dane Johnson recalled, "was a fast-paced, very explosive, high-octane team." They averaged 50 points per game. Vernon coach Brittain said later, "I think more than anything else, their offense was so confusing. Their kids are so smart, and they just ran that offense to a T. They did things that made us make mistakes, made us give up easy scores." These Dragons are celebrating the 1992 quarterfinals win, 61-0, against Alpine.

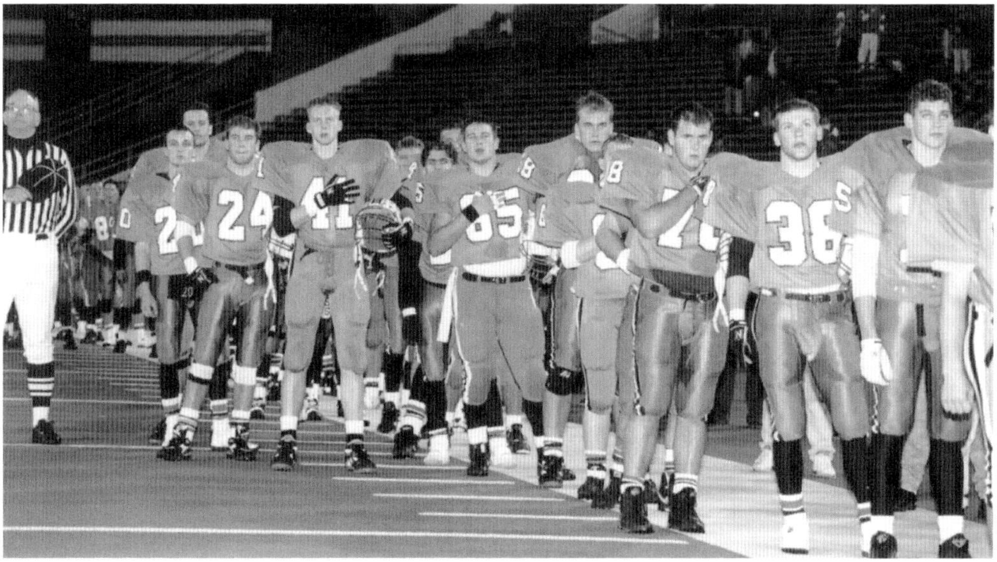

The Dragons advanced to the state finals against an unranked Coldspring. A power outage delayed the start of the game. The team is on the field singing the national anthem here. The player with his gloved hand over his heart is senior Jeff Croy (No. 41). Jeff's Dragon roots run deep: he is the son of Sheila and Larry Croy and grandson of Modean and Jack Johnson.

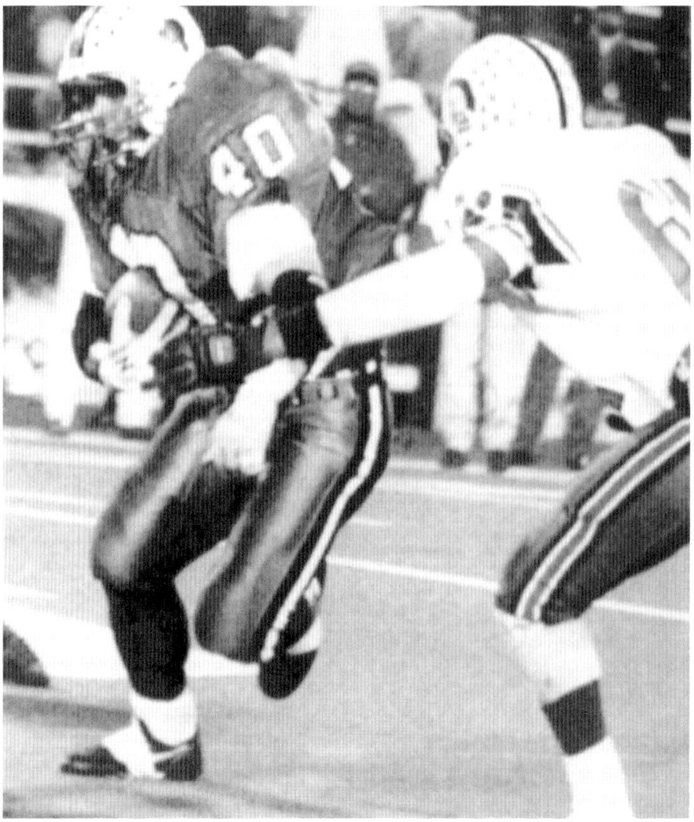

The Dragons led Coldspring 42-0 at the half after Dane Johnson scored five touchdowns. Signal caller Mantooth credited the win to the speed of Johnson, Mark Byarlay, and Brent Bohnsack—all capable of a 4.5-second 40-yard dash. "It was kind of weird," Mantooth said, "because you got the feeling sometimes that it was just a matter of who would score for us." Byarlay runs toward the end zone in this photograph from the state finals. (Photograph by Joel Harrison.)

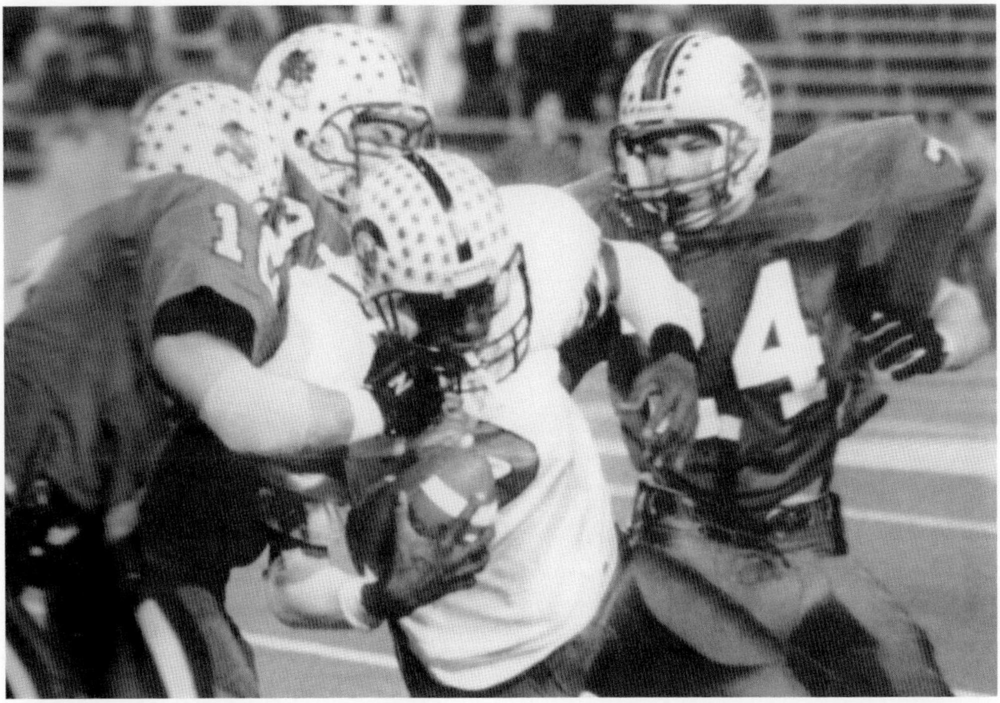

"You don't score that many points with just offense," Ledbetter said at the time. Nods were given to defenders Mark Herron, Jeff Croy, Stephen Moreland, and Craig Frost while David Reck, Joel Holmes, and Joseph Stanyer played key roles on both sides of the ball. Here, Dane Johnson and Moreland bring down a Coldspring ball carrier. (Photograph by Joel Harrison.)

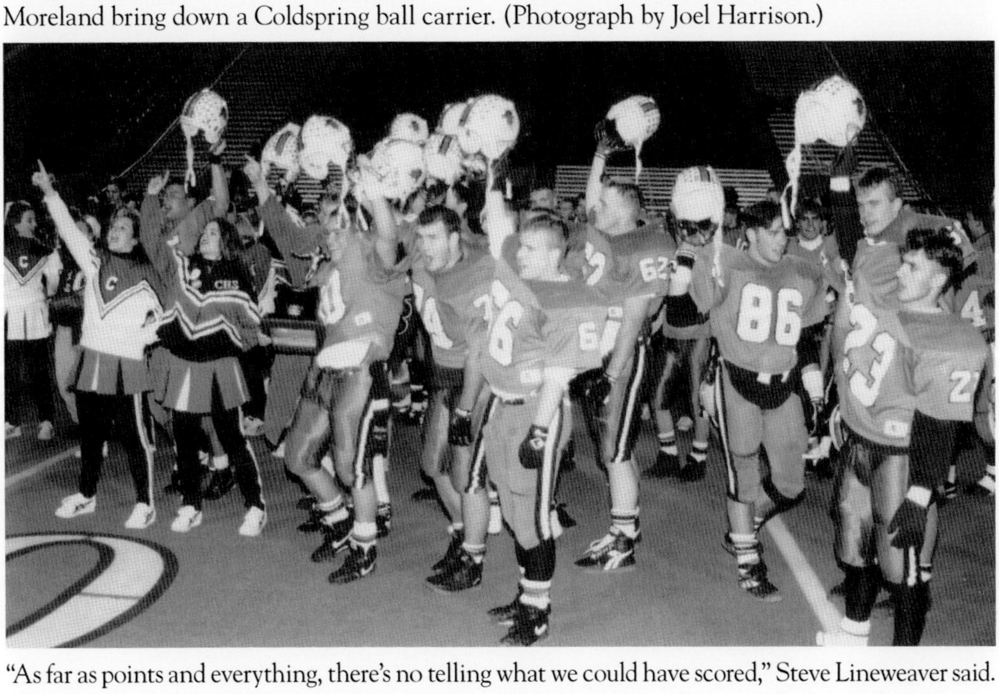

"As far as points and everything, there's no telling what we could have scored," Steve Lineweaver said. The Dragons beat Coldspring, 48-0, and these players celebrate the state championship win.

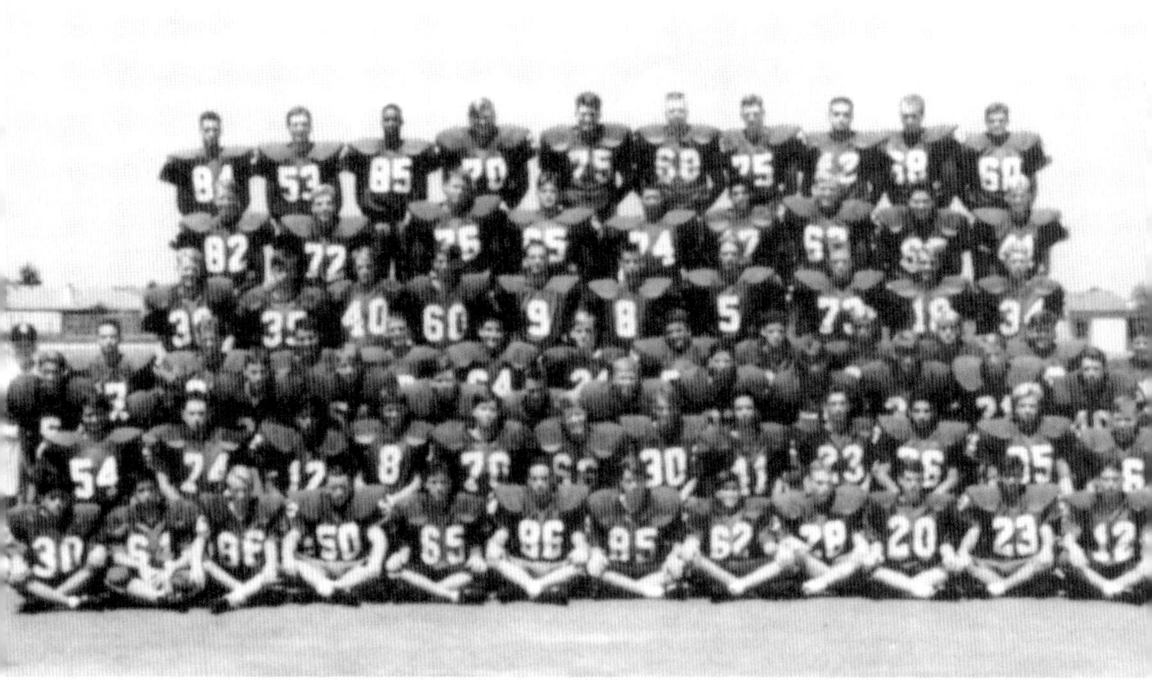

The 1992 team included, from left to right, (first row) M. Rabie, G. Hazzard, D. Kreps, C. Sisk, H. Carpenter, J. Edgington, M. McCabe, J. McCutcheon, D. Walton, E. Higgins, C. Pinson, and J. Stratton; (second row) J. Fox, M. Placencia, L. Mendoza, J. Boyd, D. Swann, T. Dyer, C. Voller, M. Stevenson, D. Sargent, L. Marquez, A. Abitz, and J. Denton; (third row) Z. Stewart, K. Brown, J. Hitchcock, T. Cotton, R. Boyle, W. Mantooth, S. Moreland, B. Kichan, R. Burgess, J. Turner, T. McGrath, M. Byarlay, and C. Gustafson; (fourth row) H. Hudson, B. Nimphius, B. Bohnsak, S. Harwell, D. Johnson, J. Baker, J. Gilbert, K. Smith, C. Heiser, J. Lineberger, M. Turner, T. Sisco, and B. Gilmore; (fifth row) T. Watkins, L. Wells, J. Jacobsen, R. Fryhover, K. Holifield, C. Frost, D. Ahlers, B. Story, S. Jacobsen, and J. Moreland; (sixth row) E. Reed, B. Hatcher, C. Story, B. LeBlanc, C. Collins, T. Sweat, D. Reck, C. Devine, and J. Croy; (seventh row) M. Herron, J. Crowder, B. Davis, J. Garrett, H. Reinmiller, S. McKean, M. Thompson, K. DeSoto, J. Stanyer, and J. Holmes.

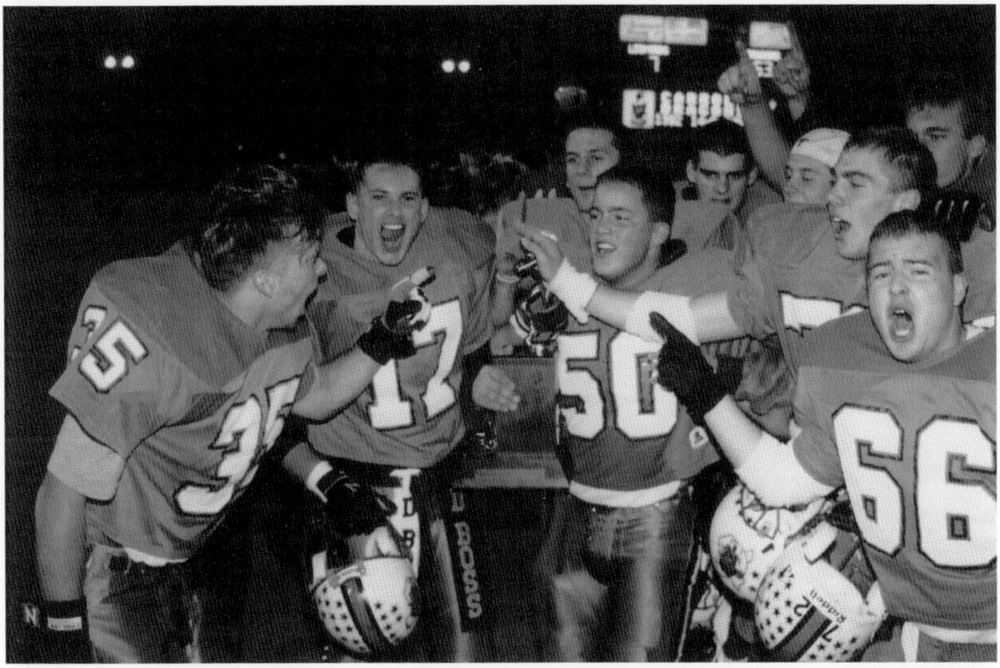

Pumped-up Dragons cheer the 3A State Championship trophy, held by Craig Sisk (No. 50). Other identified players are, from left to right, Adam Abitz (No. 35), Brian Nimphius (No. 17), and Jeromy Denton (No. 66).

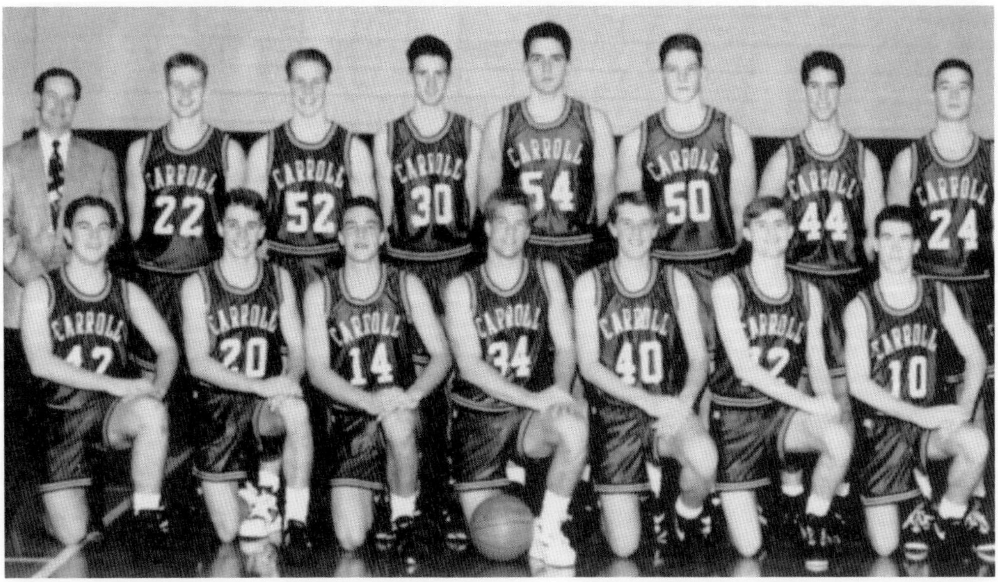

Earlier in the year, head boys' basketball coach Ken Cook and his team brought home CISD's fifth state title: the 1992 3A Boys' Basketball Championship. Team members are, from left to right, (kneeling) Chad Collins, Chad Voller, Jason Weddel, Dane Johnson, Chris Chupp, Thomas Thomas, and Bradley Drake; (standing) Cook, Jeff Croy, Jason Ayers, Juston Dobbs, Marc Thompson, Bradley Holmes, and Jamie DeBruin.

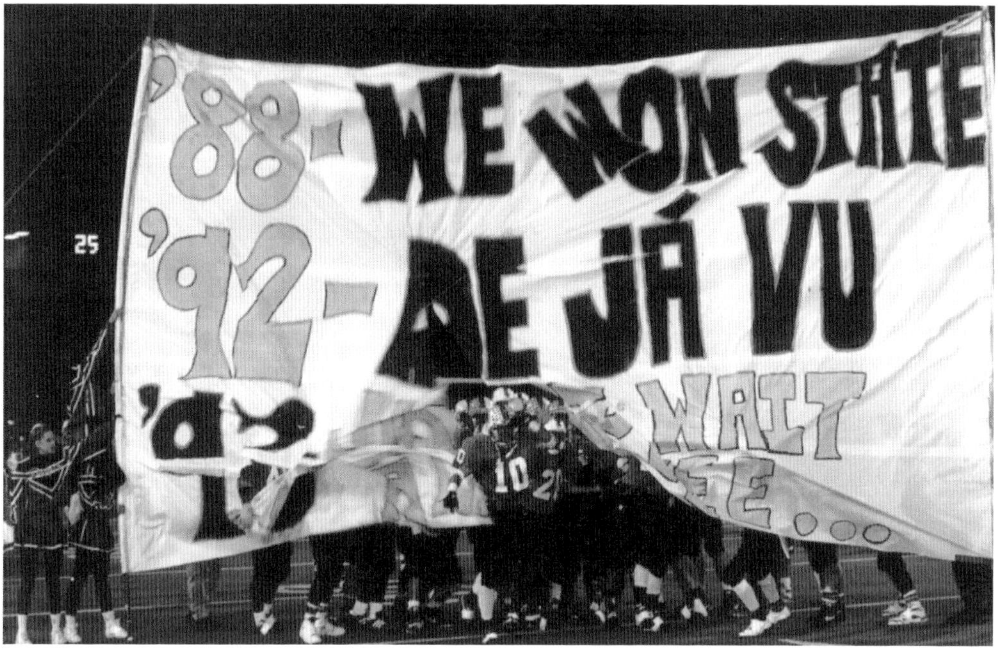

The Dragons' accumulated 61 consecutive regular season wins in 1993 were the most in the history of Texas high school football. Back-to-back state titles, as this banner calls for, were not out of the realm of possibility. Lineweaver left for the head coach position at Commerce; replacing him was Duke Christian. The new million-dollar Carroll High School, built at the corner of FM 1709 and Peytonville Road, was completed that year, and the athletic facilities behind it were state of the art. (Courtesy of Bob Ledbetter.)

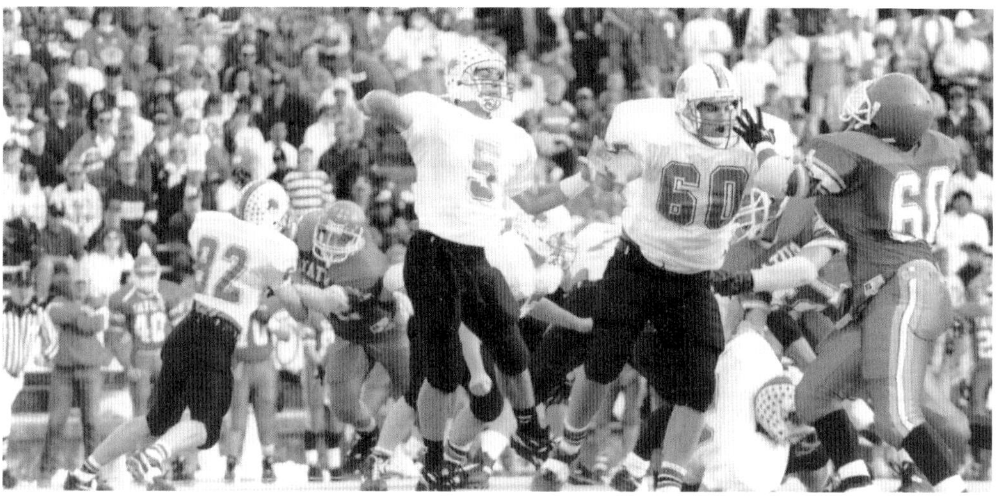

The first game in the 1993 season against rival Coppell was so close that, with only 1 second on the clock, Kris Brown kicked a 27-yard field goal to win the game. The game would later be dubbed the one that came close to ending the streak. It was also Brown's first varsity start as the Carroll quarterback; he (No. 5) is seen here with teammates Eric Reed (No. 82) and Joel Holmes (No. 60).

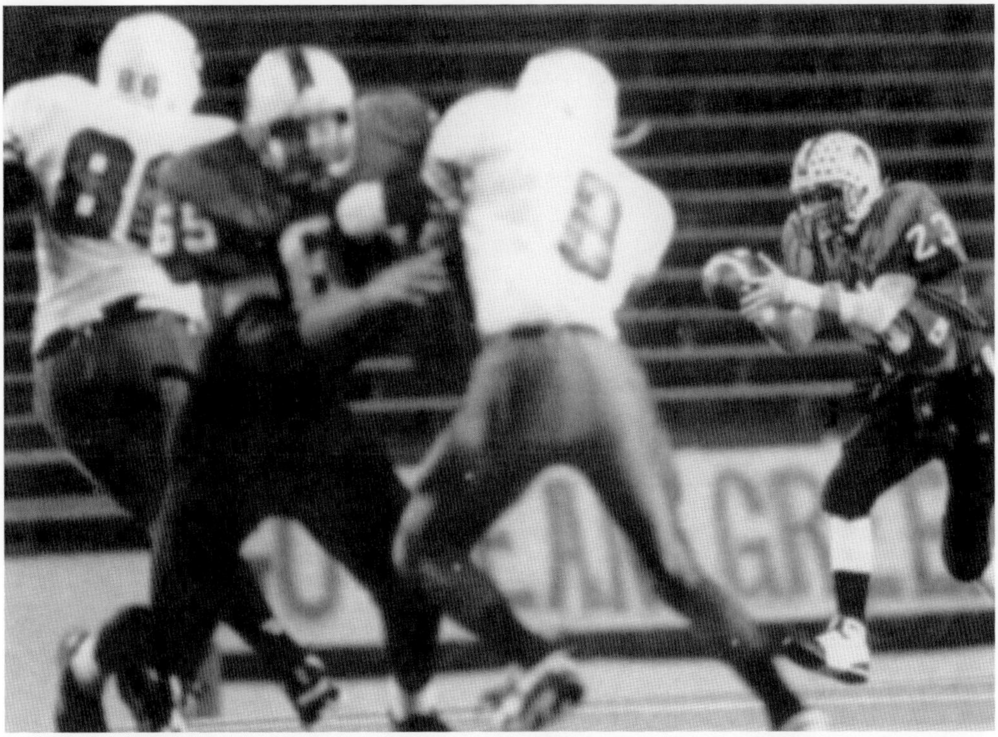

After the close call with Coppell, Ledbetter was philosophical: "That's the biggest plus in that ballgame, knowing we can come from behind. If you've never been behind, you don't know." The next week the Dragons beat No. 4 Gainesville, 44-13. Christian said after the win, "You could sense they were more focused. They'd beaten so many people for so long, I think that [the Coppell game] was just kind of a wake-up call." Running back Derek Sargent (No. 23) certainly looks focused here.

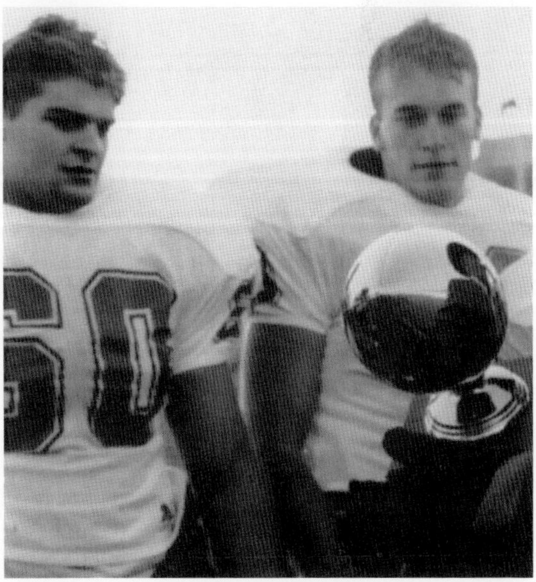

The Dragons beat their opponents in the remaining games by an average of 41 points, finishing the season with a perfect 16-0. Watching as the 1993 district trophy is presented to the team are seniors Joel Holmes (No. 60) and Joseph Stanyer.

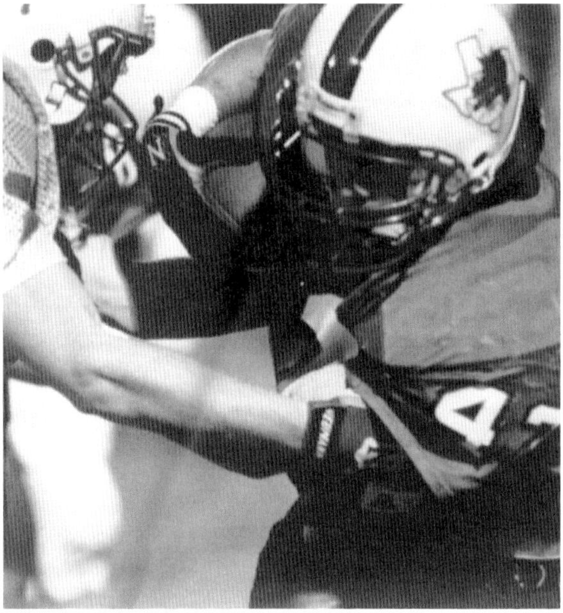

The Dragons played the Cuero Gobblers for the 1993 state title. "It was tougher," admitted Dane Johnson. "It's always tougher the second time." At the half, for the first time any Carroll coach could remember, the Dragons were shut out. But Carroll scored in the second half, Brown made an extra point that gave the Dragons the lead, and the defense held. The final score was Dragons 14, Cuero 6. "The intensity level was there in the second half," defensive coordinator Tom Rapp said. Here, running back Jon Lineberger holds onto the ball despite the efforts of a Gobbler defender.

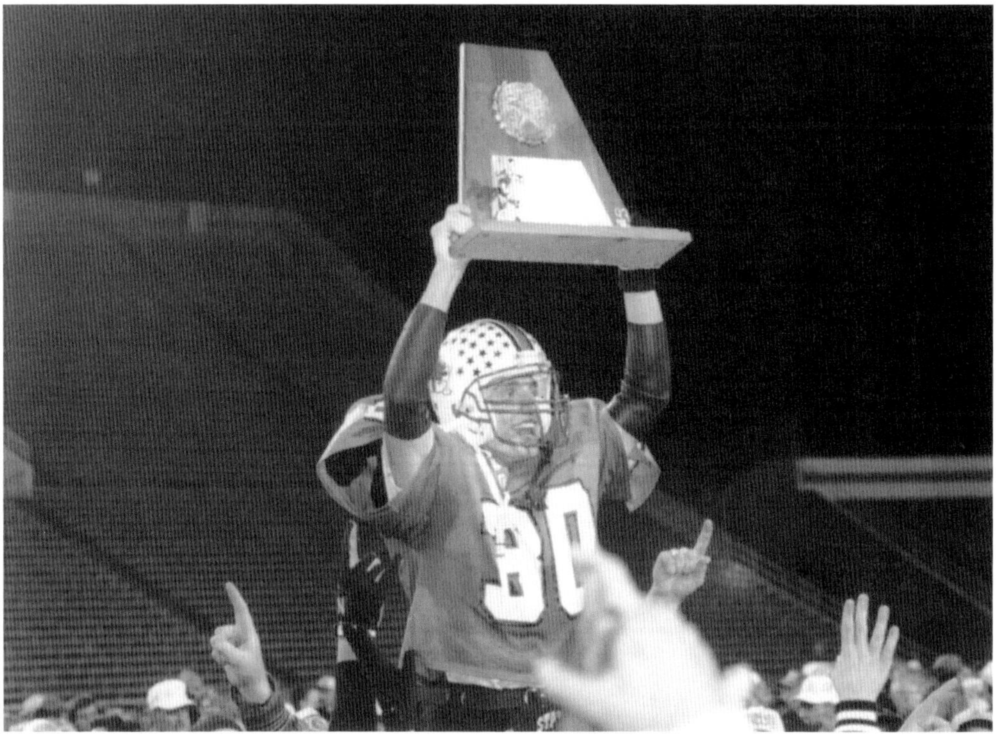

Ledbetter summed up the win: "That's the way a state championship game should be." After the win, Dragon Brian Hatch told reporters what Ledbetter said before the players took the field: "There are over 600,000 hours in your life and 48 minutes of that you're going to remember for the rest of your life. That's this game here." Holding up the state trophy for all to see is senior Chad Voller.

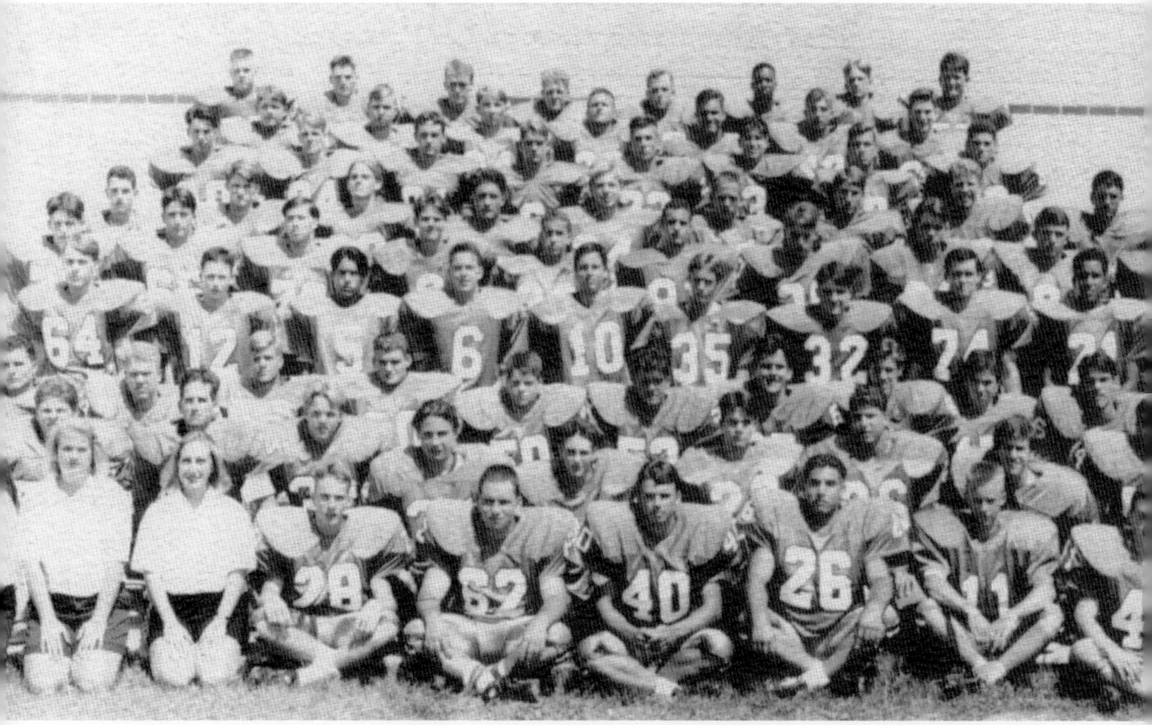

The 1993 Class 3A State Championship team members included, from left to right, (first row) Kaci Parker, Michelle Hoefar, Kristi Edwards (managers), Derek Walton, Michael Placencia, Mark Byarlay, Larry Marquez, Danny Kreps, and Eric Higgins; (second row) Bryan Gilmore, Todd Pietzsch, Tim Lawlor, Michael Morris, Steve Giancotti, Sam Leflar, Chase Brown, John McClendon, and Ricky Sanchez; (third row) Shawn Harwell, Jason Moreland, Dane Johnson, Joel Holmes, Paul Samartin, Ian Knox, Gerald White, Chance Caple, Josh Packard, and Mike Largent; (fourth row) Sean Kelly, Andy Wood, Danny Trevino, Jason Cook, Zack Vinson, Jon Mills, Chris Stankiewicz, Chad Swann, and Luis Mendoza; (fifth row) Zach Poling, Daron Wood, David Swann, Andy Hall, Matt Travis, Tim Trudell, Chad Voller, Mike McCabe, Jayson Boyd, and Jarrod Pipher; (sixth row) James Miller, Joel Turner, Jason Gilbert, Isaac Gregory, Mike Sims, Heath Brophy, David Janbaz, Eric Reed, and Corey Clay; (seventh row) Rex Fryhover, John Jacobsen, John Hitchock, Zack Stewart, Derek Sargent, Jeff McCutcheon, Ryan Boyle, and Chad Heiser; (eighth row) Toby Cotton, Chris Johnson, Todd McGrath, Kyle Smith, Kris Brown, Jon Lineberger, and Rob Hamilton; (ninth row) Shannon McKean, Marc Thompson, Joseph Stanyer, Tim Watkins, Brandon Story, Brad Davis, Matt Perry, and Hamel Reinmiller.

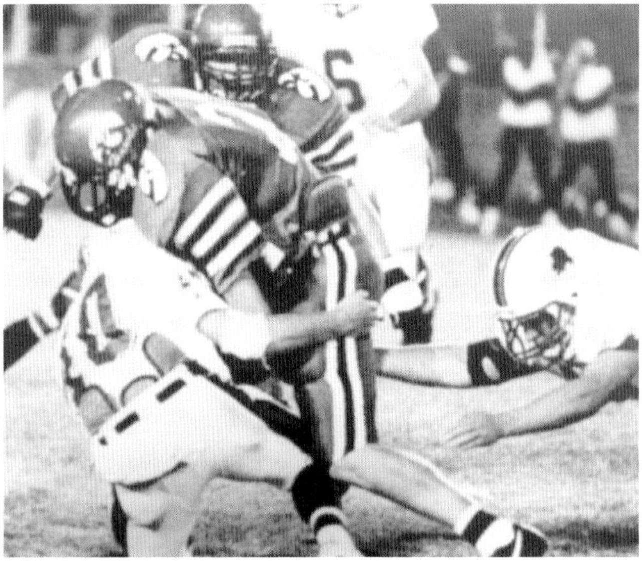

In 1994, the Dragons moved into Class 4A, the same year their unprecedented 72-game regular season winning streak came to an end. "What happened to us tonight was the best thing that could happen to this football team," Ledbetter said after the loss. "We got beat, but now we can strap it back on and get ready for district." Junior Matt Travis tackles an opponent as senior Tim Watkins assists. (Photograph by Jensen Walker.)

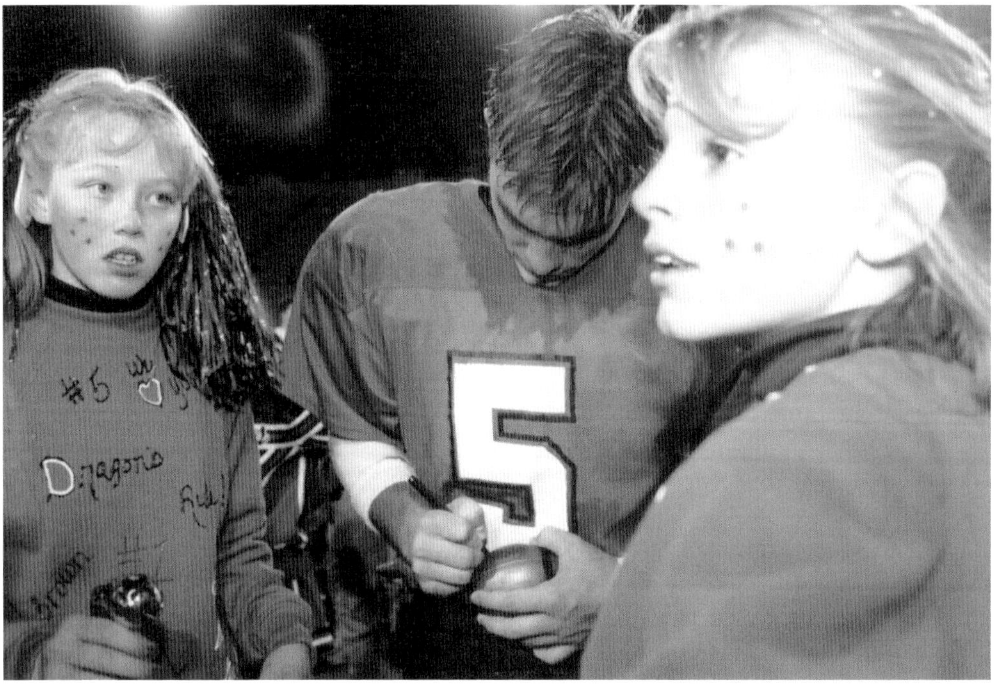

The Dragons finished the season 5-4, and senior quarterback Kris Brown (No. 5) led his team to its first 4A playoff win, over Waxahachie. But Carroll lost in the second-round playoffs to Dallas Spruce. In 1999, Brown was drafted by the Pittsburgh Steelers and played eight years for the Houston Texans before finishing with the San Diego Chargers in 2010. (Photograph by Jensen Walker.)

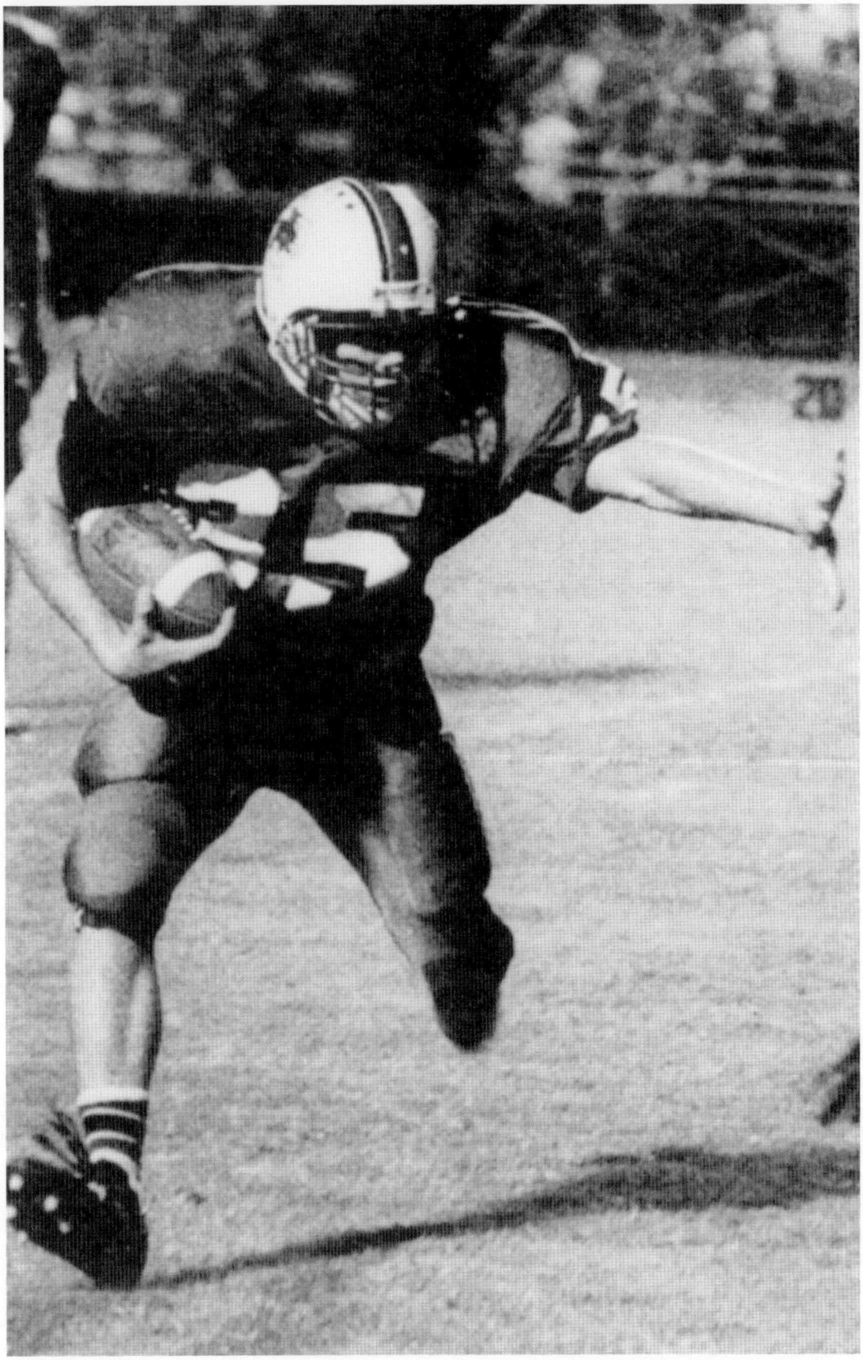

Fittingly, in the second game of the 1995 season, the Dragons beat out Gainesville—the team that stopped the streak the year before—and gave Bob Ledbetter his 200th career win. The offense was slow to take off. But the defense held opponents to fewer than two touchdowns per game, and the season ended 10-0. Seen here in regular season play is running back James Miller. (Photograph by Justin Mellen.)

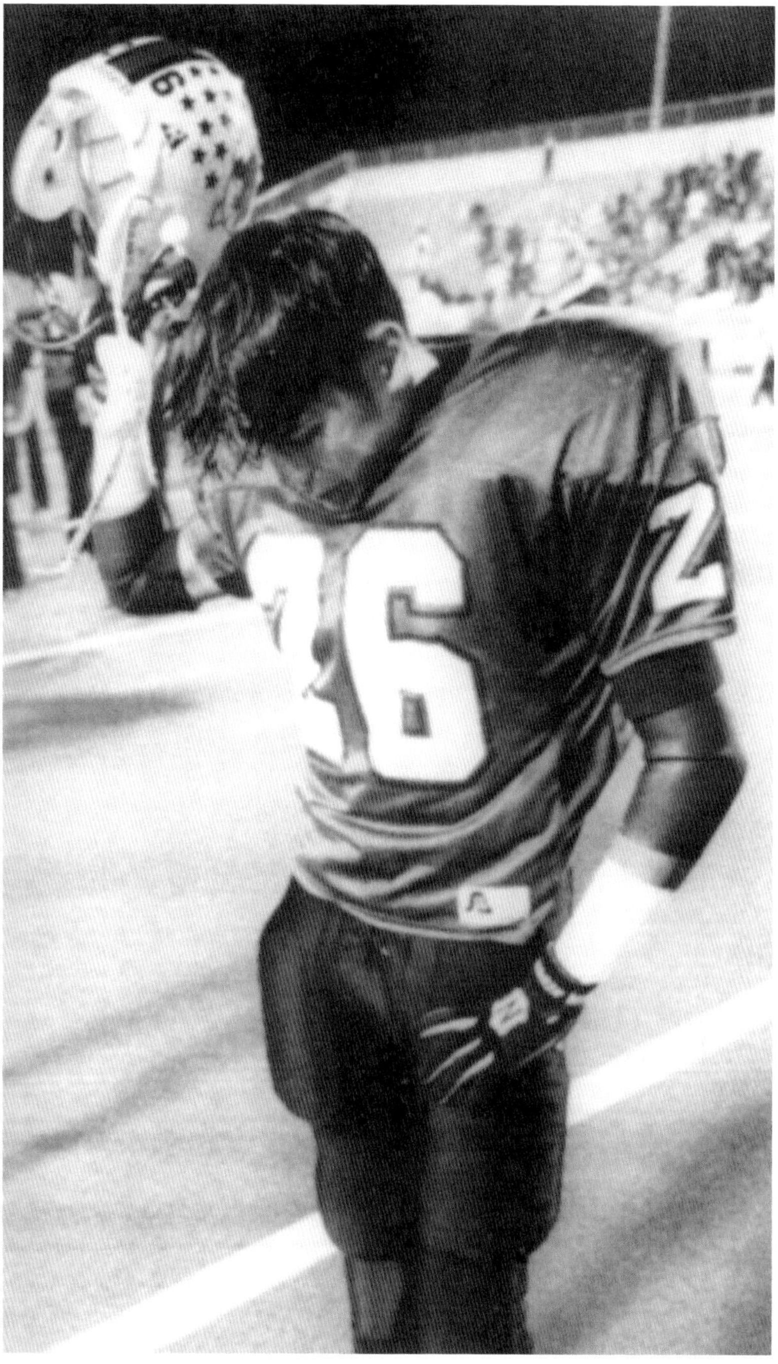

The playoff season was a short one, as the Dragons lost their first-round game against Everman. Senior Manuel Trevino is pictured here on the sidelines after that loss. At the close of the 1995 season, Bob Ledbetter stepped down as the Dragons' longest-serving head coach and became the first full-time CISD athletic director. Ledbetter's overall record at Carroll when he hung up his whistle was 172-32-3. (Photograph by Justin Mellen.)

4

Protecting the Tradition

By the mid-1990s, Southlake's population was taking off. New families were bringing an estimated 650 students to Carroll schools each year. To no one's surprise, the Dragons had outgrown their stadium. "We were going to move into Class 5A," CISD superintendent Dr. Ted Gillum said in 2015. "The first time I drove up Carroll Avenue, I knew that stadium was not going to work."

Meanwhile, Bob Ledbetter had problems of his own. "I had to replace myself as head coach," he explained. He tapped Tom Rapp for the job.

Rapp grew up in Des Moines, Iowa, playing high school football and baseball and running track. He graduated from Iowa State, received his master's degree from the University of Iowa, and began his coaching career southwest of his hometown. Rapp's first Texas coaching job was in the Northwest ISD before joining Ledbetter's staff in 1988.

Rapp's first season as head coach ended 3-6-1. Two years later, the Dragons made it to the 1998 4A state finals, losing to Stephenville by three points. The next year, the Dragons went 6-4, and it was the coach's last at Carroll. "Coach Rapp did a great job," Ledbetter said. "But it didn't matter. He would have had to go 15-0 or 16-0 to be successful [here]."

The next coach hired was Todd Dodge.

Dodge grew up in Port Arthur, Texas, where he played quarterback for his high school. "I grew up in a town that had tradition," Dodge said, "and I had an opportunity to play at the University of Texas, where there is a lot of tradition." Dodge's early coaching career was spent in high schools in the Dallas–Fort Worth area and as an assistant coach at the University of North Texas in Denton.

"When I had the opportunity in 2000 to be the head coach at Carroll," Dodge said recently, "that was the highlight of my career." Early on, a booster club member asked Dodge, "What's your motto, Coach? What do you want us to put on the T-shirts?" Dodge had one thing in mind. "The one thing I couldn't get out of my head was I was so proud to be a part of this place. So I told him to put on the T-shirts: Protect the Tradition."

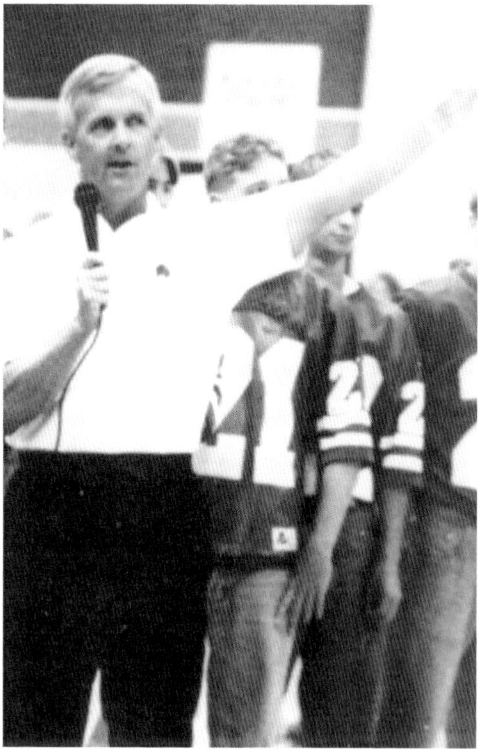

"When you're following somebody like Coach Ledbetter," Tom Rapp said in 2015, "those are gigantic shoes that you are trying to fill. I was very fortunate to get the head coaching job." Here, Rapp addresses students at a 1996 football pep rally. (Photograph by Caroline Fitzgerald.)

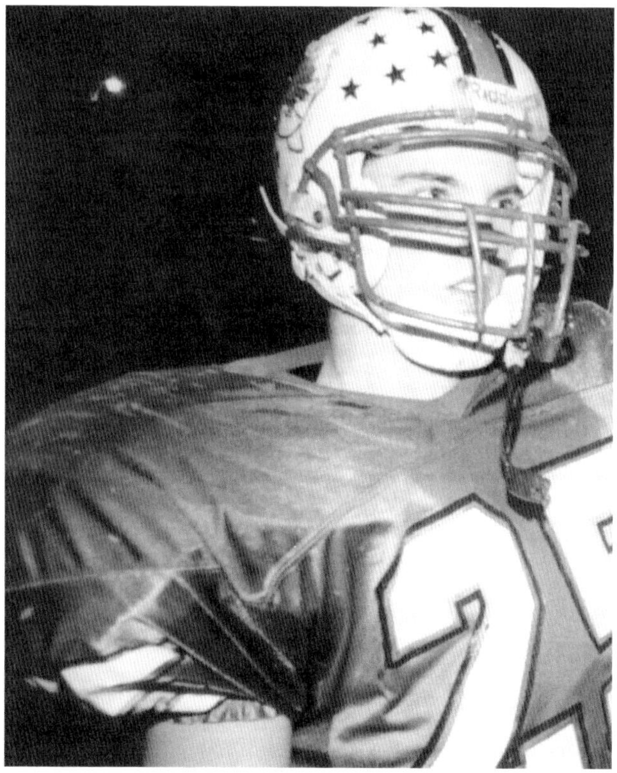

The 1996 season began with two losses, one win, and a tie; next up was the Dragon homecoming game against Denton. The teams were tied 17-17 with 1:57 remaining on the clock. The Dragons were lined up on Denton's one-yard line when running back Blake Poindexter, shown here, took the ball over the goal line and scored to win the game. (Photograph by Justin Mellen.)

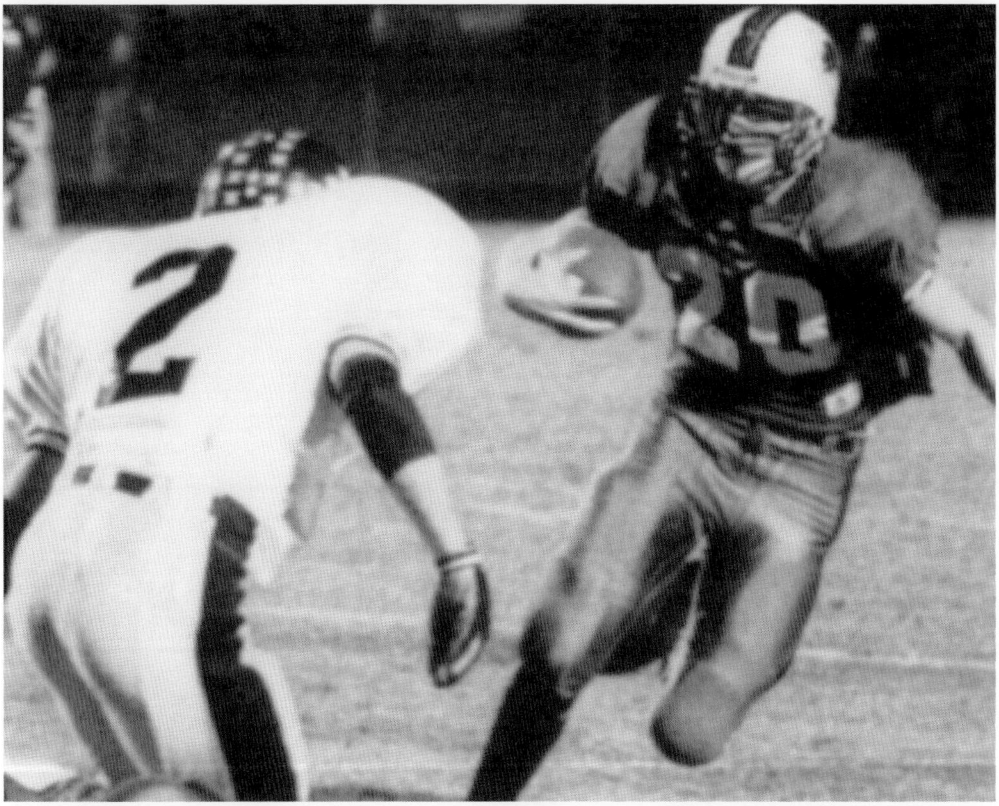

Anticipation of the first official game between the Dragons and the Grapevine Mustangs went beyond the players and coaches. Grapevine mayor Bill Tate and Southlake mayor Rick Stacy—also third cousins and good friends—wagered a meal on the outcome. The Dragons lost to Grapevine, 28-14, and the season ended 3-6-1, the worst in 27 years. Here, in a game against Highland Park late in the 1996 season, wide receiver Tyler Brown jinks around a Scot player. (Photograph by Justin Mellen.)

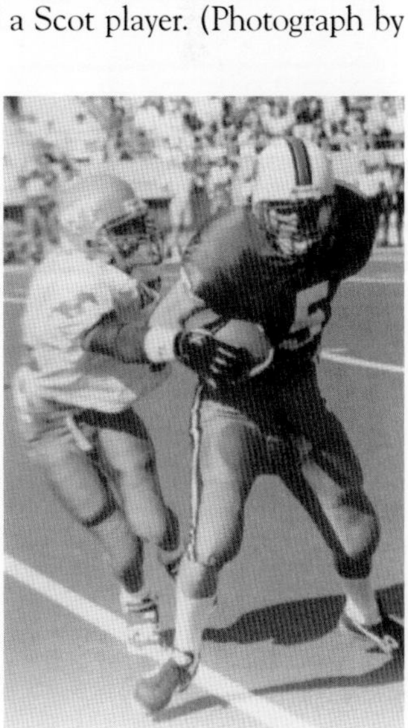

Carroll lost again to Grapevine in 1997. "They had some great players," Rapp said. "But that [loss] really became a rallying cry for our kids. We decided if we're going to stay in the same district as Grapevine, we're going to do everything we need to do so we can beat Grapevine." Here, Dragon sophomore Justin Turner avoids a Coppell Cowboy later that season. (Photograph by Justin Mellen.)

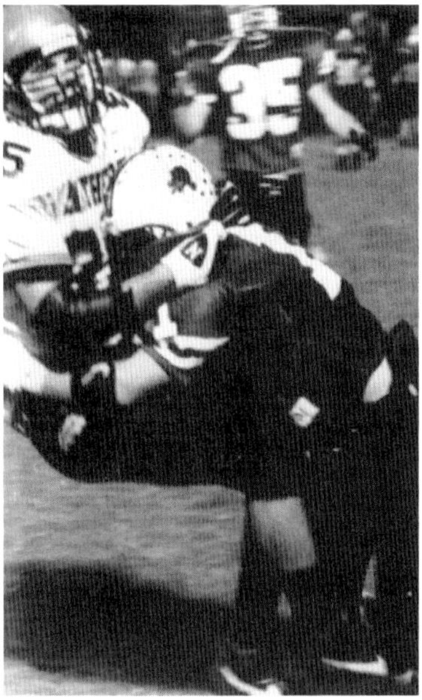

The Dragons pulled out a 6-4 season in 1997 and went into the 4A playoffs against Dallas Lincoln in the Cotton Bowl. With the Carroll 21-6 win, the Dragons "knocked the door down," Rapp said. "The kids learned that we could be successful at the 4A level." A loss in the second playoff game closed out the season. Here, in the game against Colleyville Heritage earlier that year, Heath Emmert takes down a Panther. (Photograph by Vince Esposito.)

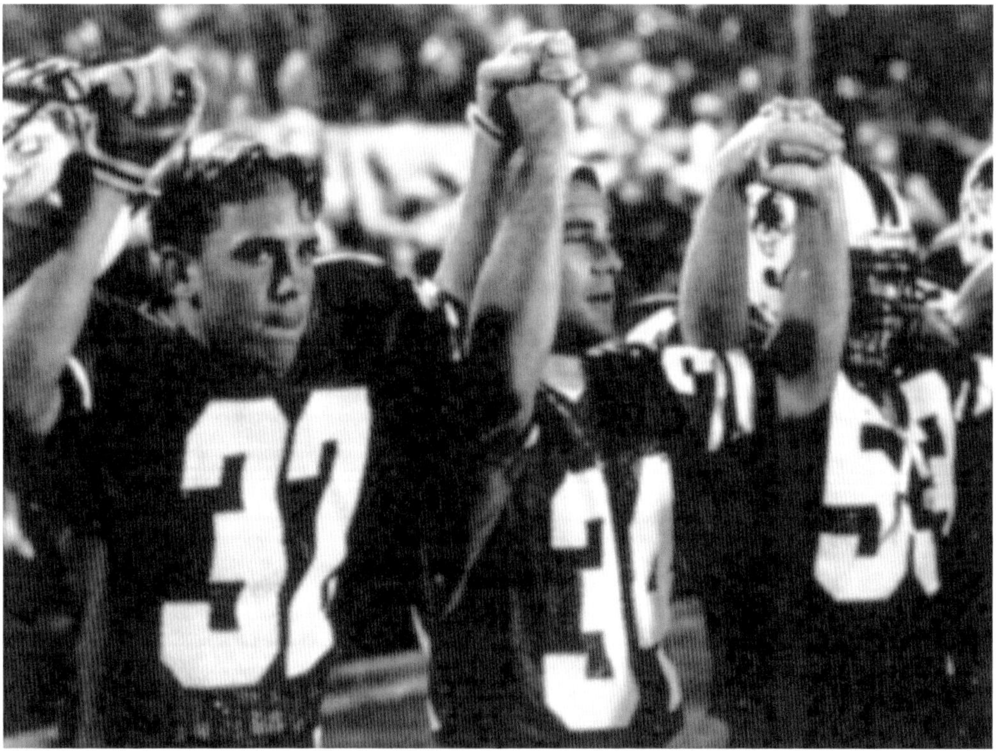

A new Dragon Stadium was in the works. The big question was where to put the stadium. "Wherever it goes, it will have some effect on some resident," committee member and former mayor Gary Fickes said. "But we need a stadium." Team members, from left to right, Ryon Skaggs, Kyle Blanco, and Andy Rumpler join hands on the sidelines for a kickoff in 1997. (Photograph by Vince Esposito.)

The 1998 Dragons went 9-1 to make it to the playoffs again. "We had a great group of kids," Rapp said. "Nathan Chandler was our quarterback. Tye Strickland and Clay McNutt were in the backfield. What really helped that team was winning the first Texas State 7on7 Championship game in College Station. That was a feather in those kids' caps." In this photograph, quarterback Chandler prepares to throw a pass as running back McNutt readies himself. (Photograph by Vince Esposito.)

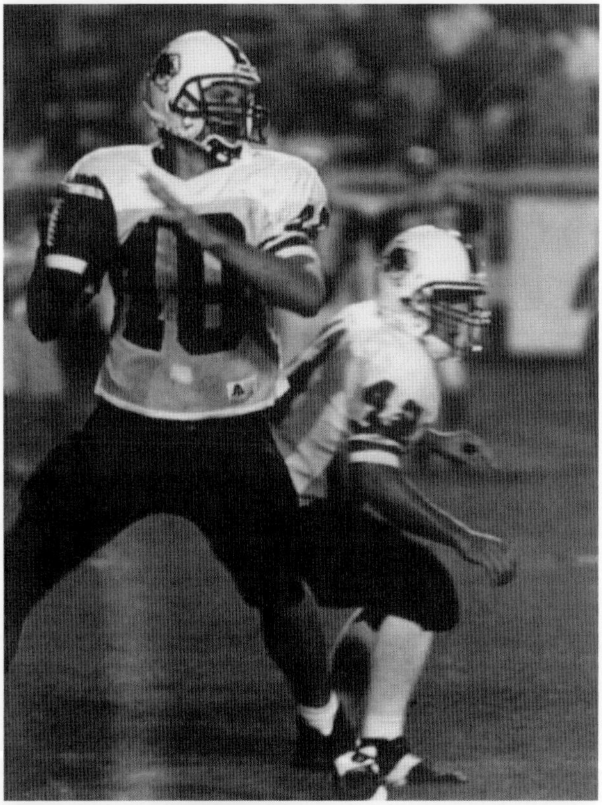

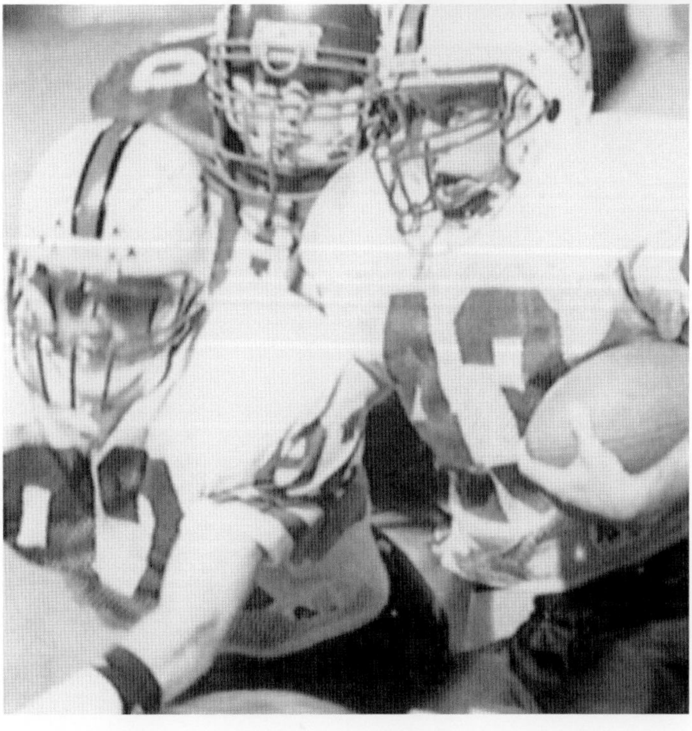

When it came time to play Grapevine again, the Dragons won, 28-23, putting them within reach of the district championship. "Our kids stepped on the field that night confident, saying, 'We're not letting you guys beat us again this year,'" Rapp recalled. Here, defenseman Justin Turner clears a path for running back Clay McNutt, who ran for more than 170 yards in the game. (Photograph by Vince Esposito.)

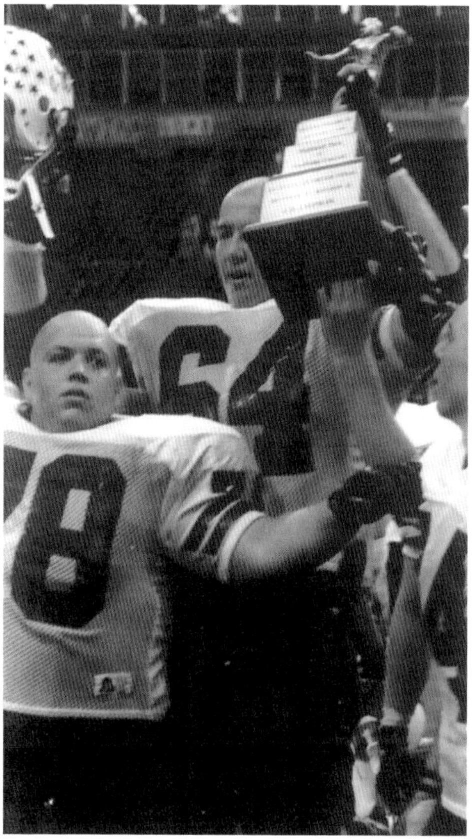

Holding the state quarterfinals trophy in this photograph is Zak West alongside Matt Robbins (No. 78). In the following week's 4A state semifinal game against Stephenville in Texas Stadium, the Yellow Jackets exchanged leads with the Dragons. In the fourth quarter with less than a minute on the clock, Carroll led, 28-24. But Stephenville quarterback Kelan Luker threw a 52-yard touchdown pass to win the game, 31-28. "The clock ran out," Rapp said. "But that's how it happens in high school football." (Photograph by Ryan Finn.)

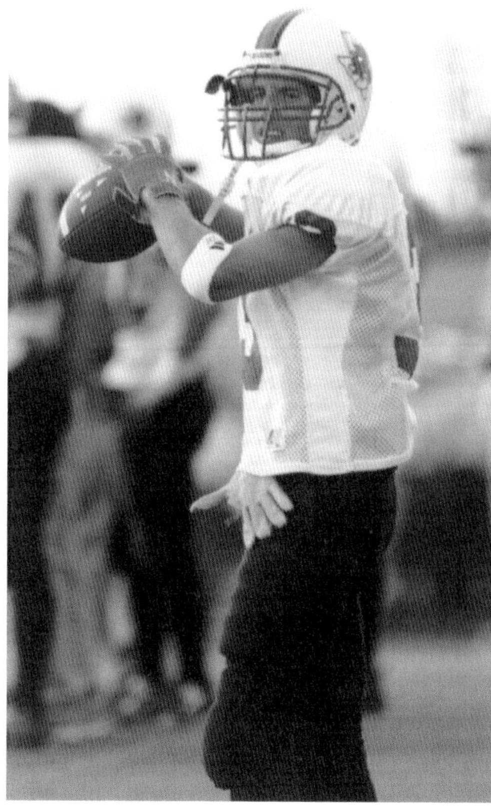

The 1999 season began with a defense that held tough and an offense that could score. After a midseason win over Colleyville Heritage, 31-20, Colleyville Heritage coach Chris Cunningham told a reporter, "The Dragons played defense the way they have all season. They're tough and disciplined." The win was the offense's best showing of the season. "We had a good idea we could move the ball," Rapp said after the game. "And quarterback T.J. Culbertson [seen here] showed he could pass the ball."

Matt Whittey (No. 65) raises his helmet during the singing of the alma mater after a successful 13-7 win over Grapevine that year. But the season ended 6-4 with no playoff games on the schedule. It would also be the last season for Rapp as the Dragons' head football coach. "I'll always have fond memories of coaching at Carroll," he said recently. (Photograph by Vince Esposito.)

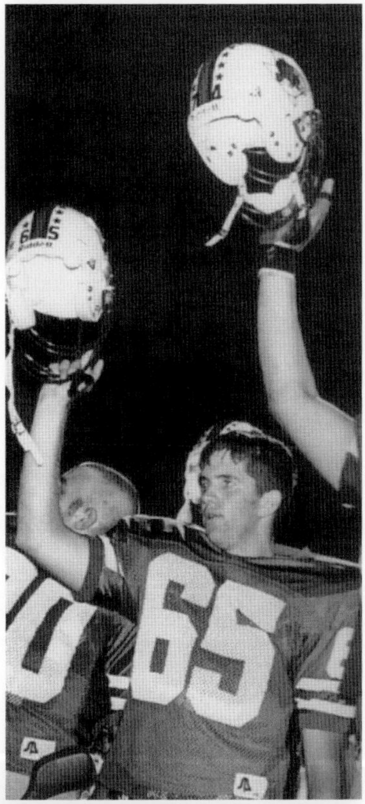

"When I had the opportunity to be the head coach at Carroll, it was the highlight of my career," Todd Dodge recalled. "We lost our first three games [in 2000]. We were at a booster club meeting and Mr. Warren Davis [Dragon booster club president] said, 'Todd, I told you that I'll always have your back. But I want you to know, they're getting awful close.'" Carroll won six of the next seven games and advanced to the playoffs. Dodge is seen here speaking to his team. (Photograph by Jeff Hillary.)

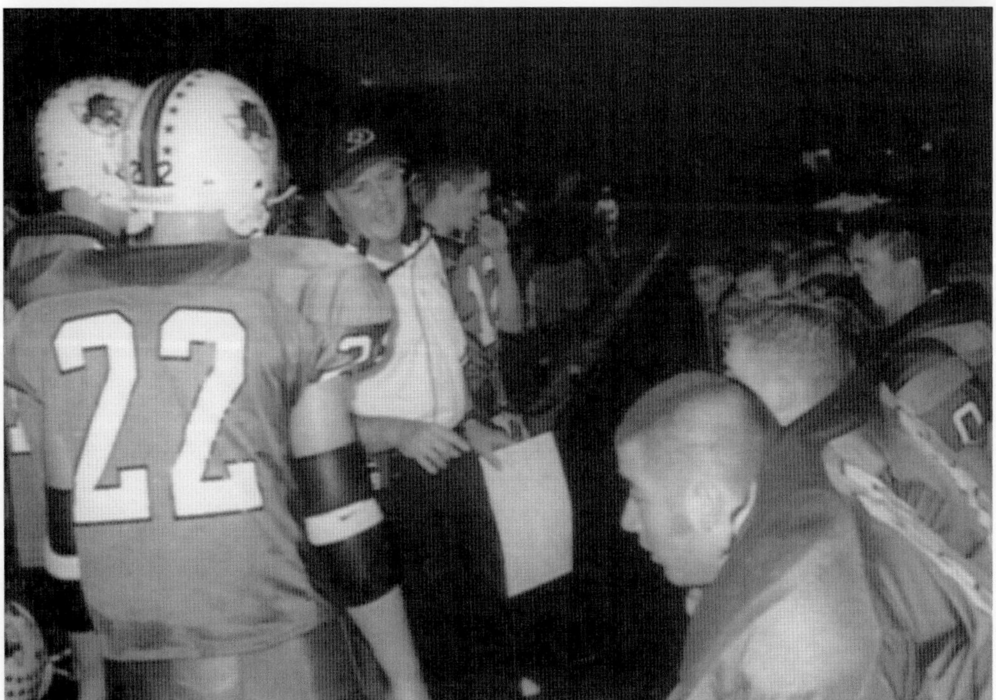

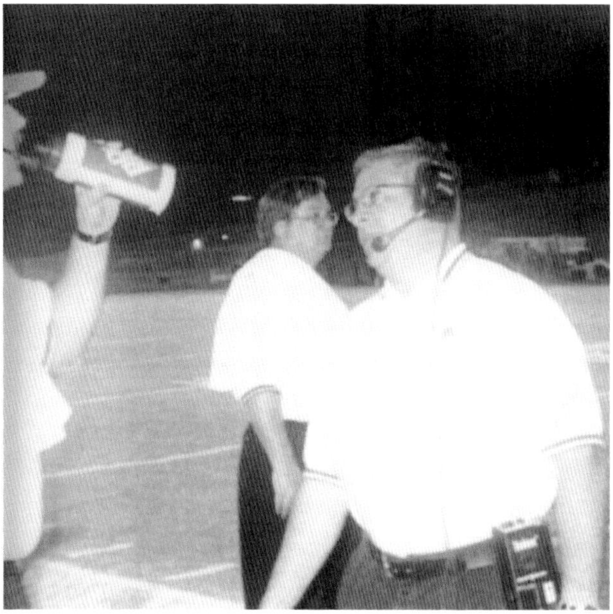

One game in particular stood out in Dodge's first season: "The Stephenville victory gave us credibility. We didn't just light it up offensively that night, the defense was churning, too." The Carroll coaches here are, from left to right, Robert Drake, Al Rushing, and Ron Mendoza. "The part of coaching that I really enjoyed," Rushing said in 2000, "was working with high school athletes and watching them improve from their freshman year to their senior year." (Photograph by Jeff Hillary.)

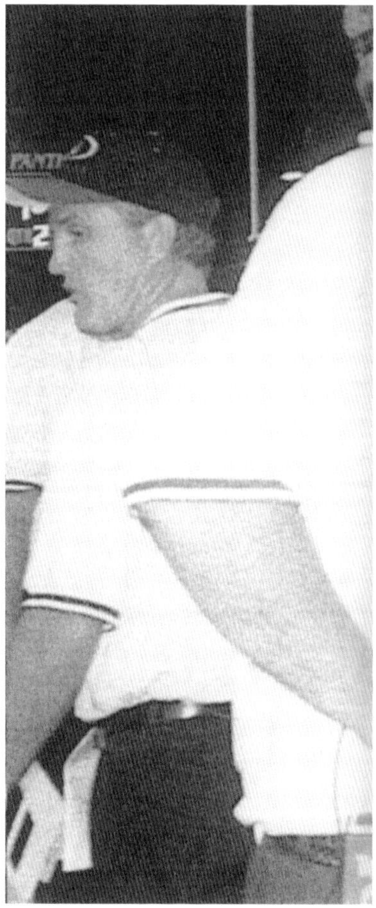

Advancing to the next round, Carroll played Andrews High School, located near Midland, Texas. "We were down 35-7," Dodge recalled. "I got the kids together and I said, 'Guys, we've got an opportunity to get beat worse than any Carroll team's gotten beat before. Or we've got the chance to make the biggest comeback in school history. Let's choose one of the two.'" The final score was Carroll 49, Andrews 37. Coach Charlie Stalcup is pictured on the sidelines. (Photograph by Jeff Hillary.)

By 2001, Dodge had established a quarterback-training program. "It all started with a player named Ricky Lay. Lots of people don't know Ricky, but he was a two-year starter. His senior year [2001], he led us to the semifinals, and several newspapers picked him as the 4A Player of the Year." Shown jumping in the air during a regular season game against Brewer that year is Matt Daniels. (Photograph by Kim Millard.)

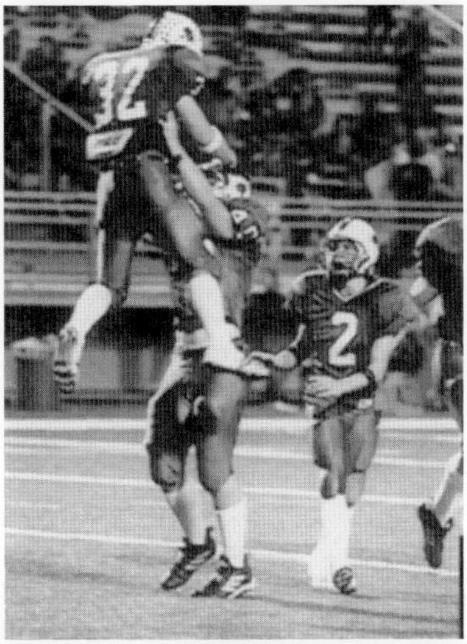

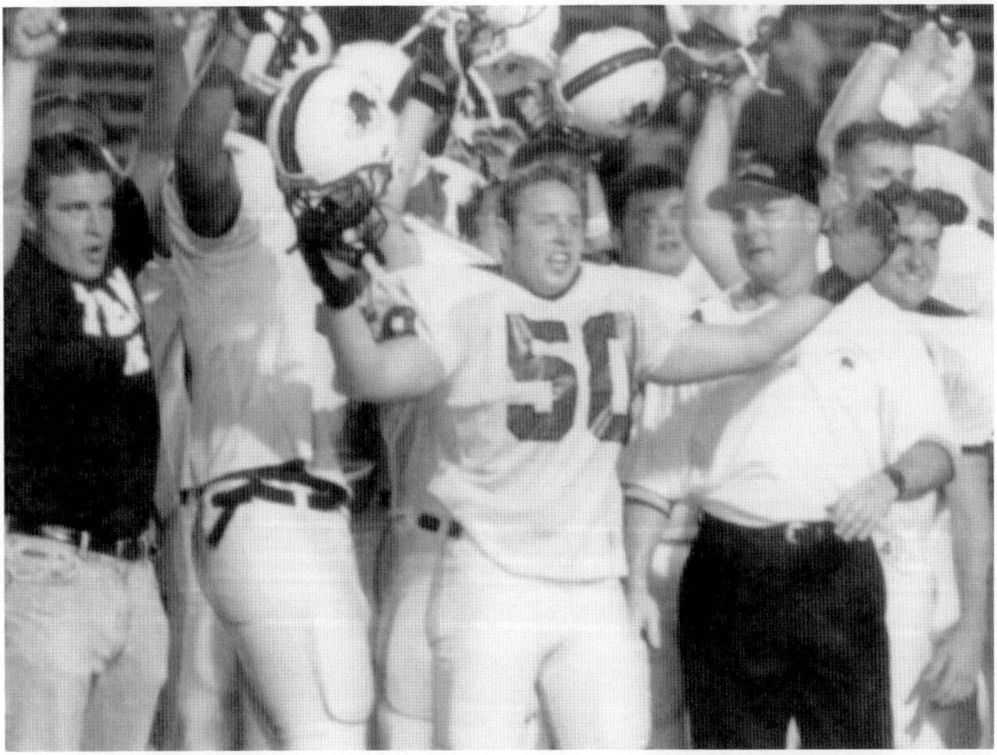

The third-round playoff match was once again against Andrews and scheduled for play in Odessa. The question came up as to the best way to get the team to the game. When Ledbetter asked Dodge what he wanted to do, Dodge said, "Well, might as well shoot for the moon. I'd like to fly." Ledbetter replied, "That's what we're gonna do." The Dragons beat Andrews, but they lost in the semifinals. Shown here celebrating a midseason win over Grapevine with Dodge (in cap), from left to right, are John Blackburn, Kyle Lochrie, Todd Salazar, Preston Jacobsen, Garrett Hartley, and Bracken Spencer. (Photograph by Kim Millard.)

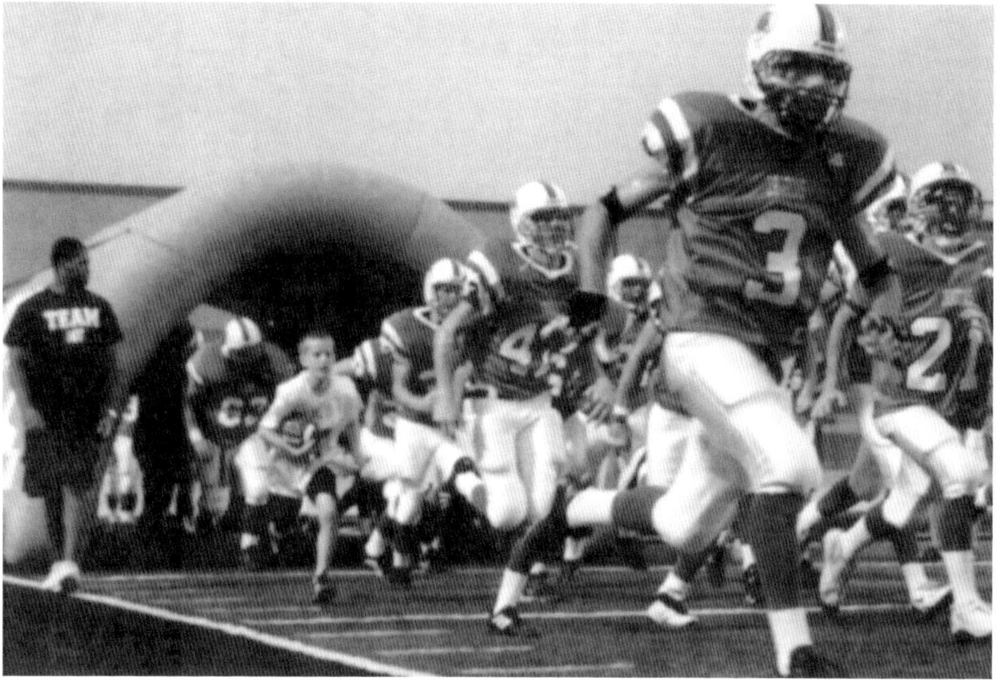

In 2002, the Dragons moved up to Class 5A. "Going into that season," Dodge explained, "we had a chance to have an outstanding football team, regardless of 4A or 5A." In this photograph, the team is running into Dragon Stadium for the season's second game, against Burleson. Quarterback Chase Wasson completed 25 of 33 passes that night for a total of 369 yards and five touchdowns. With the Carroll win, 47-7, fans caught a glimpse of what the rest of the season would bring. (Photograph by Matt Hutcheson.)

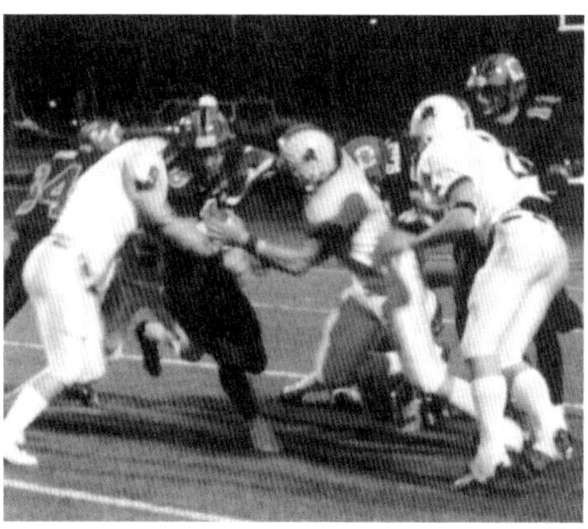

At midseason, when asked who would win district, Lewisville coach Ronnie Gage said, "You have to go with Southlake. They're playing well and their quarterback [Wasson], he's the key." Dodge's "shotgun, no-huddle, pass and dash offense," as one reporter described it, was working. And the Dragon defense was quick to take advantage of their opponents' mistakes. Members of that defense, seen here, include Christian Merritt, Jake Benoist, and Chase Hargis. (Photograph by Kyle Grice.)

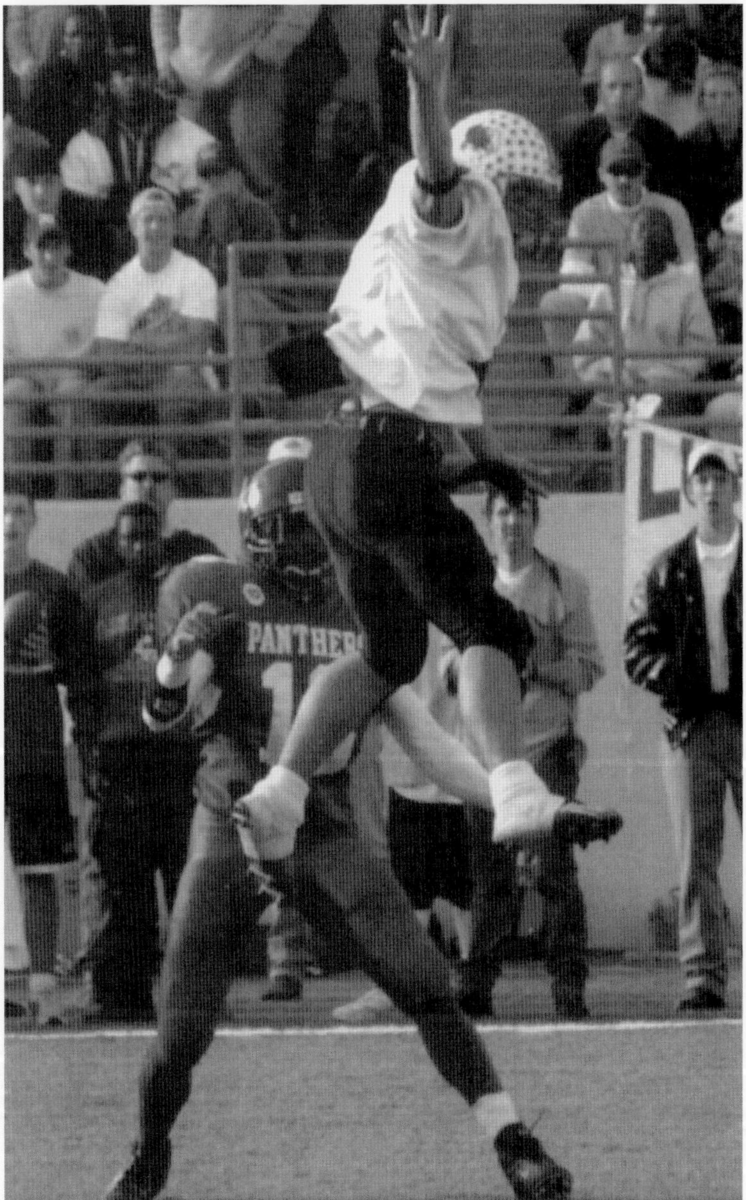

Carroll's perfect 10-0 season took the team to the playoffs. "We had some tremendous players on that team," Dodge recently said. Standout players included kicker Garrett Hartley, who set a state record that year with 90 points after touchdown. Hartley played at Oklahoma University and has played for the New Orleans Saints and the Cleveland Browns. Scott Chandler (whose older brother Nathan quarterbacked for the 1998 Dragons) played at Iowa and went on to play for the Dallas Cowboys and the Buffalo Bills. In the 2002 state semifinal game against Lufkin, Tre Sellari (shown here defending a play earlier in the game) caught a deflected fourth-down pass to keep a game-tying drive going. The Dragons then made an interception and kicked a last-minute field goal to win the game, 33-30. (Photograph by Matt Hutcheson.)

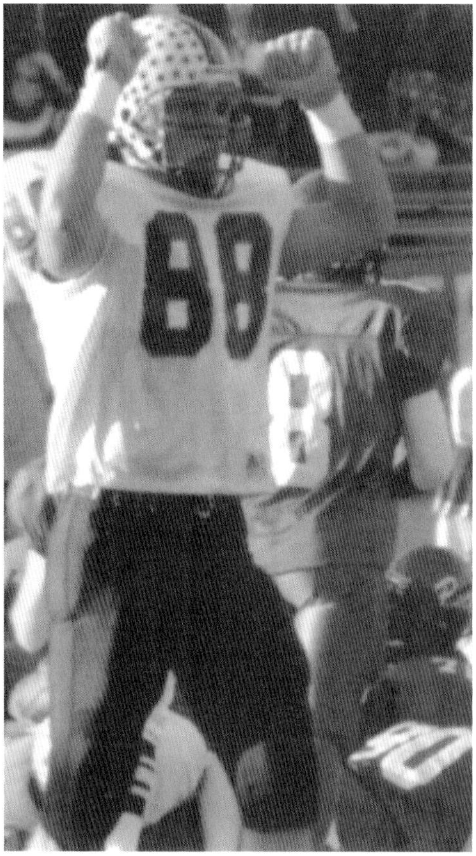

The 2002 state finals matched Carroll against Smithson Valley at the Alamodome in San Antonio. The Dragons won, 45-14, and broke the record for winning a state championship in the first year of moving up in classification. Dragon Jake Benoist is shown here celebrating a play during that state finals game. (Photograph by Matt Hutcheson.)

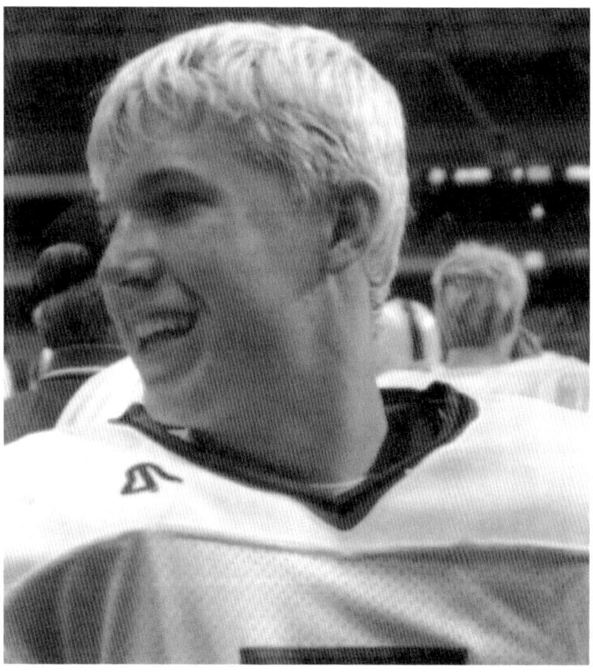

"When we went into 5A, those players didn't want to just go 6 and 4," Dodge said. "They had plans on winning the state championship. And we did." Quarterback Chase Wasson, seen here, broke the passing record for yardage thrown in a season and was named the 5A Offensive Player of the Year. (Photograph by Matt Hutcheson.)

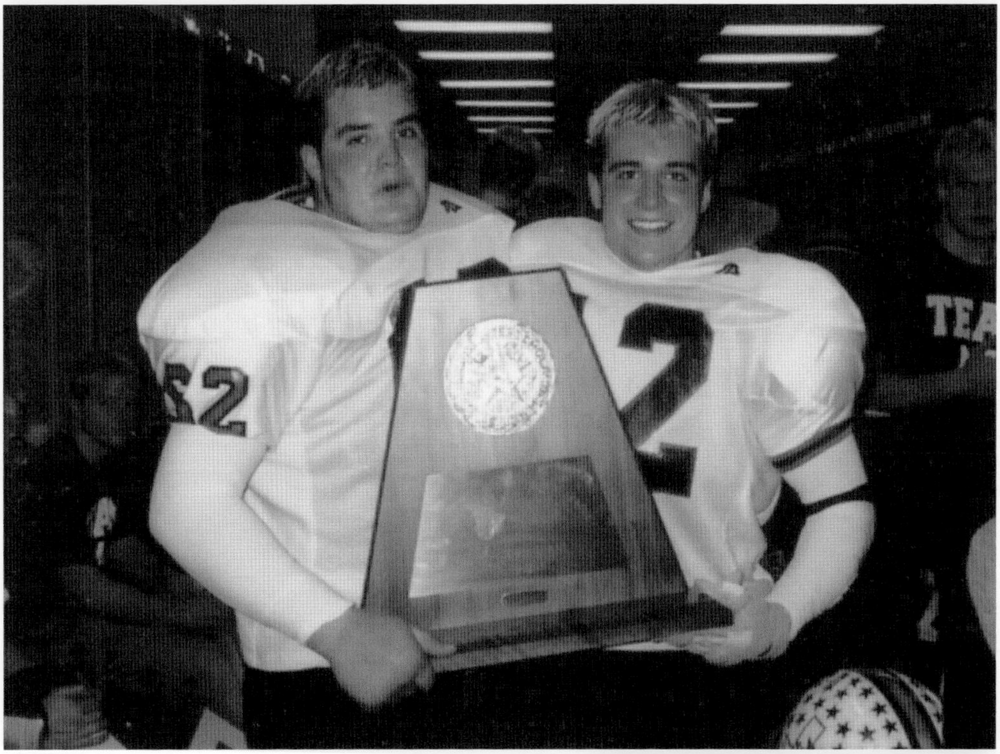

Todd Salazar (left) and John Blackburn show off the 2002 state championship trophy in the Alamodome locker room after the win. (Courtesy of John Blackburn Jr.)

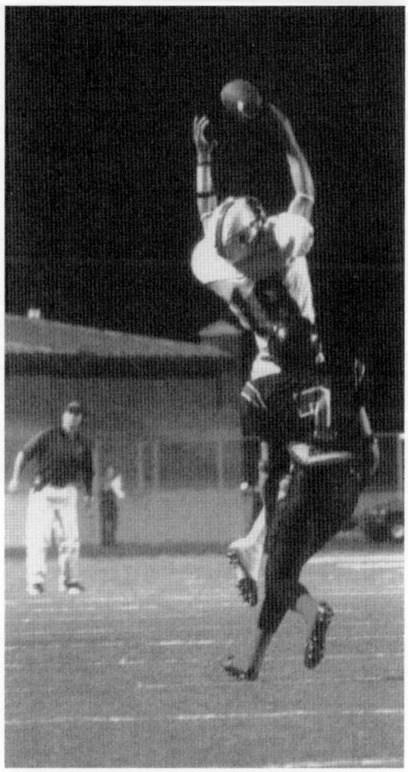

The Dragons were the team to beat in 2003. "I have so much respect for that entire team," Dodge recalled, "because they definitely had a bull's-eye on their chests. Everybody was shooting for us." In this photograph, Dragon Gary Richardson jumps to make a catch in a regular season game against Burleson. (Photograph by Kyle Grice.)

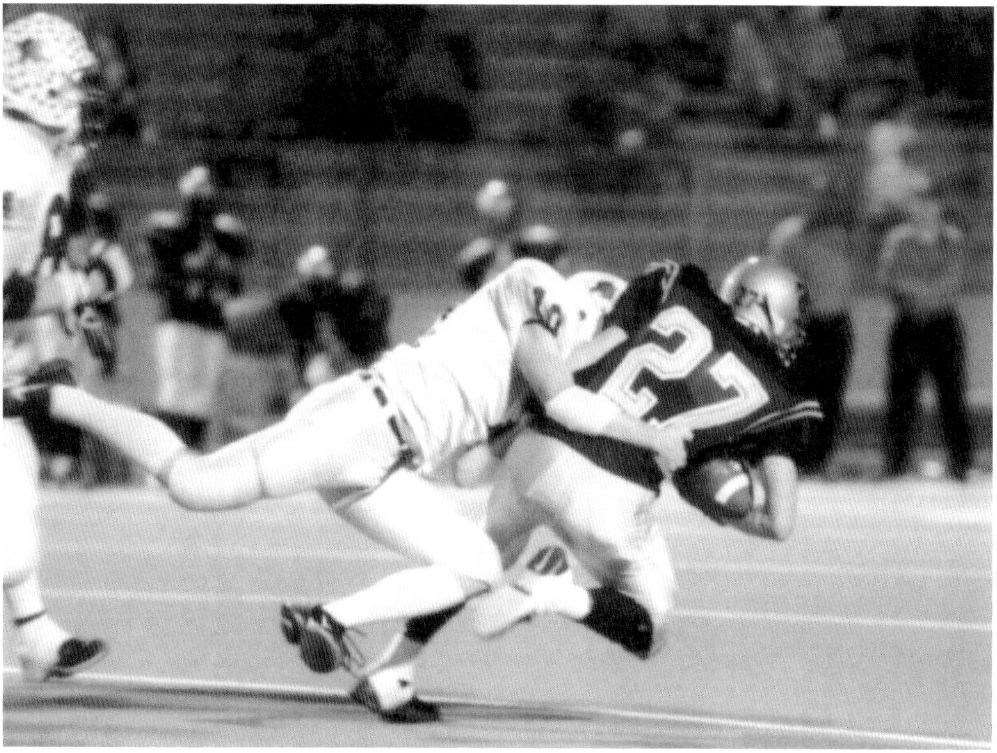

Carroll's 52-13 victory over the Colony secured the Dragons' district championship. The offense scored more than 500 points, and the defense allowed only 13 touchdowns in regular season play. The team was once again headed to the playoffs. Here, safety Beau Galbraith tackles a Colony player. (Photograph by Matt Gatto.)

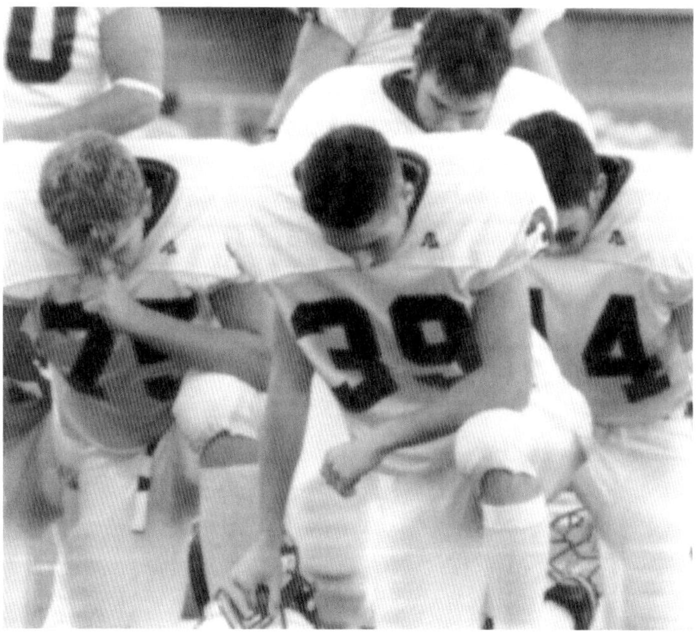

A traditional part of Dragon pregame routine includes taking a knee in the end zone after running onto the field. These players, from left to right, Michael Boydston, Brad Keiser, and Kenton Gedwed, do just that. (Photograph by Kyle Grice.)

"It was tremendous to get back to the state championship [2003]," Dodge said. One local sportswriter wrote, "Carroll coach Todd Dodge did not start the no-huddle, spread offense craze in Texas but the Dragons' overwhelming success in their first two seasons in Class 5A has put the program at the forefront of football's newest trend." The Dragons in this play include Ben Hixson, Adam Hansen, Tres Reagin, Michael Agnew, and Trever Johnson. (Photograph by Kyle Grice.)

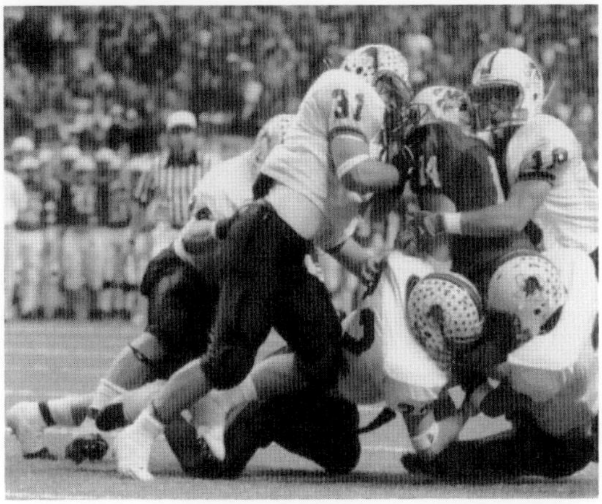

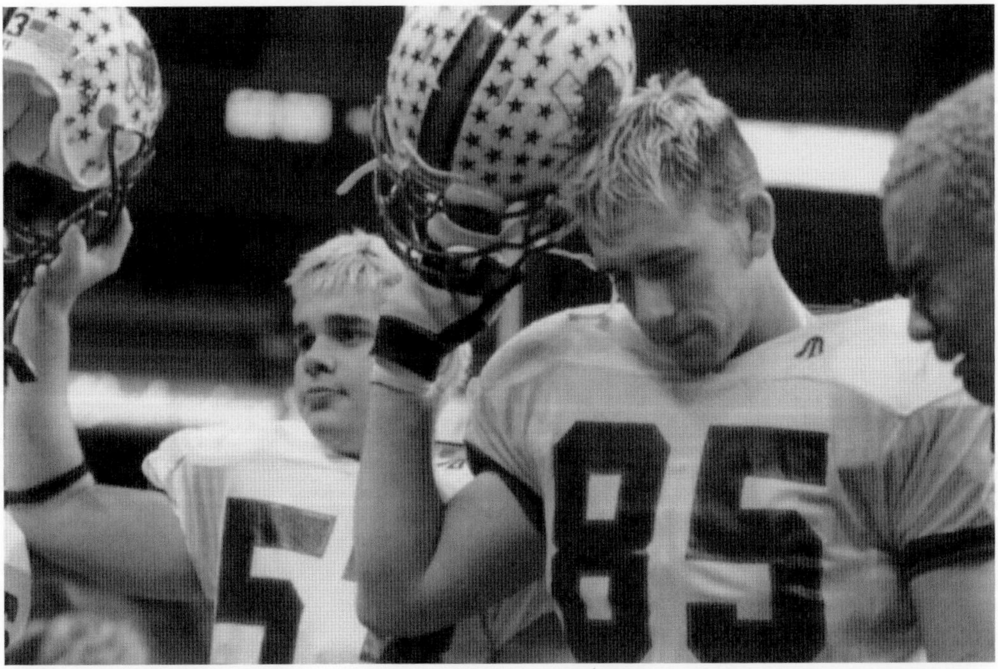

Area coaches took notice. Irving MacArthur head coach David Beaty said, "I will tell you this, I've never seen the butts in the seats like they have since [putting] that ball . . . in the air." But despite it all, the Katy Tigers defeated the Dragons in the final moments of the game, 16-15, for the 2003 state title. The loss ended the Dragons' longest winning streak in 5A history (31 wins). Here, Dragons Bill Lacava, Adam Boydston, and Joseph Huggins react to the loss. (Photograph by Kyle Grice.)

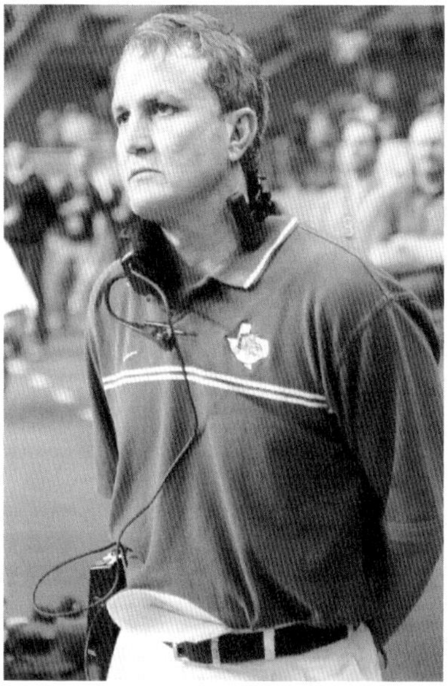

"Going into the [2004] season," Dodge said, "players and coaches made a pact to do everything in the memory of Charlie [Stalcup]," seen here. The Dragons' defensive coordinator had lost his two-year battle to melanoma before the start of the season. After a big win in the season opener against Midland Lee, the Dragons beat longtime rival Coppell, 70-21. Quarterback Chase Daniel threw for 392 yards and six touchdowns that night.

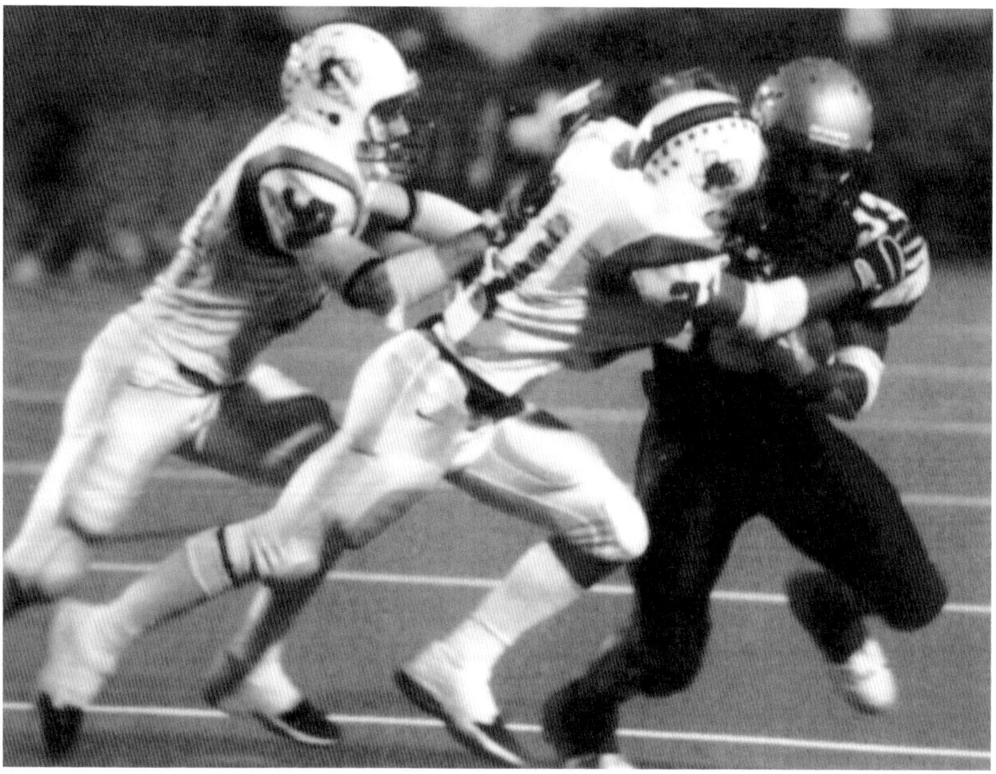

The midseason game against Denton Ryan was the first in Texas high school football history to be televised. "ESPN put that game on national television," Dodge said. "We had a huge win [52-27]." The Dragons went on to finish the season undefeated. In their game against Plano East earlier in the season, senior Beau Galbraith and sophomore Arius Ford, pictured, stop their opponent. (Photograph by Matt Gatto.)

The Dragons' third-round game against Abilene was a close one. A key interception by linebacker Patrick Benoist "sealed the deal," said Dodge, and gave the Dragons a 35-30 win. Carroll won the next week's game against Denton Ryan, 28-7. The semifinal game against Lufkin in Waco's Floyd Casey Stadium was played before a crowd of more than 40,000 fans. The Dragons pulled out the 37-30 win. Here, running back Aaron Luna powers through three Plano East Panthers in a game earlier that season. (Photograph by Matt Gatto.)

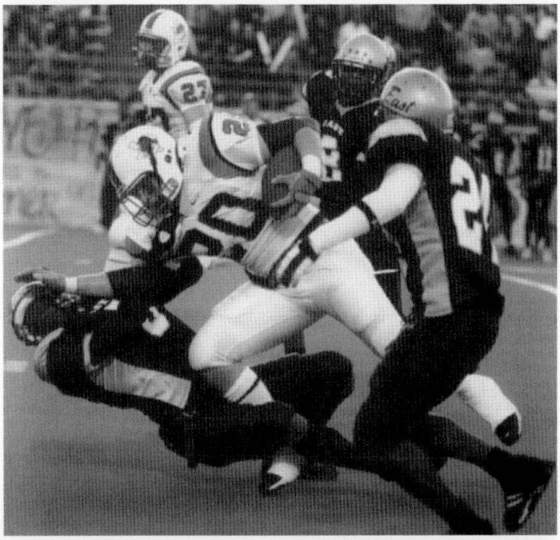

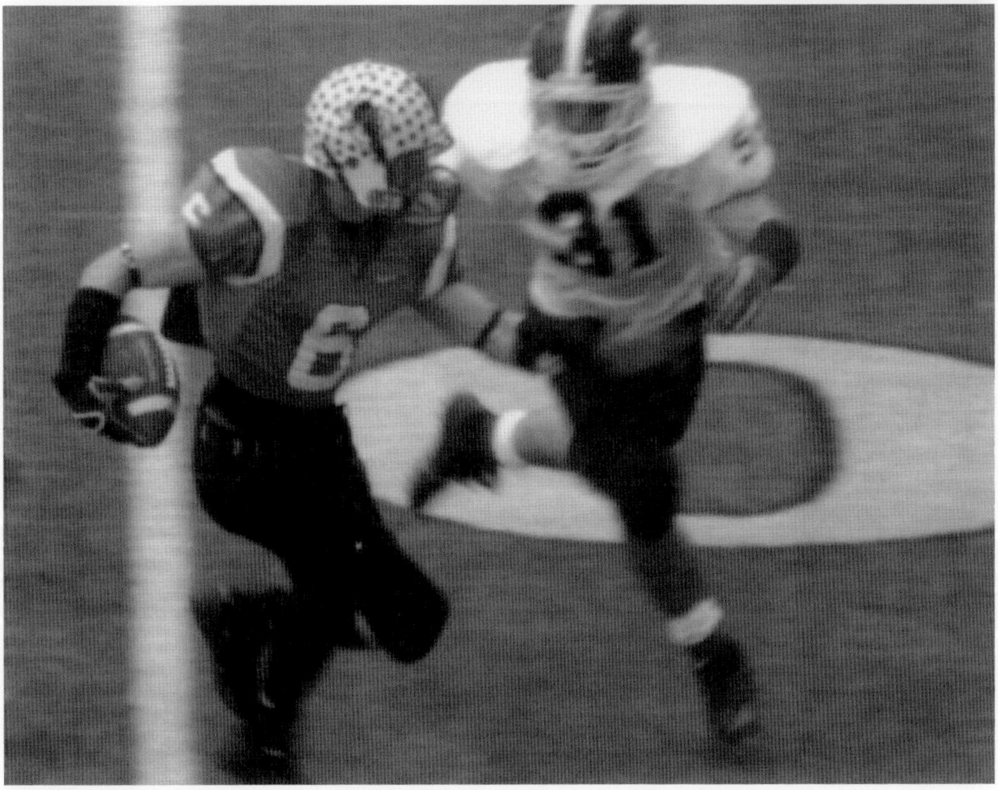

Receiver McKay Jacobson (No. 6) makes a run in the state finals against Smithson Valley—a nip-and-tuck game: the Dragons kicked a field goal with four seconds on the clock to win it, 27-24, for their second 5A state title. The Associated Press and *USA Today* named them the National High School Champions. Senior quarterback Chase Daniel finished the season with 5,981 yards and 69 touchdowns. He played at the University of Missouri, went on to play for the New Orleans Saints, and currently plays for the Kansas City Chiefs. (Photograph by Robyn Krogman.)

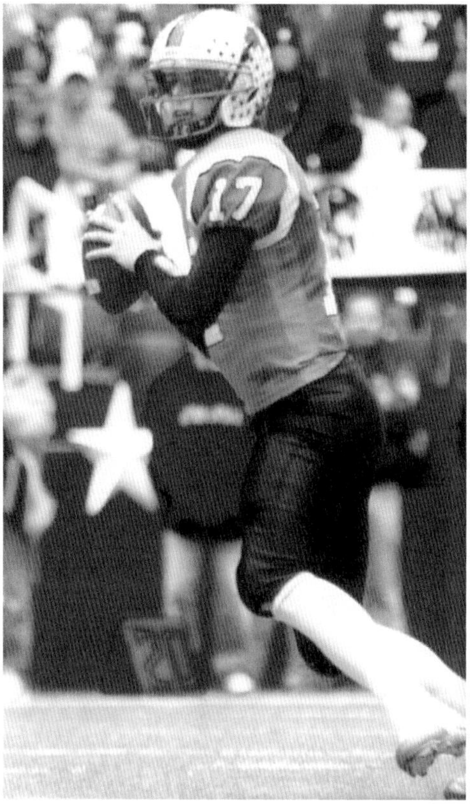

The 2005 starting quarterback, senior Greg McElroy (No. 17), had backed up Chase Daniel. "He was ready," Dodge said. A lot of players returned from the 2004 team. "We had talent throughout our roster." The Dragons beat Midland Lee, 48-25, in their season opener. (Photograph by Mallorie Seebeck.)

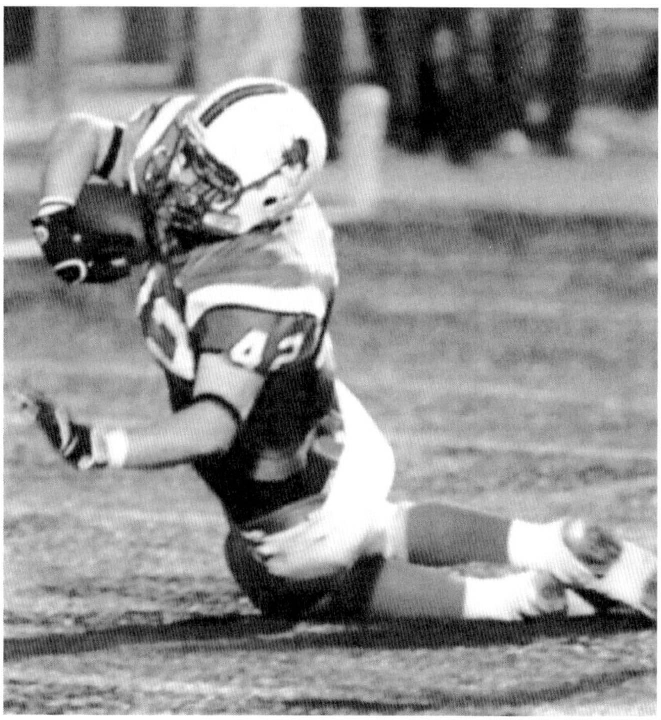

The Dragons beat their remaining non-district opponents handily, and the first district game against Denton Ryan was again nationally televised. The Dragons put up numbers as big as they ever had. But the last district game against Grapevine was a nail-biter. "They gave us all we wanted," Dodge said. "We had to really hold on to win that one." The final score was 28-23. Here, Dragon defenseman junior Kyle Russo recovers a fumble in a game that season. (Photograph by Jay McPhail.)

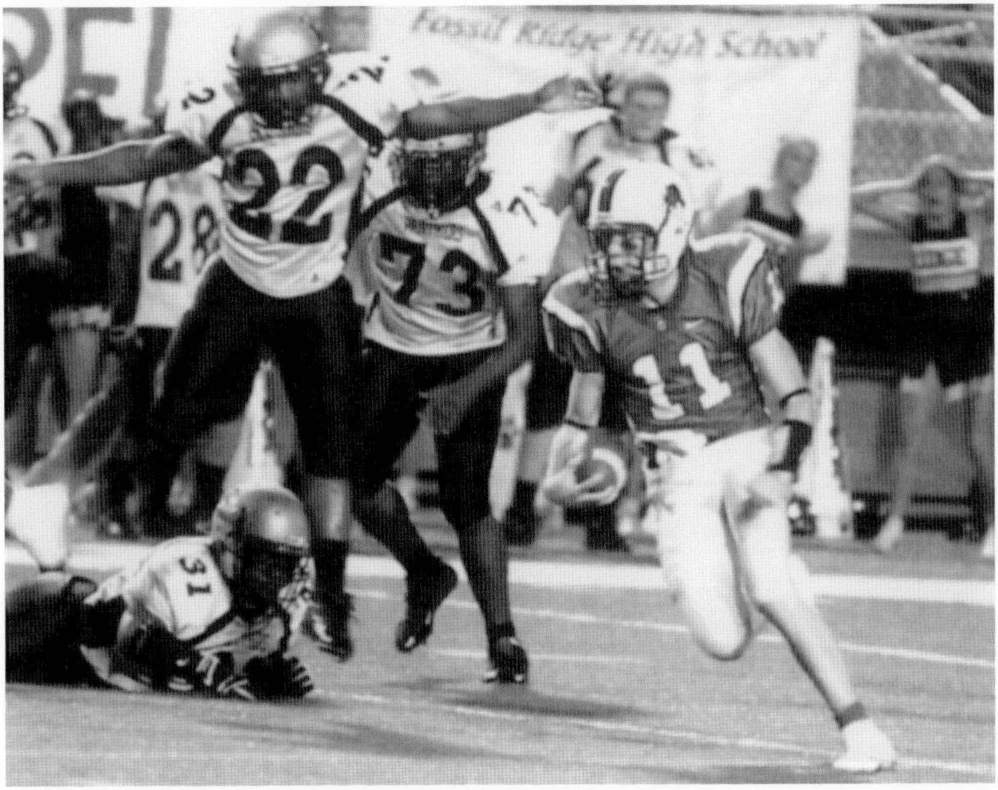

"Defensively," Dodge remembered, "we were led by Patrick Benoist and Joseph Agnew in the back end. We just had a lot of really good players." Included on the roster were two sophomores, running back Tre Newton and Dodge's son, wide receiver Riley Dodge. Here, Dodge heads toward the end zone to score against Fossil Ridge. (Photograph by Jay McPhail.)

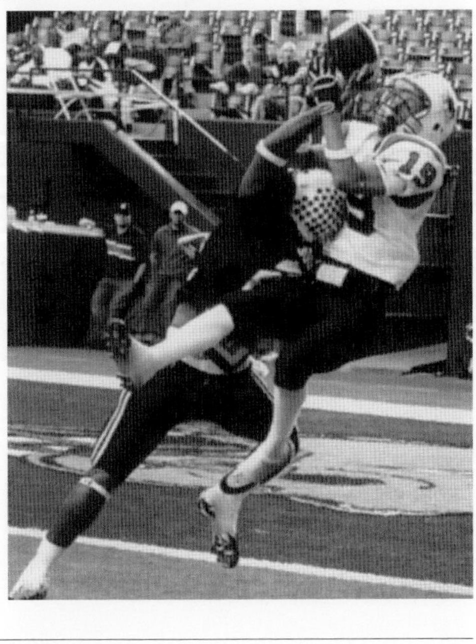

"We had probably the greatest six-game playoff run that maybe the history of Texas had ever seen. Every team we played in the first five rounds was undefeated," Dodge said. In this photograph taken during the fourth-round playoff game against Plano, senior Clint Renfro (whose father Mike Renfro played for the Dallas Cowboys in the 1980s) jumps to make a catch. (Photograph by Mallorie Seebeck.)

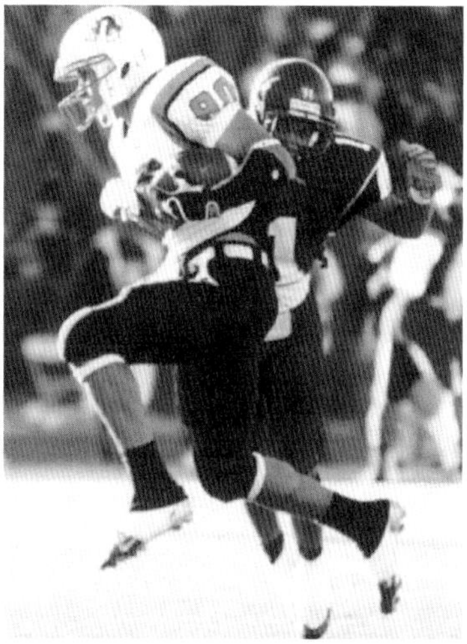

"We lost the flip with Lufkin for week five of the playoffs," Dodge recalled, "so we took our team on the road to East Texas. That's when [Dallas Cowboy] Dez Bryant was a junior at Lufkin, and they had a very good first half. But we blew them out in the second half." Final score: 46-28. Here, senior Corbin Smiter tries to break away from a Lufkin defender. (Photograph by Mallorie Seebeck.)

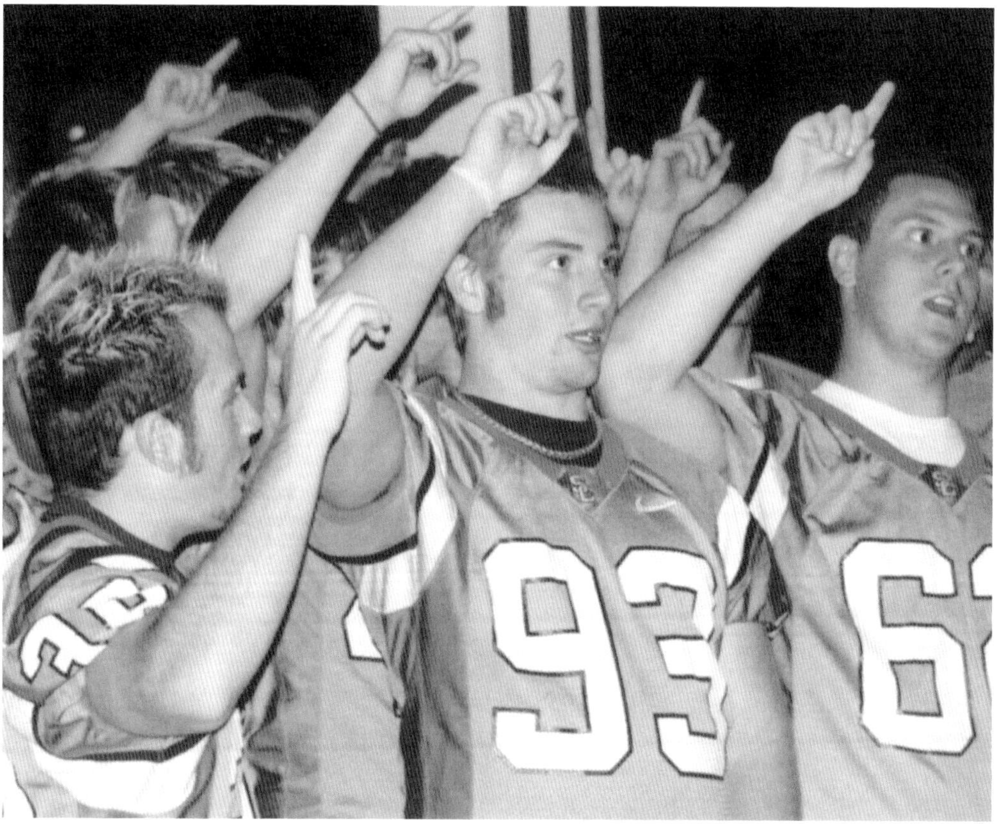

The Dragons played Katy in the 2005 state championship game. "Katy had a great team," Dodge said. But the Dragons beat them, 34-20. *USA Today* named the Dragons the National High School Champions for a second year. The team had a 32-game winning streak going. "I think we had 10 guys sign Division I scholarships from that team," Dodge recalled. At a community-wide pep rally held in Southlake Town Square, seniors Alex Haitz, Joe Graff, and Blake West sing the alma mater. (Photograph by Jay McPhail.)

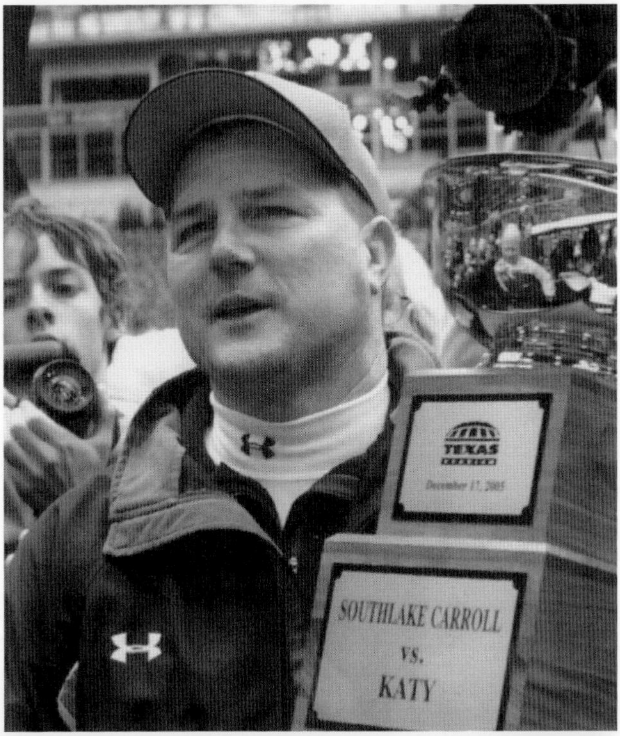

"This win had Charlie's [Stalcup] fingerprints all over it because of the relationship he formed with these players," Dodge said after winning the state championship. It was Dodge's fourth consecutive trip to the 5A state finals and his third state title as Carroll head coach. McElroy went on to play for Alabama, was drafted by the New York Jets, played with the Cincinnati Bengals, and is a college football analyst on ESPN's SEC Network. (Photograph by Jay McPhail.)

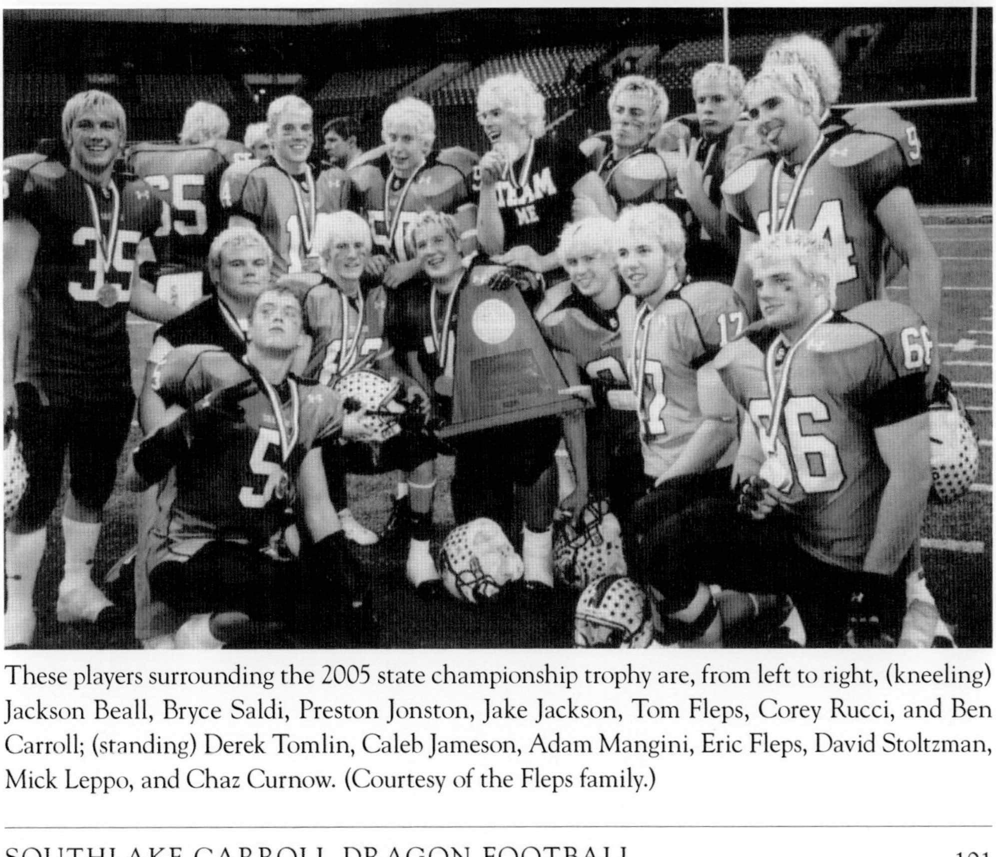

These players surrounding the 2005 state championship trophy are, from left to right, (kneeling) Jackson Beall, Bryce Saldi, Preston Jonston, Jake Jackson, Tom Fleps, Corey Rucci, and Ben Carroll; (standing) Derek Tomlin, Caleb Jameson, Adam Mangini, Eric Fleps, David Stoltzman, Mick Leppo, and Chaz Curnow. (Courtesy of the Fleps family.)

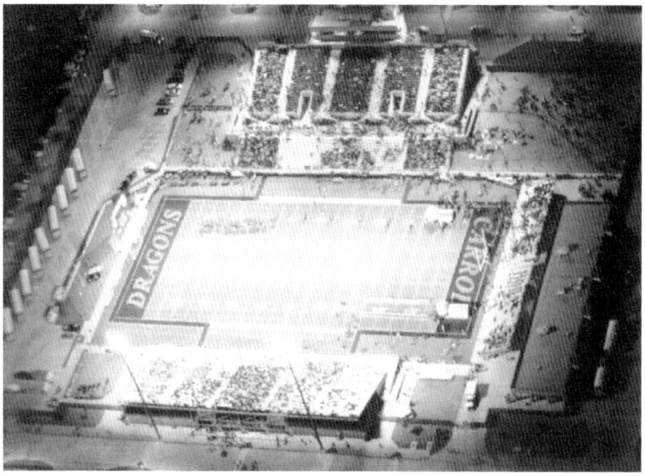

Before the game against Grapevine in the 2006 season, the US Army Golden Knights parachute team flew over Dragon Stadium and jumped onto the field. In the airplane was Carroll Senior High School yearbook photography editor Mallorie Seebeck, who snapped the stadium's first-ever aerial photograph. (Photograph by Mallorie Seebeck.)

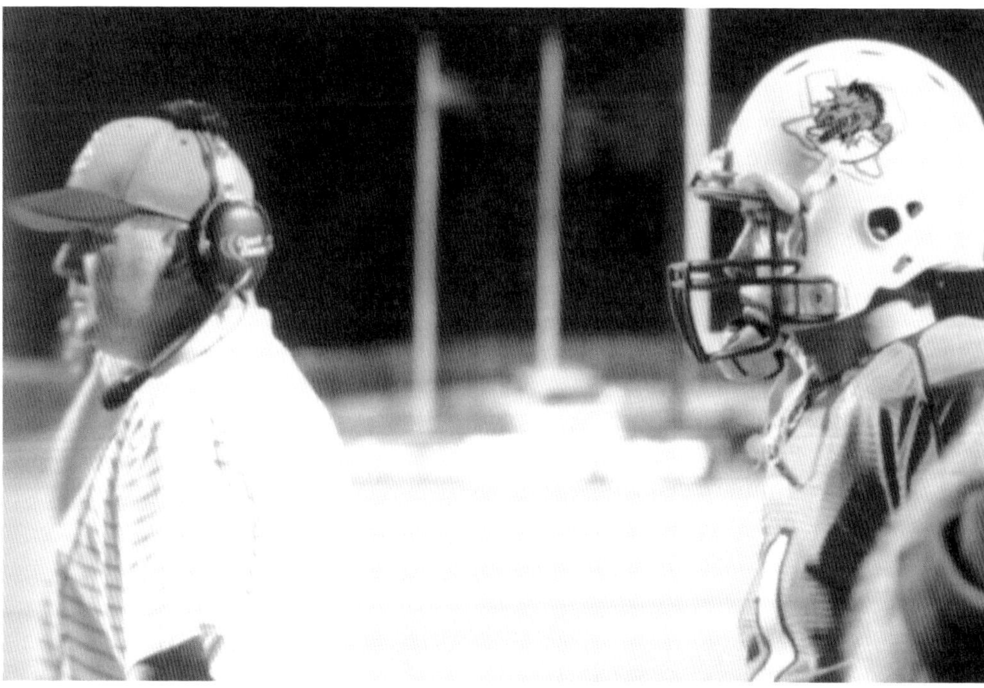

Only three starters returned for the 2006 season. "Our offensive line was pretty much the junior varsity line from the year before," Dodge explained. The second game of the season was in Dragon Stadium against Evangel Christian Academy, considered by many to be one of Louisiana's top programs. It was the Dragons' third nationally televised game in three seasons. The Dragons won, 43-16. Seen here standing on the sidelines are Todd Dodge and his son Riley. (Photograph by Mallorie Seebeck.)

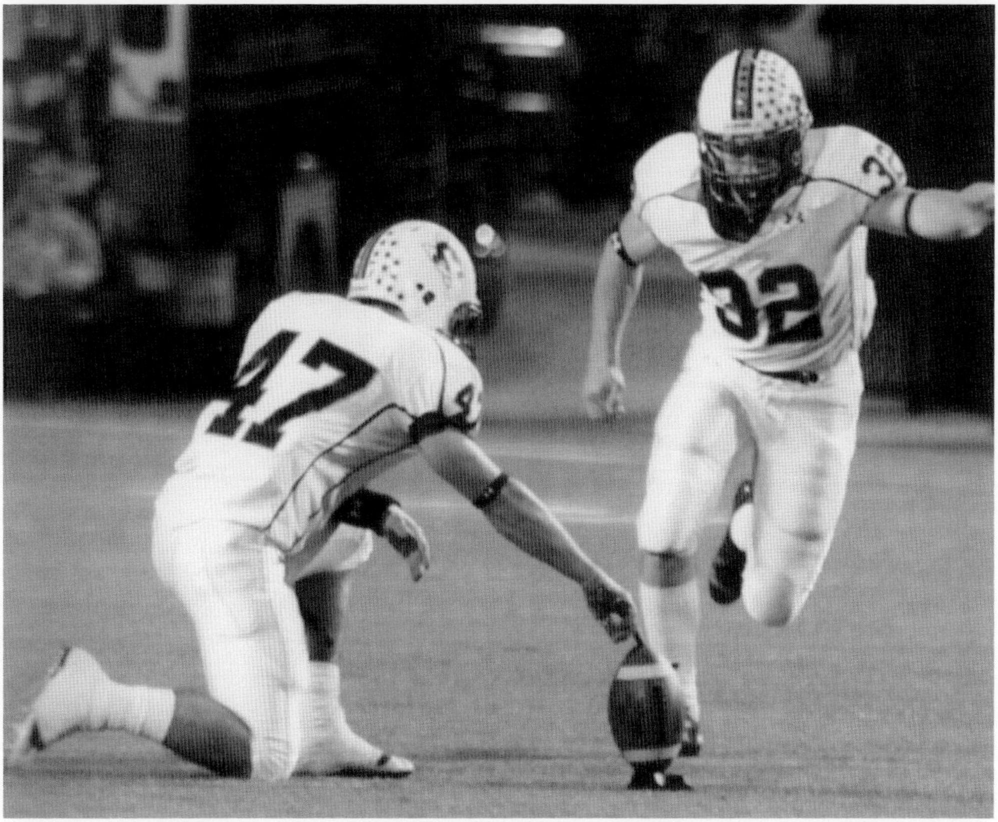

"That team [2006] had the best and most productive defense the entire time I was at Carroll," Dodge said. Undefeated in the regular season, the Dragons headed to the playoffs. Senior kicker Cade Foster, who made varsity as a freshman, prepares to kick as Greg Lehane holds the ball during the last regular season game. (Photograph by Mallorie Seebeck.)

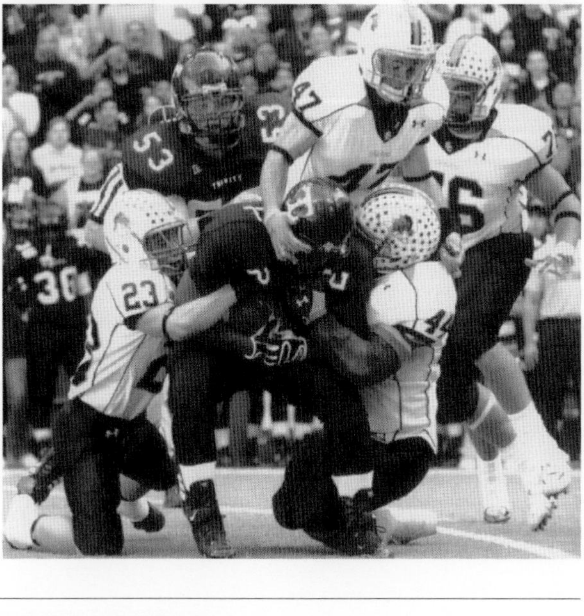

Round two of the playoffs created lots of buzz as the No. 1 Dragons met No. 2 Euless Trinity. "We played in front of 50,000 people there in Texas Stadium. One of the real classics of all time in Texas high school football history," Dodge said. Carroll won, 22-21, with nine seconds left. "Probably the most electric atmosphere any of us had ever been in," Dodge said. Dragons in that game included Luke Anderson, Greg Lehane, Justin Padron, and Kevin Swanson. (Photograph by Mallorie Seebeck.)

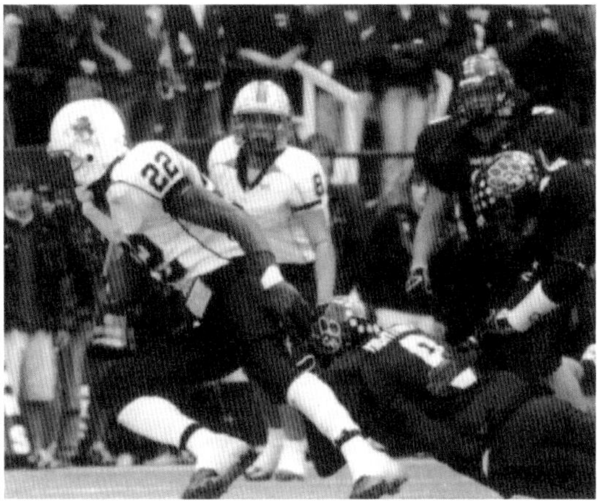

The third-round playoff game was against Odessa-Permian. "The thing I was most worried about in that game," Dodge said, "was coming off the huge emotional win against Trinity. But our kids just answered the bell big time [42-6]." Carroll beat fourth-round Colleyville Heritage, 33-7. Here, Dragon Tre Newton (No. 22) (whose father Nate Newton played for the Dallas Cowboys in the 1990s) avoids Colleyville Heritage defenders. (Photograph by Mallorie Seebeck.)

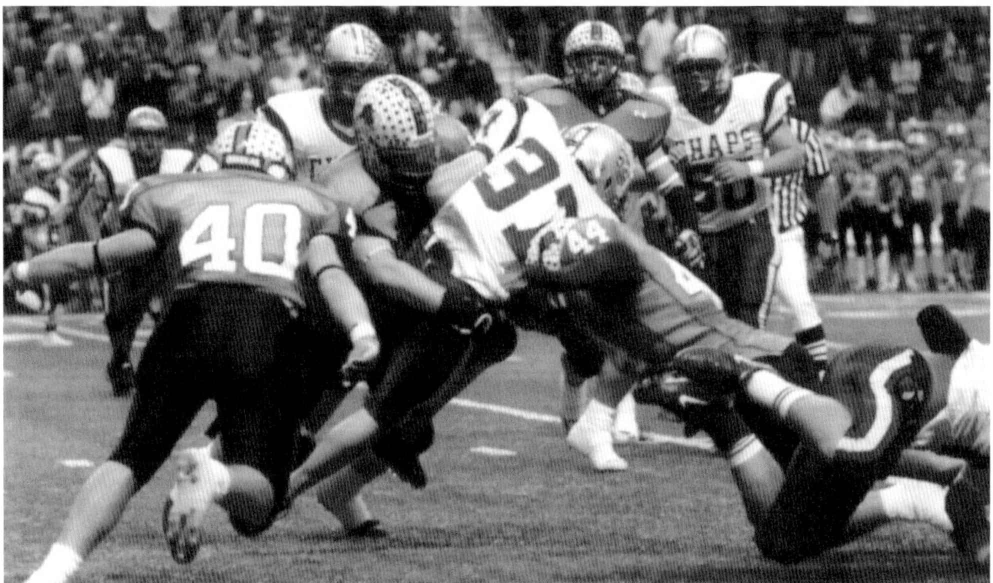

The Dragons beat their fifth-round opponents, Allen, 38-0 for the team's 47th win in a row. The state final game was against Austin Westlake. The Dragons were losing at halftime. "We had a come-to-Jesus meeting at halftime, and those kids came out and scored on the first two possessions to get the lead back," Dodge said. Carroll won the Class 5A State Championship—a three-peat—42-29. Here, Dragons, including Justin Padron, tackle an Austin Westlake player as Austin Shrum (No. 40) moves in to assist.

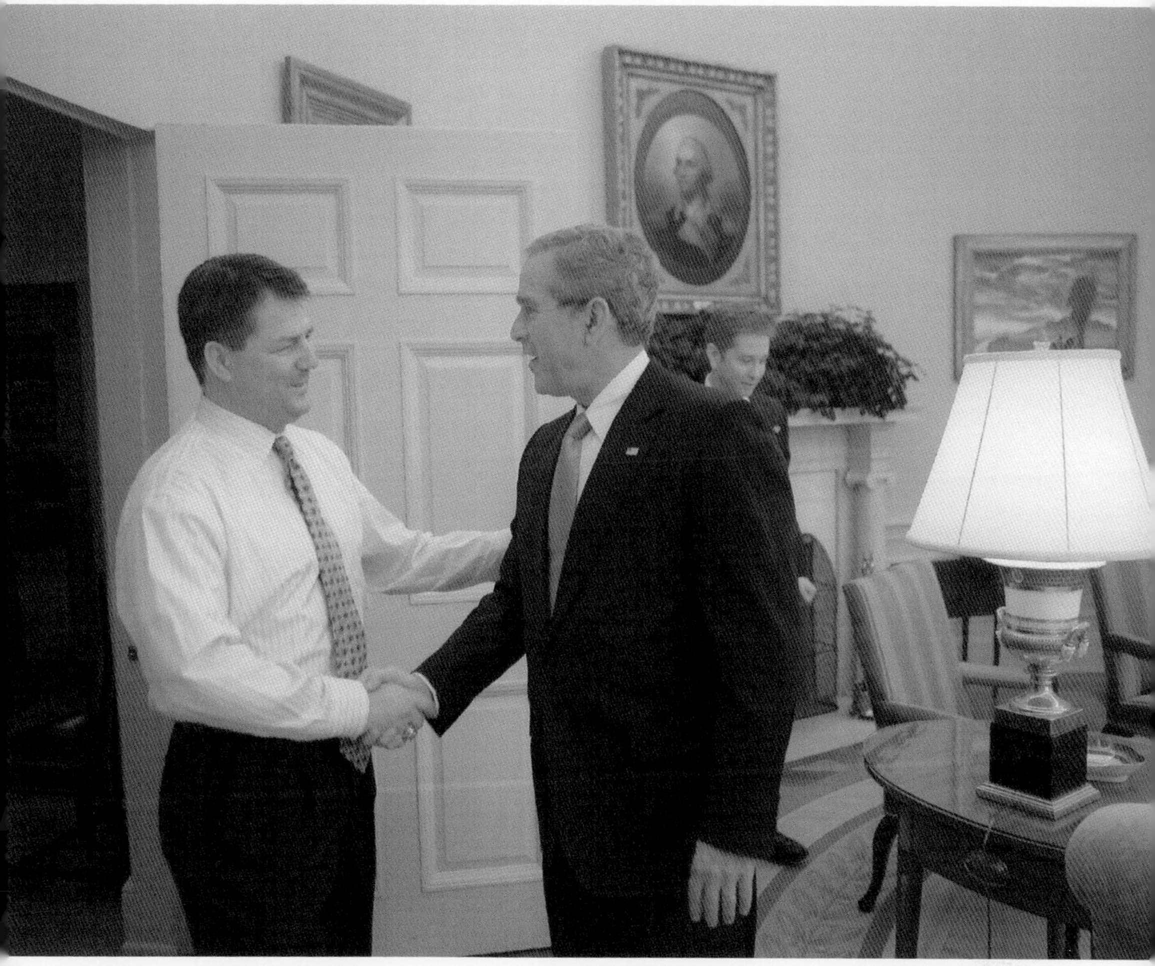

"That was the famous game where Riley threw up and then threw a touchdown pass," Todd Dodge said. Stories about the incident include a Westlake player who admitted he could not take his eyes off the young quarterback as he threw up. As a result, the defender missed covering the Dragon who caught Dodge's pass for the touchdown. President George W. Bush watched the game on television. Several months later, while on a visit to Washington, DC, the Dodge family was invited to the Oval Office to meet the president. "The first thing the president said was, 'Hey, Riley, I've never seen anyone throw up and then throw a touchdown pass,'" the coach, seen here with the president, said. Later he recalled, "Personally, it was my most gratifying win because we did it when no one expected us to." For a third time, *USA Today* named the Dragons the National High School Champions. (Photograph by Eric Draper, courtesy of the George W. Bush Library and Museum, Dallas, Texas.)

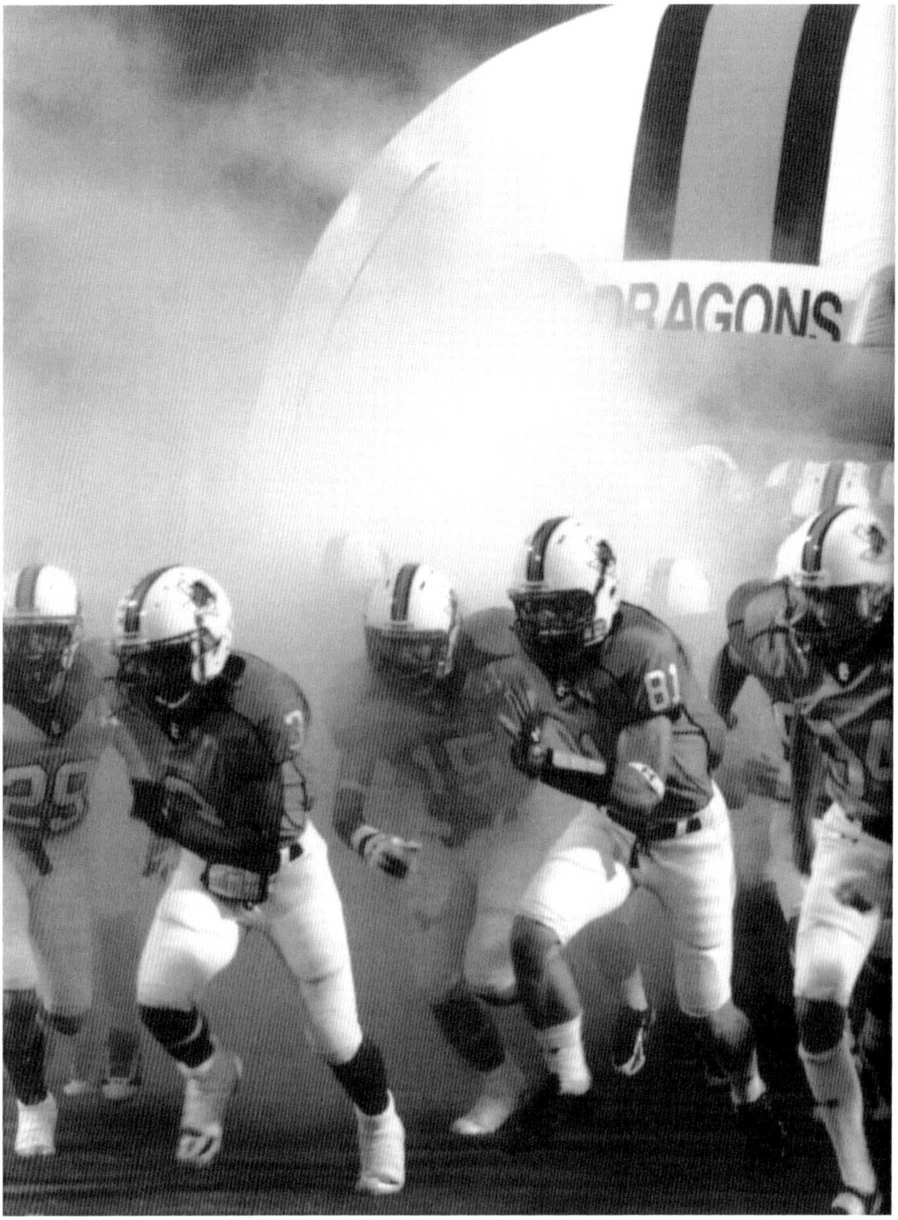

While the Dragons were making history in their playoff run, Coach Dodge had accepted the head coach position at the University of North Texas in Denton. The championship game against Austin Westlake was played on December 23. "I spent Christmas Day with my family and started there [UNT] on December 26. It wasn't until the team banquet in January that I was able to be with the team and celebrate all the great things that had happened that season." As for his replacement, Dodge said, "You never know when you leave somewhere whether or not you will be asked for your opinion on who should be hired. Well, they asked me, and I recommended Hal Wasson." This photograph is a familiar scene for all Dragon fans as the players run out of the inflatable helmet onto the field in Dragon Stadium. (Photograph by Mallorie Seebeck.)

5

The Tradition Continues

When Hal Wasson took over as Carroll's head coach in 2007, he had already been part of the Dragon tradition. In 2002, Todd Dodge hired Wasson as his running backs coach, and that year the Dragons won the 2002 Class 5A State Championship. Wasson stayed two years, then left to be the head coach at Keller Fossil Ridge.

Wasson grew up on a cotton farm in Kerens, 65 miles southeast of Dallas, and played sports in high school and college. After graduating from Abilene Christian University, his job in Groesbeck was the first in a long line of coaching positions he held in small-town Texas high schools, including Ennis, Corsicana, Italy, San Saba, Pittsburg, Kerens, Mexia, and Liberty Hill. Wasson said the key to his success in each assignment was the relationships he and his family made in the community. "Everywhere we've been, it's been a remarkable journey," he said.

After Dodge announced his departure in 2006, CISD athletic director Ronnie Tipps phoned Wasson at Fossil Ridge. "Next thing I knew, they offered me the job," Wasson said. "I got to come back because I understood the culture of the Dragon Nation. And it wasn't a tough decision, but it was a decision. We're all competitive and we all want to make a difference. I told Todd that every place I'd coached, we were able to raise the bar. But there was no possible way to raise the bar at Carroll."

Dodge encouraged Wasson to take the job and just "get through the first year." When Wasson and his wife, Sally, decided to take the position, they knew it was "gonna be a ride. But either you jump in or you don't. No testing the waters." They knew the Carroll staff. They knew the community. "But," the new head coach told his wife, "we've got to win. It's gonna be really hard, I'm telling you. So, just hang on."

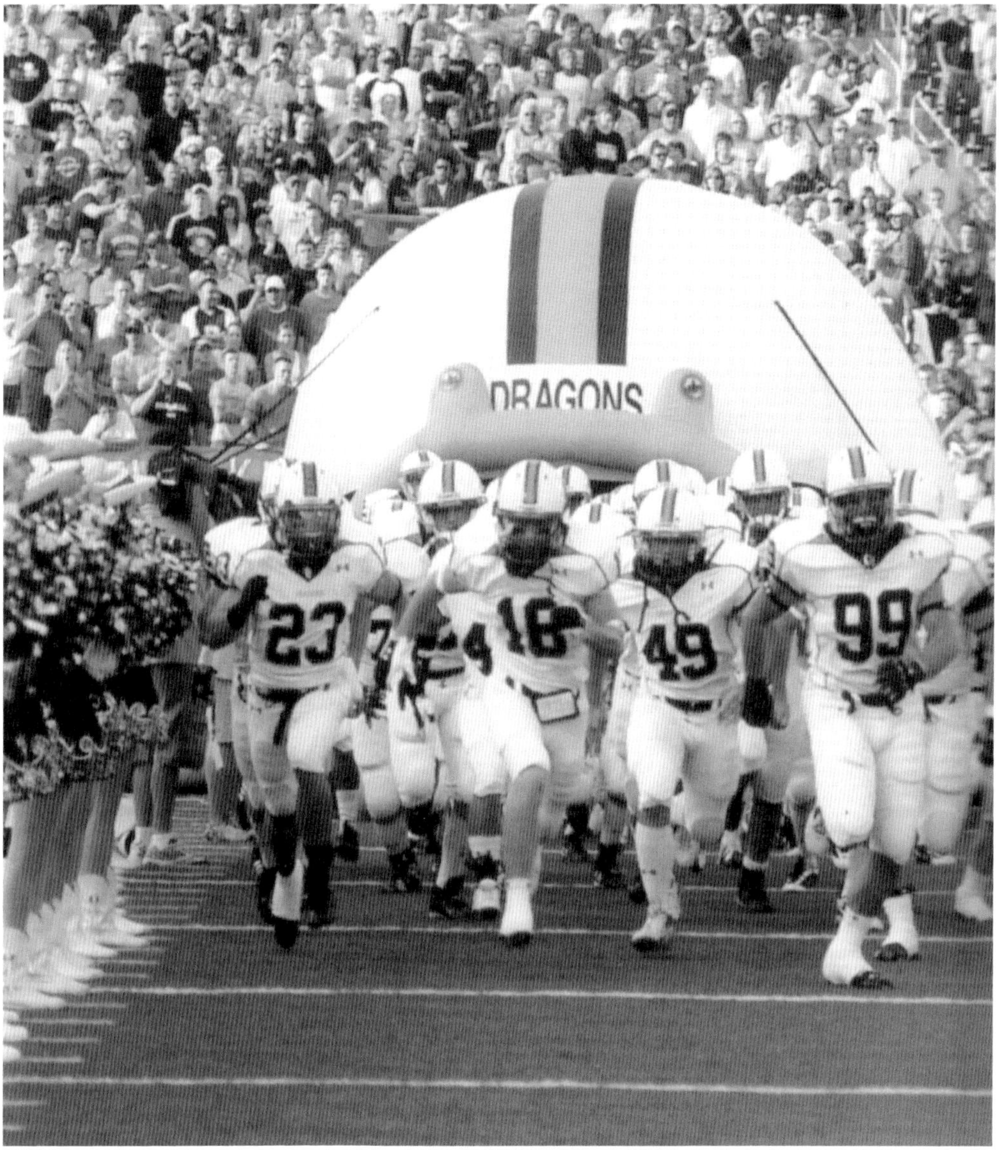

In 2007, Hal Wasson took over as head coach in a hot media spotlight. The reigning 5A state champion Dragons had won four titles in five years. The Associated Press ranked the team No. 1 for the fourth consecutive season. Wasson's starting quarterback was Todd Dodge's son, Riley. And Wasson would coach his team's second game on national television: the "Clash of the Champions" matched Carroll against the defending Florida state champion, the Miami Northwestern Bulls. Northwestern was coming into the game with its own media attention—the football season was almost cancelled after a grand jury reported the school had tried to cover up a sex scandal involving several players. The Miami Dade School District fired the head coach and his eight assistants, but the team was allowed to play. Here, the Dragons enter the Southern Methodist University Gerald J. Ford Stadium for the game before a crowd of more than 31,000—the highest regular season high school football attendance in the history of Texas. (Photograph by Charlie Mills.)

Before halftime, the score was 21-21, then quarterback Dodge threw a completed pass to receiver Tre Newton (No. 22) on the Bulls' six-yard line, but a fumble allowed Northwestern to recover. The Bulls made a safety in the second half to take the lead and held onto it. The final score was Bulls 29, Dragons 21. The loss ended a Dragon 49-game winning streak and was the team's first defeat since 2003. (Photograph by Charlie Mills.)

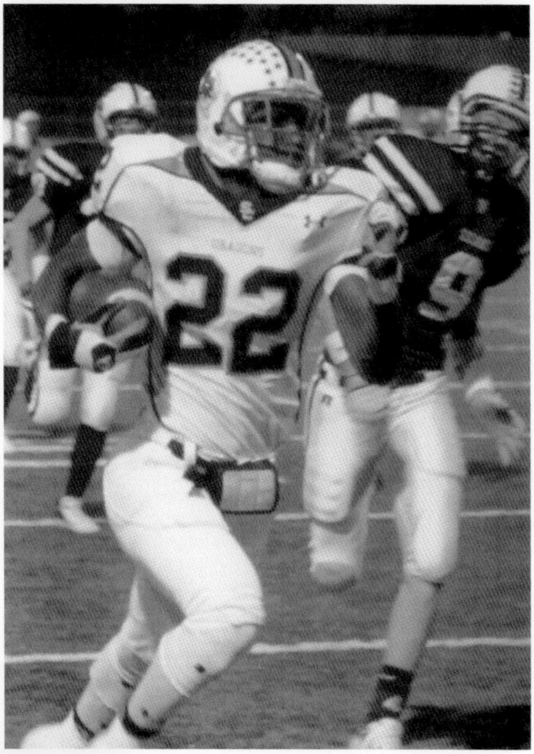

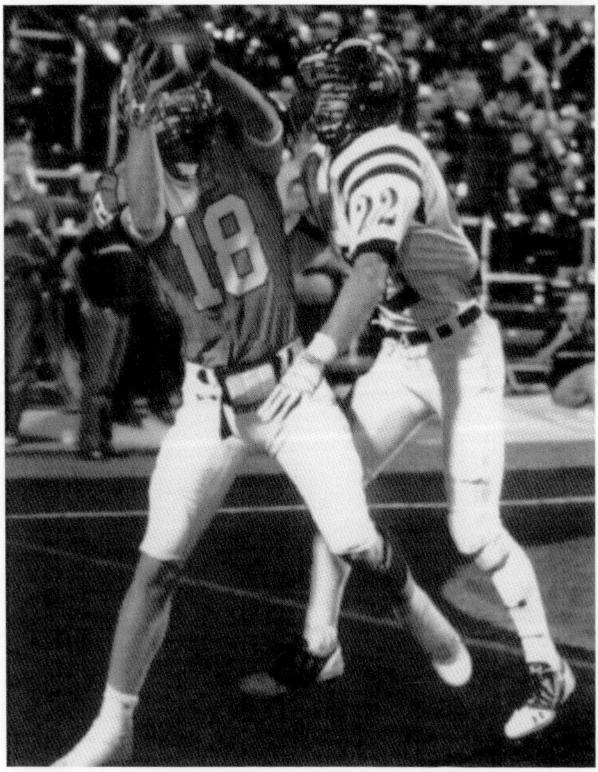

The team's seniors, including Ethan Cunningham (No. 18), were in the eighth grade the last time the Dragons had lost a game. The record-winning streak began in 2004 and ended with the Northwestern loss. "I hurt for our kids. I hurt for our coaches," CISD athletic director Tipps said. "You hate to see it end, especially with the big-game atmosphere we had." (Photograph by Erin Murphy.)

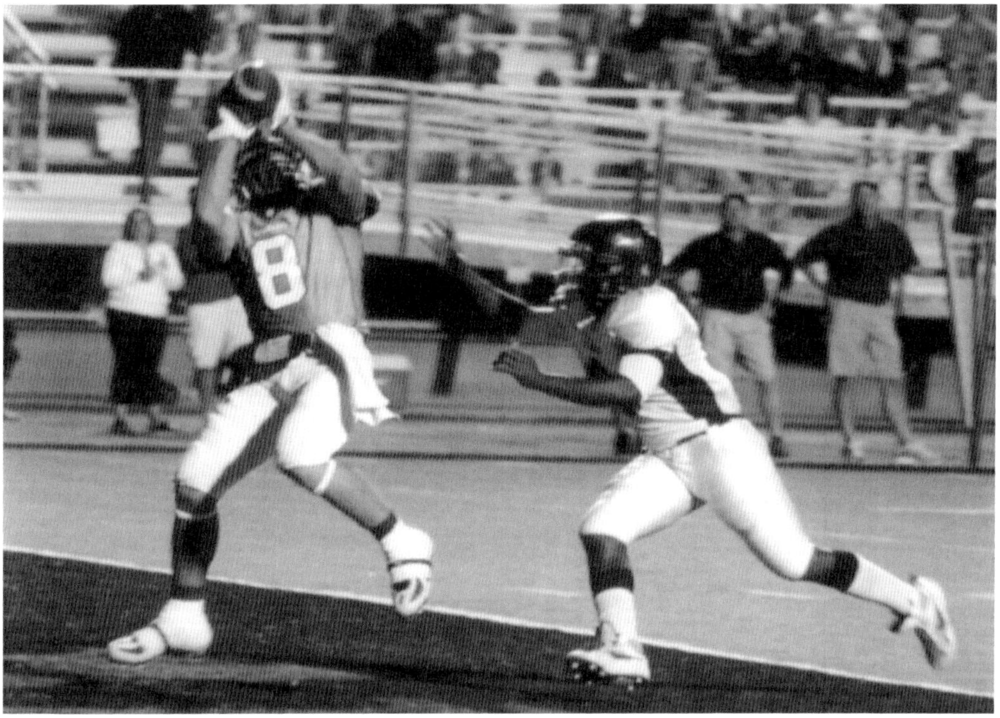

By the time the midseason Haltom game rolled around, eight players were out with various injuries. Despite that, the Dragons led the Buffalos 51-0 at halftime. Running back Newton, nursing a hurt ankle from the Northwestern game, had 12 carries for 153 yards. Sophomore kicker Cade Foster booted a pair of field goals, the second one a 42-yarder. Senior receiver Blake Cantu (No. 8) makes this catch as he outruns his Haltom opponent. (Photograph by Charlie Mills.)

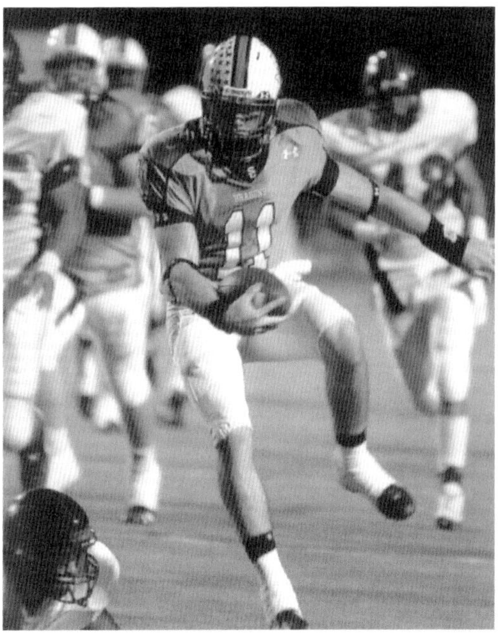

The Dragons outscored their remaining opponents that season, 207-72. The team had the area's top-ranked offense when it came time to play their first-round playoff game against Flower Mound in Texas Stadium. But the injuries continued. "I told Riley (No. 11) with Tre nicked up, we were going to put the ball in his hands," Wasson told reporters before the game. "When we put the ball in his hands, magic happens." (Photograph by Charlie Mills.)

By halftime Carroll was ahead, 21-17, and Flower Mound never regained the lead. The Dragons won, 35-24. Carroll beat their second-round opponent, Cedar Hill, 38-17, and advanced to the third round against Abilene. But, with a 14-2 lead over the Eagles in the second quarter, Dodge suffered a shoulder separation. Backup quarterback Kyle Padron stepped in and completed a pass to put Carroll up 21-9. But Abilene took the lead, 22-21, and held on to win the game. Here, senior Chris Brainard makes a run in an earlier game that season. (Photograph by Charlie Mills.)

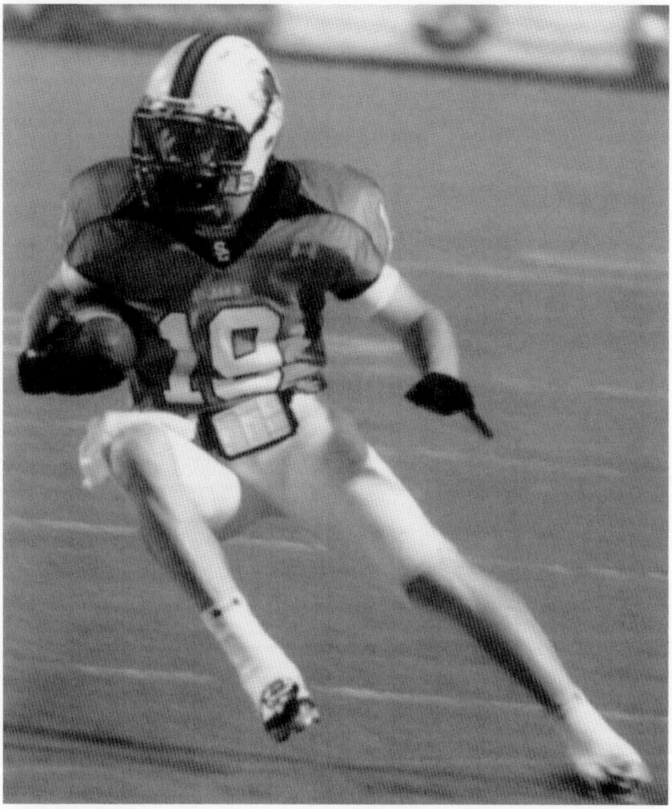

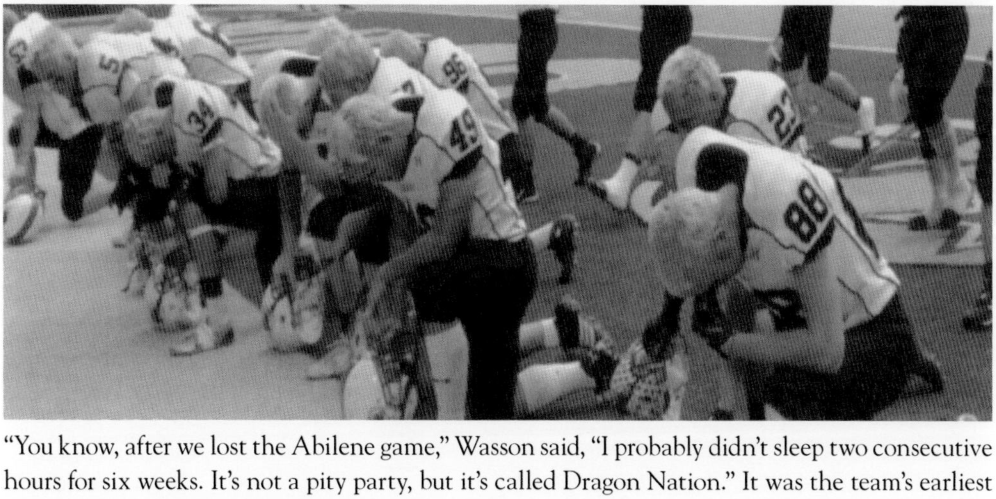

"You know, after we lost the Abilene game," Wasson said, "I probably didn't sleep two consecutive hours for six weeks. It's not a pity party, but it's called Dragon Nation." It was the team's earliest post-season exit since 2000. The loss for injured senior Dodge was bittersweet. "Best four years of my life. But I felt like I let my team down a little bit not being able to play for them," Dodge said. Here, the Dragons take a knee. (Photograph by Charlie Mills.)

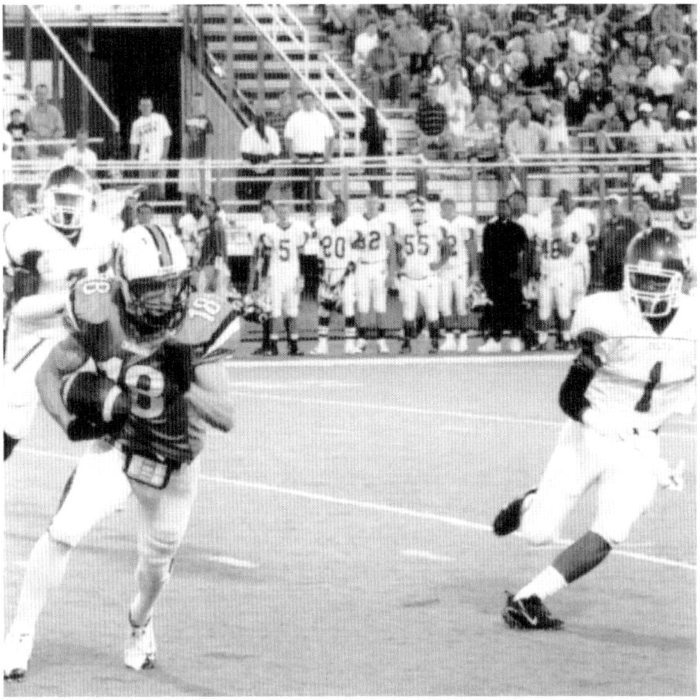

Senior Josh Popkin (No. 18) avoids this Arlington Colt defender in the second game of the 2008 season. The Dragons outscored their non-district opponents that season, 156-53. But that mattered little when they lost their district opener to Coppell in double-overtime. The Cowboys had not defeated the Dragons in seven years. And in their game against Flower Mound, quarterback Kyle Padron was injured. (Photograph by Erick Cruz.)

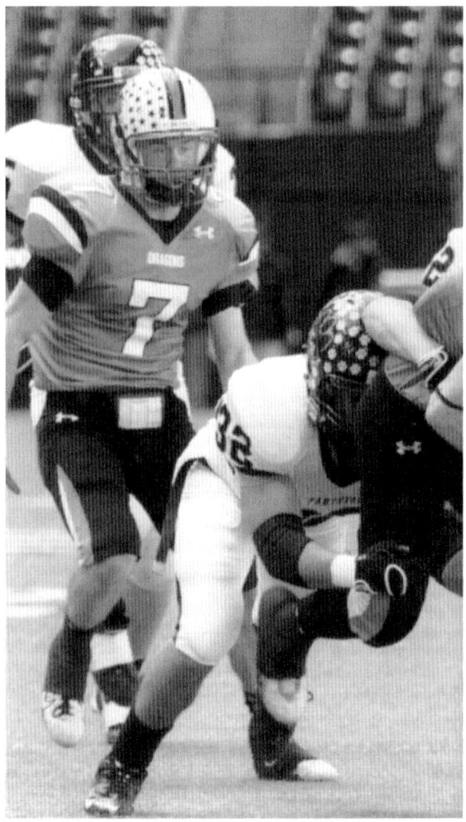

"David Piland and Kyle Williamson had alternated as Padron's backups," Wasson said recently, "and it just so happened that Piland was the backup that night [against Flower Mound]." The Dragons won, 38-14, and entered the playoffs. Pictured here running to help his teammate in Carroll's round-one win against Colleyville Heritage is Dragon Joshua Rake (No. 7) . Second-round opponent Cedar Hill brought the Dragon playoffs to a close, winning 31-18. "There was a lot of soul searching at that point," reflected Wasson. (Photograph by Kenny Thacker.)

The Dragons opened their 2009 season in the Gerald J. Ford Stadium at Southern Methodist University against Plano West and beat the Wolves, 35-9. Junior Alex Latimer and senior Greg Stoltzman force a third down in this photograph taken at the game. The defense was key in the next week's 44-10 win over Arlington. "When you are swarming to the football and you're confident, you make things happen," Wasson said. (Photograph by Leigh Campbell.)

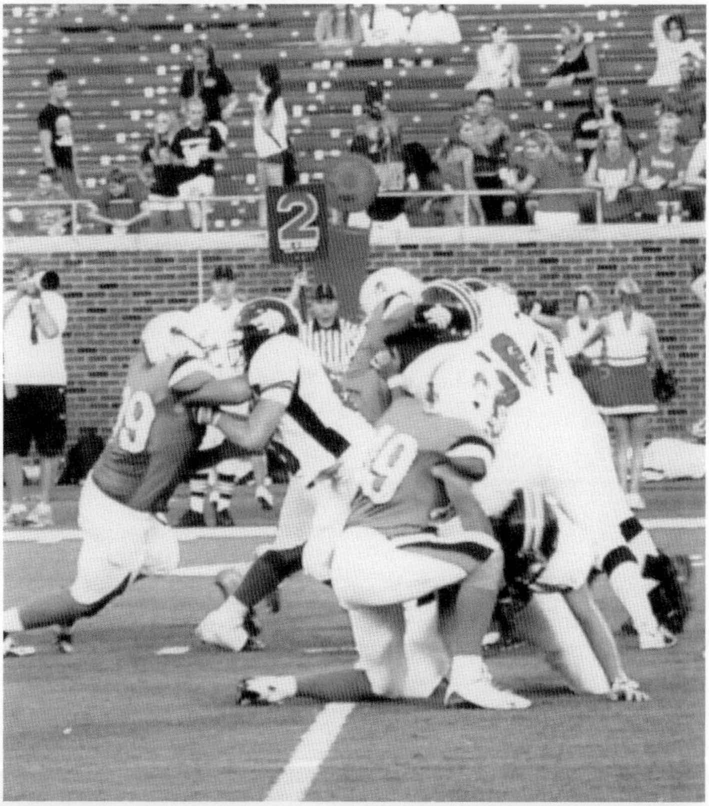

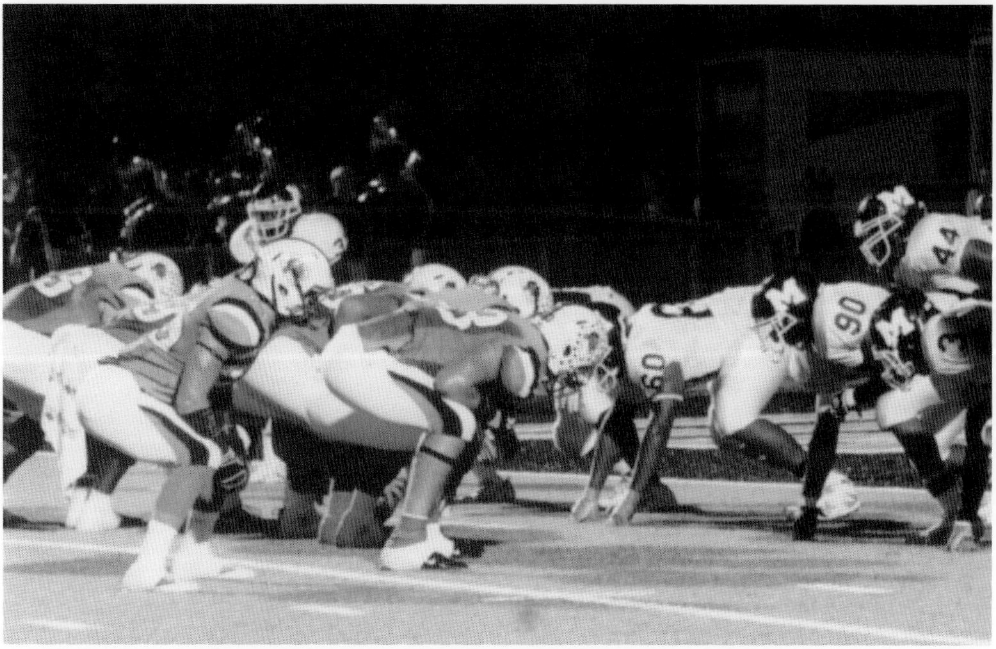

The Dragons played Mesquite in Dragon Stadium on brand new turf that year. Here, the teams are ready to try it out. The Dragons finished the regular season 9-1. (Photograph by Dani Cole.)

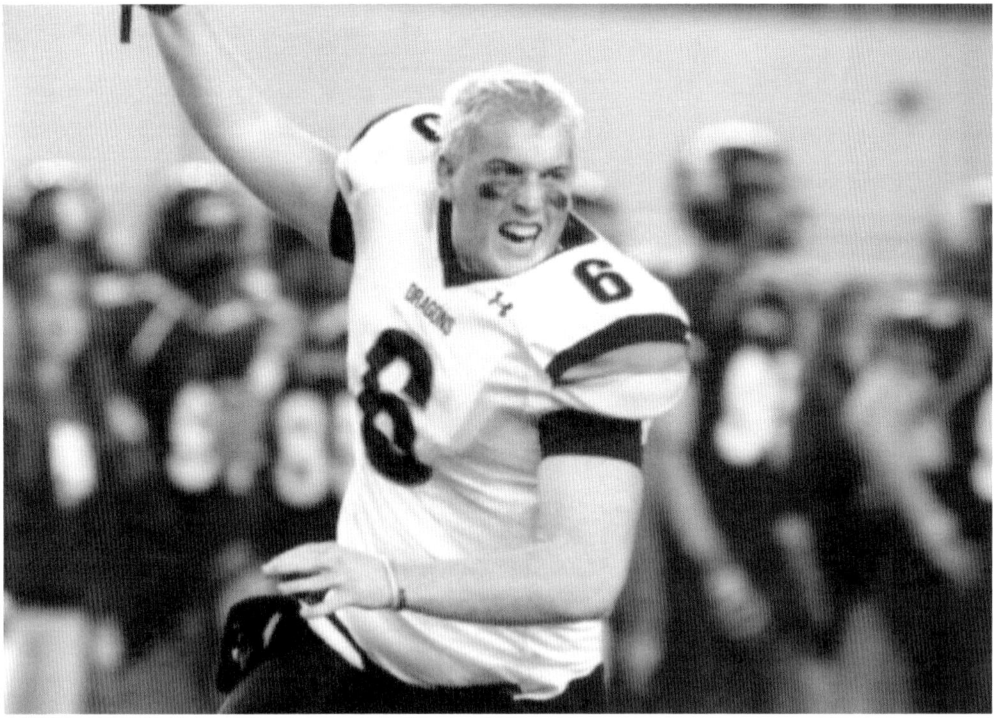

The Dragons won their first-round playoff game against Colleyville Heritage, 55-7. In round two, a fourth-quarter 21-21 tie against defending state champion Allen forced the game into two overtimes. But the Dragons were able to win, 35-34. Quarterback Kyle Williamson celebrates the victory. (Photograph by Dani Cole.)

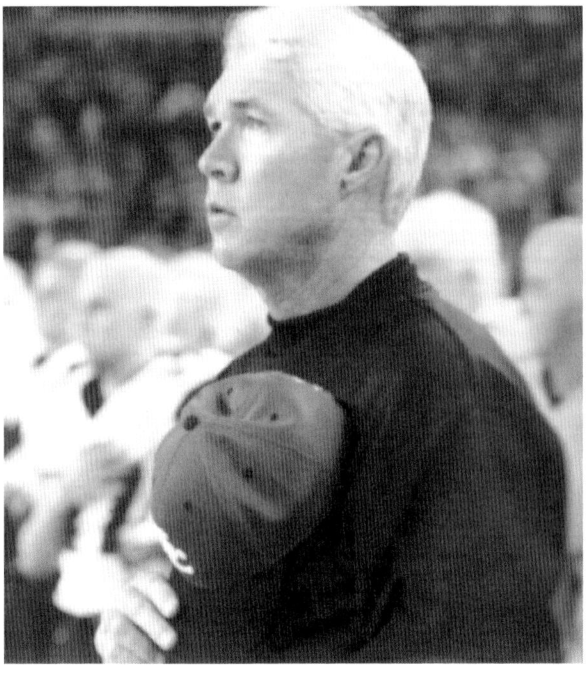

Coach Hal Wasson listens to the national anthem before the start of the third-round game against Arlington Bowie. The Volunteers beat the Dragons, 45-21. "The football team went three rounds deep in the playoffs," CISD athletic director Kevin Ozee remembered, "and people actually wanted our head coach removed. We all want to win every game, but that unrealistic expectation put undue pressure on the players and coaches." (Photograph by Carley Callahan.)

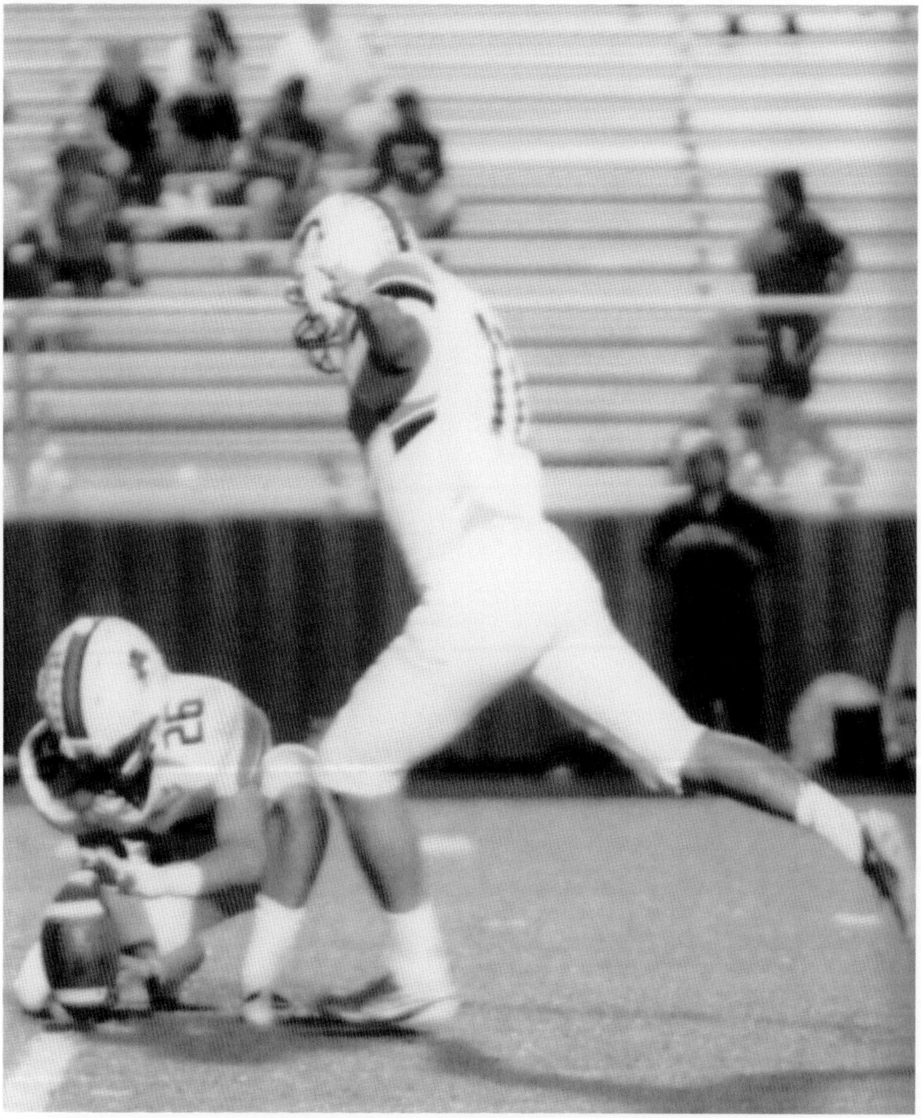

"That's when I fell in love with the mental conditioning part of the game," Wasson said recently. "You've really got to stay focused. You choose to get better or get worse. Don't let the clutter get in your head." In spring 2010, junior Daxx Garman registered in CISD and took practice with the varsity. Garman was tapped as the Dragon quarterback. But in late August, within days of the Dragons' season opener, an eight-minute television news report questioned the student's eligibility to play. After a series of UIL meetings, decisions, and appeals, Garman was ruled ineligible to play—only hours before kickoff. "You can imagine the devastation to the young man and the hurt on your team," Wasson said recently. Following the UIL ruling, the media coverage was intense. "They [reporters] were jumping out of bushes, pulling cameras from their lunch pails. You don't train for this as a coach." The Dragons lost their season opener against Copperas Cove. Here, Dragon Zach Thomason kicks an extra point in the Fossil Ridge game, while Mac McGuire holds the football. (Photograph by Connie Tam.)

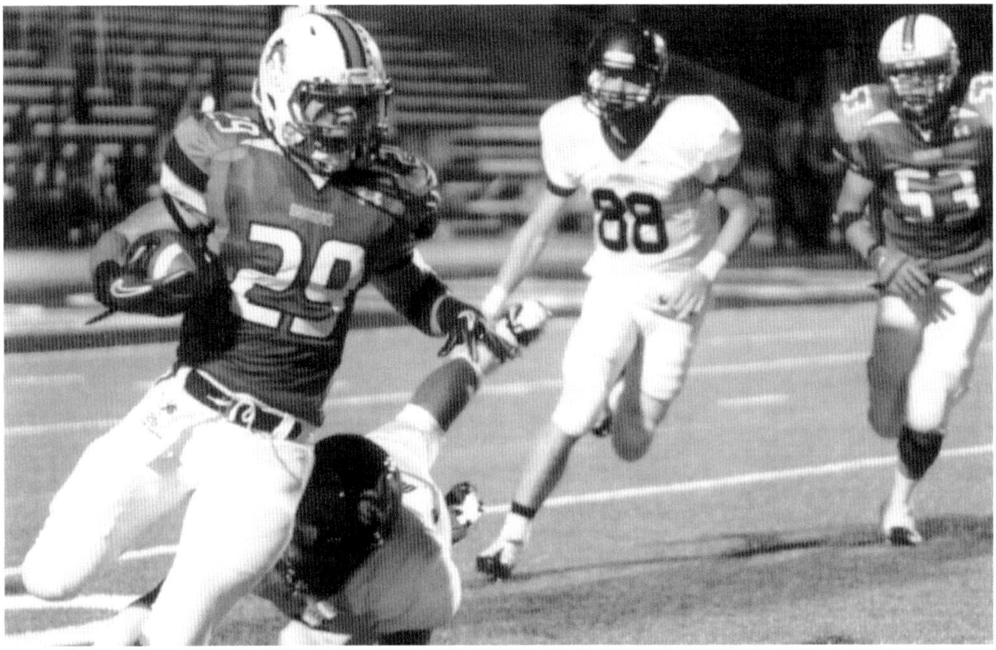

After losing their season opener, the Dragons won their next five games. Here, senior Paul Stevenson (No. 29) gets past an opponent in the Richardson Berkner game as junior J. J. Prince (No. 53) runs up to assist. The 2010 season ended 7-3, and the Dragons moved into the playoffs. (Photograph by Connie Tam.)

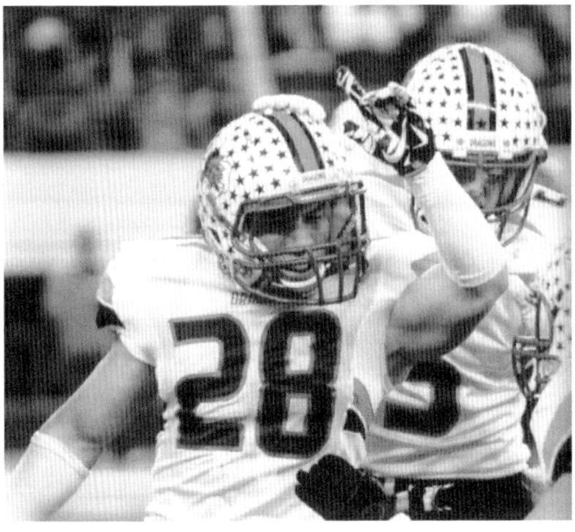

The Dragon defense held off first-round opponent Flower Mound's passing game to win, 50-27. They played second-round opponent Colleyville Heritage in the new AT&T Cowboys Stadium in Arlington. Here, defenseman Shawn Hoagland celebrates picking off a Heritage pass in the game; the Dragons won, 34-17. The Dragons pressured third-round Abilene's offense for two turnovers and a sack the next week, kept the Eagles scoreless in the first quarter, and won, 38-24. (Photograph by Victoria Raines.)

The Denton Guyer Wildcats beat the Dragons in the state quarterfinals round, 23-14. "That was a real rallying cry. 2010 set up 2011," Wasson said recently. Senior Scott Crawford gives Dragon assistant coach Tim Wasson (Hal Wasson's brother) a hug after the Denton Guyer loss. (Photograph by Harvey Dunn.)

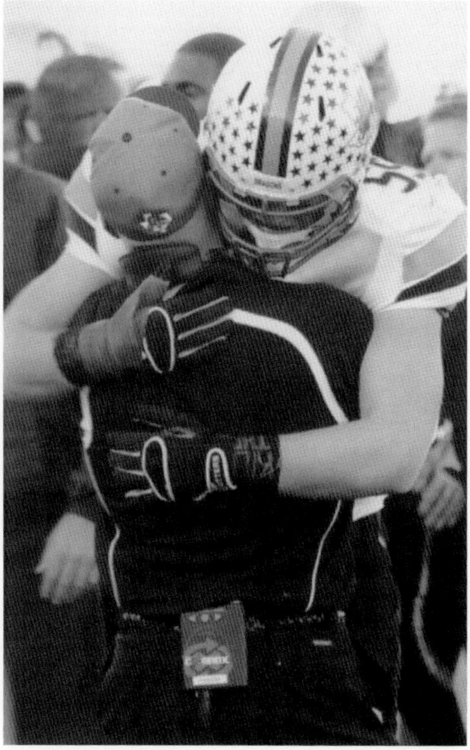

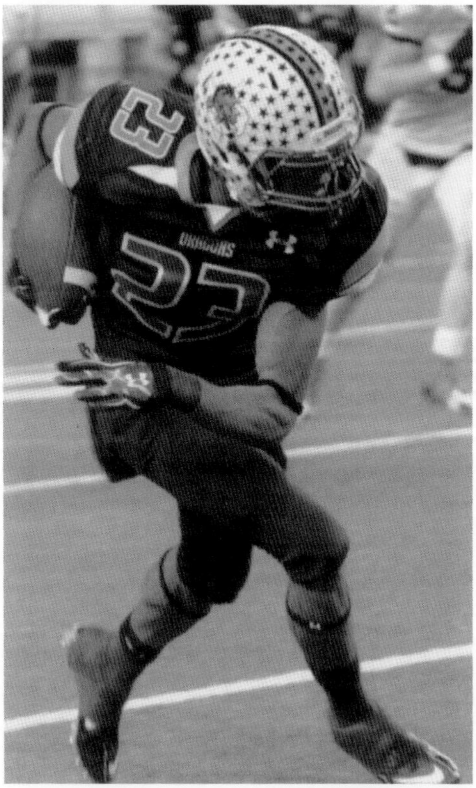

Many of the returning seniors on the 2011 team had played together since seventh grade and remembered Carroll winning its 2006 state title. "Some really young guys stepped up," Wasson said, "and they parlayed that [Denton Guyer loss] into a state championship season." Sabian Holmes (No. 23) makes this run during the first-round playoffs against Plano East. The Dragons won, 23-16. (Photograph by Sasha Lowich.)

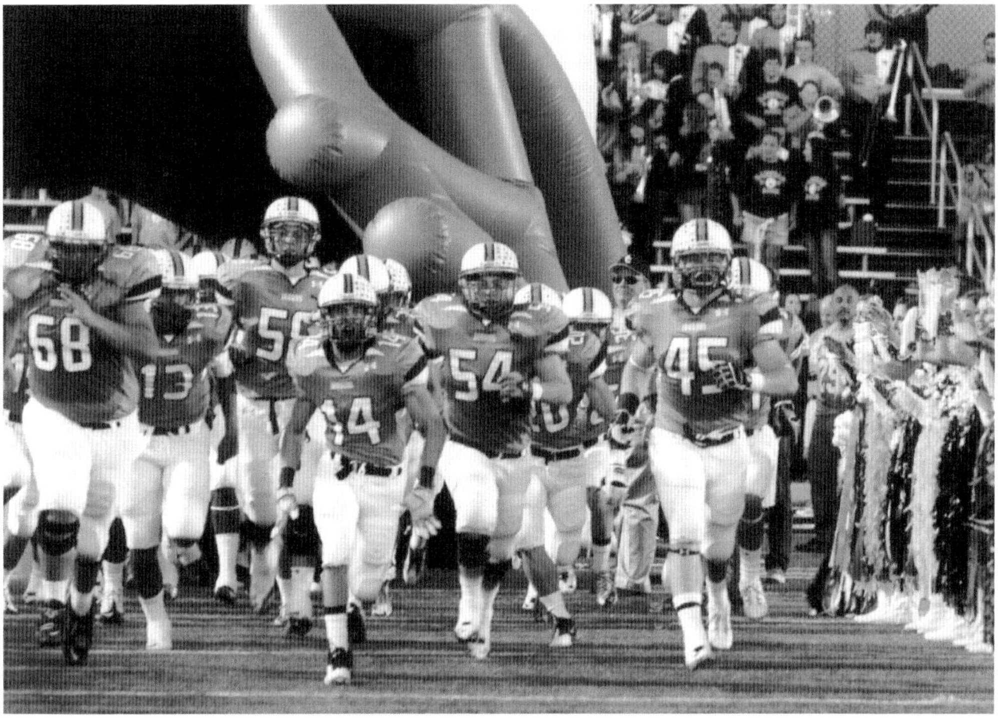

"We didn't even know how good we were," Wasson said. "That team chose to get a little better and better each week." Senior linebacker Will Davis said at the time, "The tradition here is really just about laying it down every day at practice. Just knowing that you're going to battle every Friday or Saturday with your brothers that you've been working for your whole life." Those brothers are seen running onto the field at Dragon Stadium. (Photograph by Victoria Raines.)

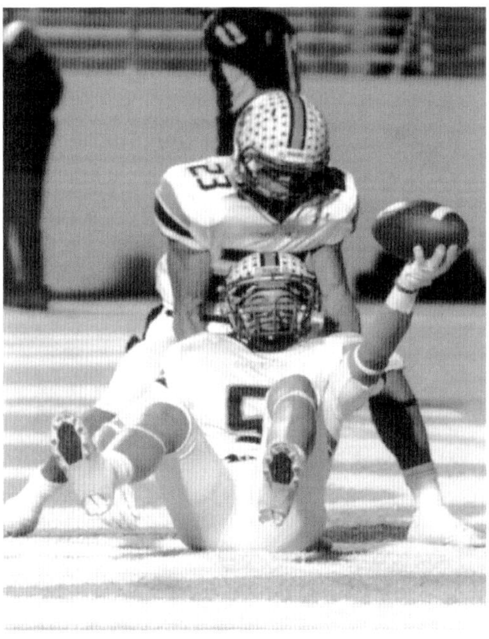

2011 was a season of fourth-quarter rallies. "I think we won six games in the last couple of minutes," Wasson remembered. "That team was at its best when it mattered the most." The Dragons won the final game of the regular season against Denton Guyer, 32-29. Peyton Williams holds up the football in that game after making one of his season-total 92 catches. Sabian Holmes backs him up. (Photograph by Connie Tam.)

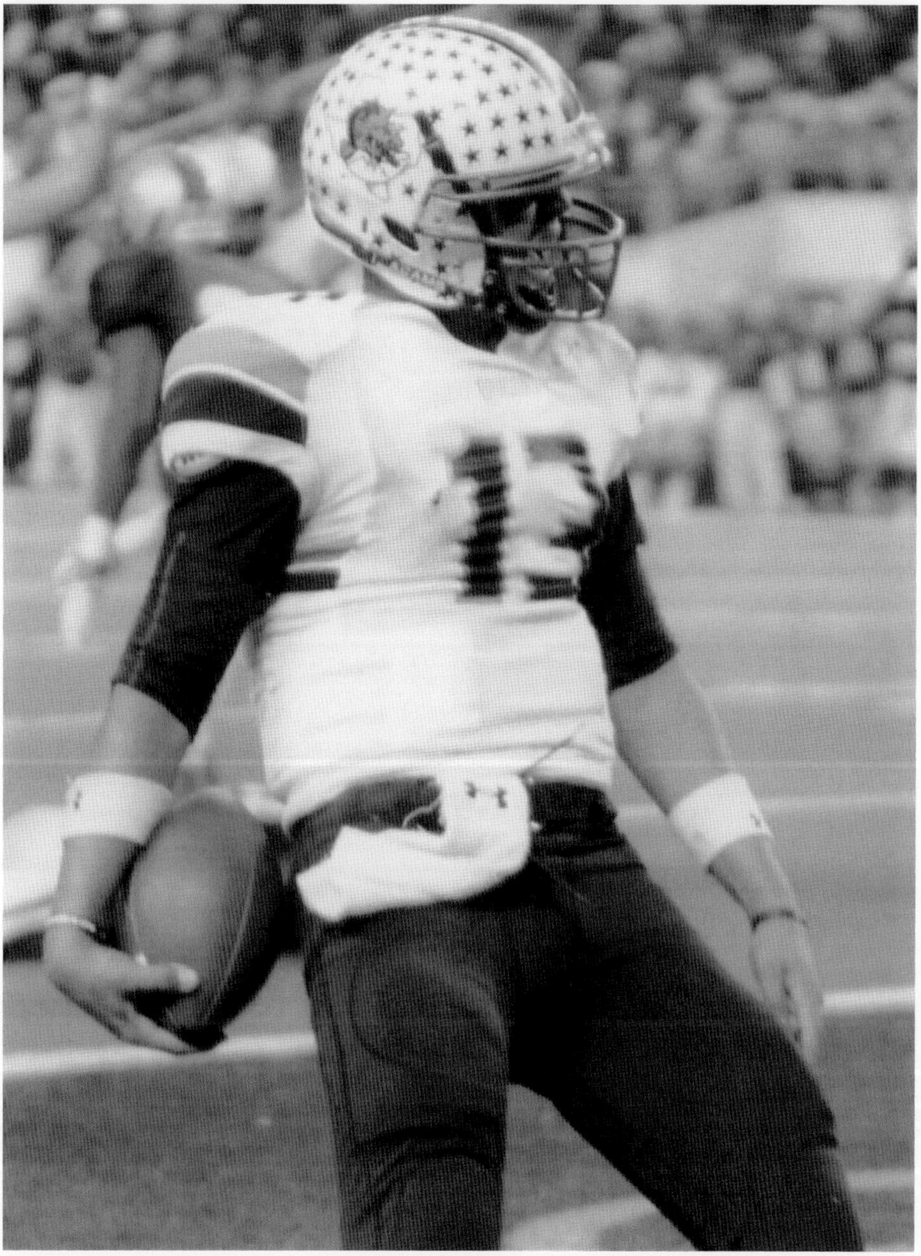

Early in the playoffs, Wasson's son, Chase, handed his dad a ball cap embroidered with the words "Silver Fox"—a reference to the elder Wasson's full head of gray hair—and the cap seemed to bring good luck. "Lo and behold, every week we'd win a playoff game," the coach said. Then the semifinal game against Dallas Skyline in Gerald J. Ford Stadium came around. "In the last play of the game with less than 30 seconds, Kenny Hill [No. 13] breaks a long run and a silver fox [others described the creature as gray and brown] runs across the field while he scores the magical winning touchdown." The final score was 28-24. Foxes had been seen previously in the area, but it is a mystery as to how that one got there. (Photograph by Connie Tam.)

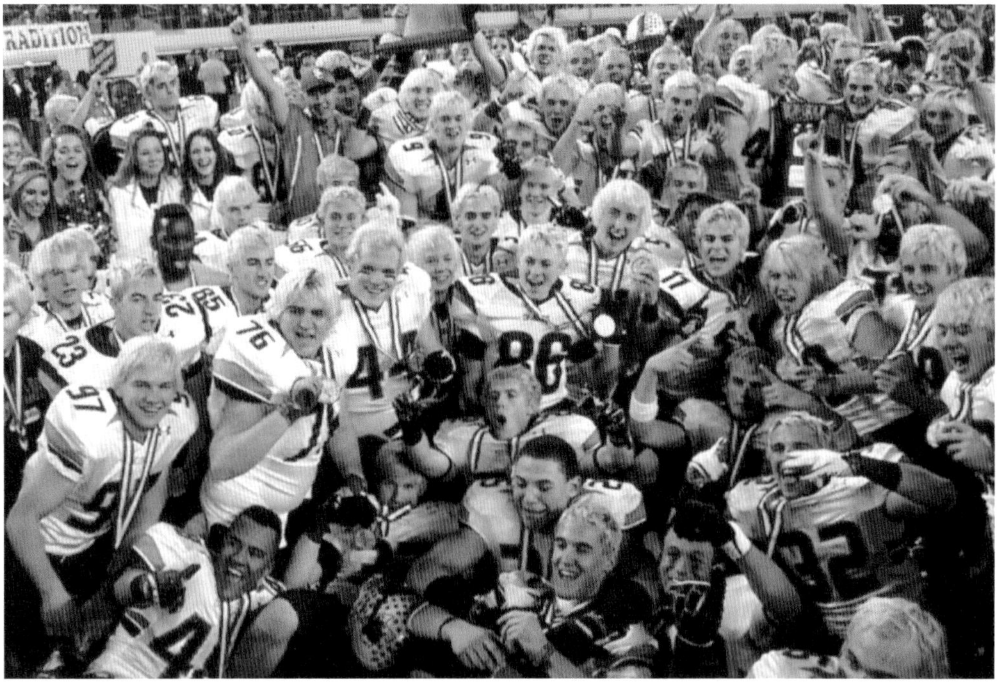

The Dragons won the 2011 state final game against Fort Bend Hightower, 29-26, and captured the program's eighth state title. "The 2011 season was a magical year," Wasson said. Hill was the game's offensive MVP, Will Davis won defensive MVP, and Wasson was named National Coach of the Year. The champions pose with their coach (upper left, with arm raised), a few fans, and the trophy (buried among the players, in the upper right). (Photograph by Sergei Veness.)

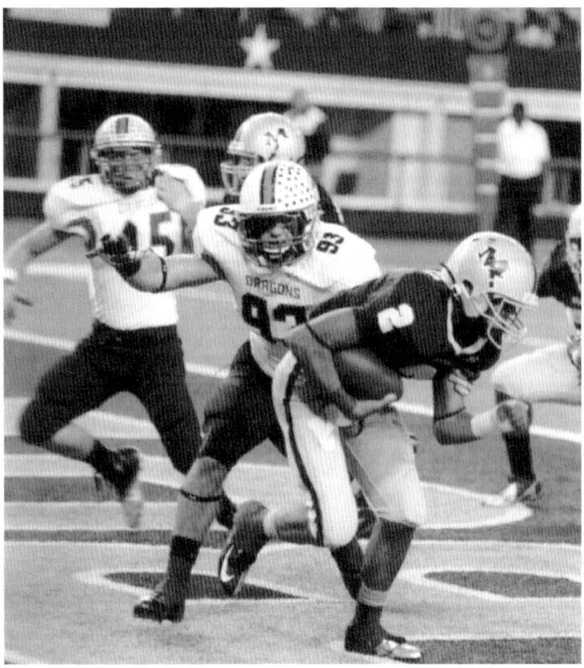

In the first game of the 2012 season, Allen shut out the state champion Dragons, 24-0. But Carroll won their remaining regular season games and headed to the playoffs. The defense held the first-round Arlington Martin quarterback, pulled down here by Dragon Connor Page, to one touchdown, and the Dragons went on to win rounds two and three. (Photograph by Will Shepherd.)

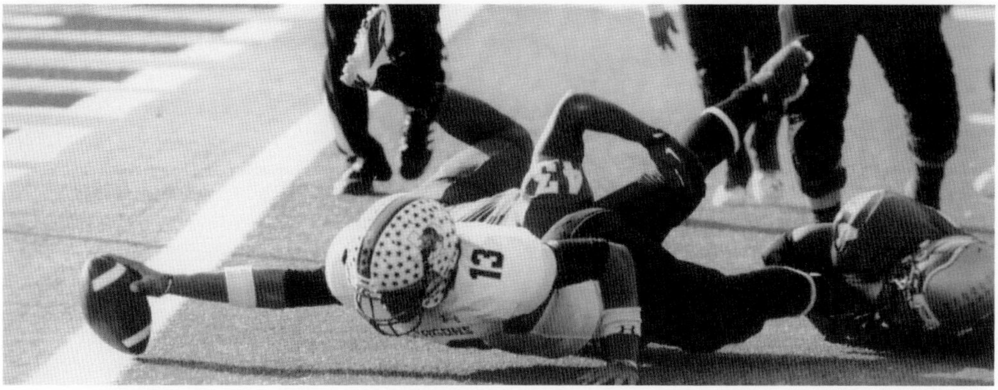

The fourth-round loss against DeSoto in Gerald J. Ford Stadium was a heartbreaker that ended with a controversial call. One year to the day since the silver fox mojo took Carroll to the state championship finals, quarterback Hill was poised to score from the three-yard line. With 12 seconds on the clock, the quarterback (seen here) stretched to try to score, but officials ruled the play short of the goal line. After the game, Hill said, "We're like brothers out there, and disappointed." (Photograph by Greg Lang.)

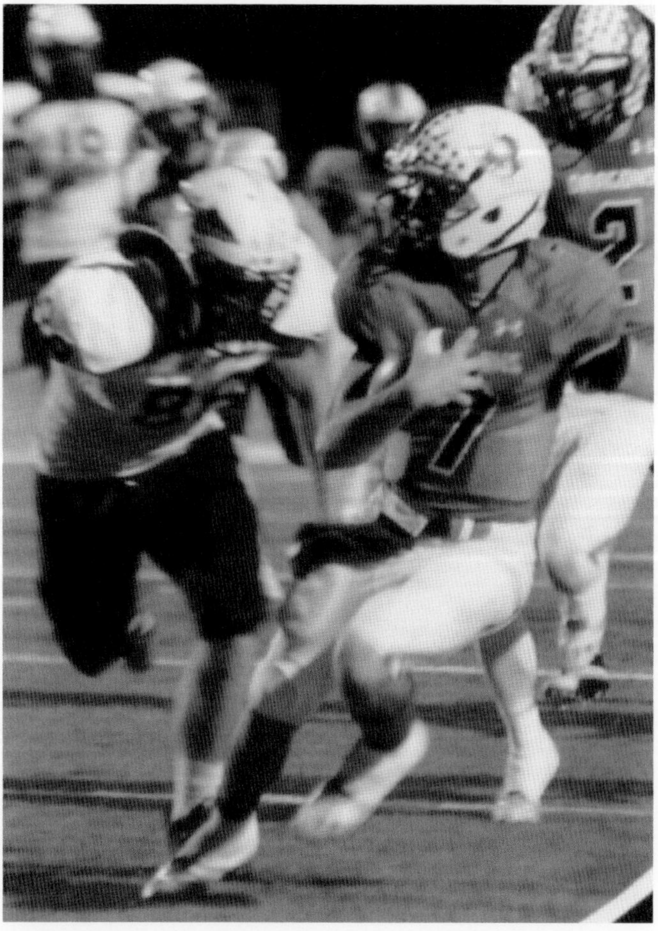

The 2013 Dragons came off regular season with a 9-1 record. Junior Ryan Agnew, seen here running past a Keller defender, moved up as starting quarterback, filling the big cleats of Kenny Hill, who graduated and went on to start for Texas A&M University. The Dragons won big against Bowie and Midland Lee in the first two playoff rounds. But in the third-round playoff game, Euless Trinity beat Carroll, 42-38, ending the 2013 football season. (Photograph by Lauren Neumann.)

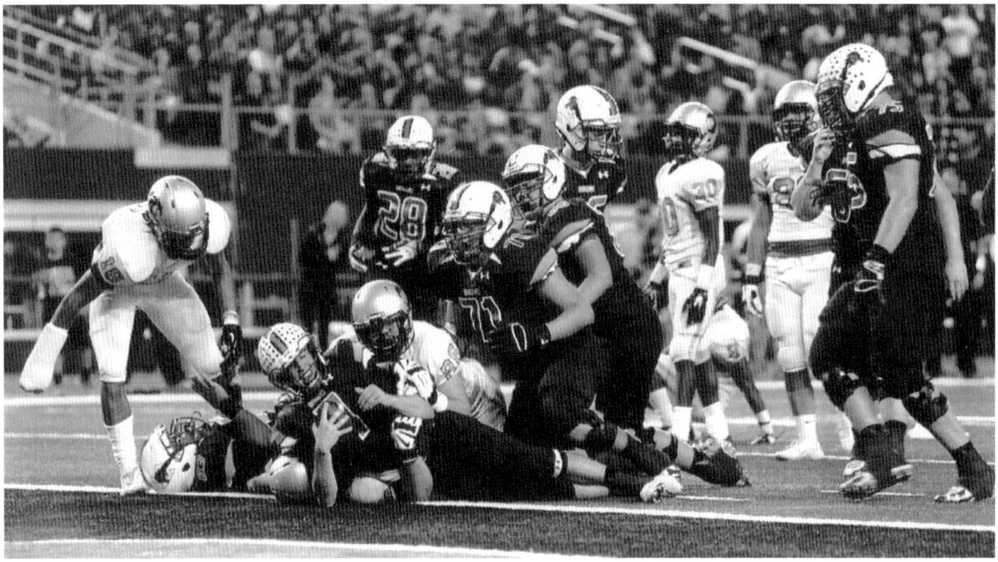

In 2014, the UIL created a new school classification, 6A, for high schools with an enrollment of 2,100 or more. The realignment landed the Dragons and the Euless Trinity Trojans in the same district, and their first-ever district game was played on October 17, before a crowd of 13,000 in Dragon Stadium. The Dragons won, and with a perfect season, headed into the playoffs winning three rounds until losing to defending state champion Cedar Hill. Ryan Agnew scores this touchdown with the help of his teammates in the second-round playoffs against Denton Guyer. (Photograph by Sydney Colon.)

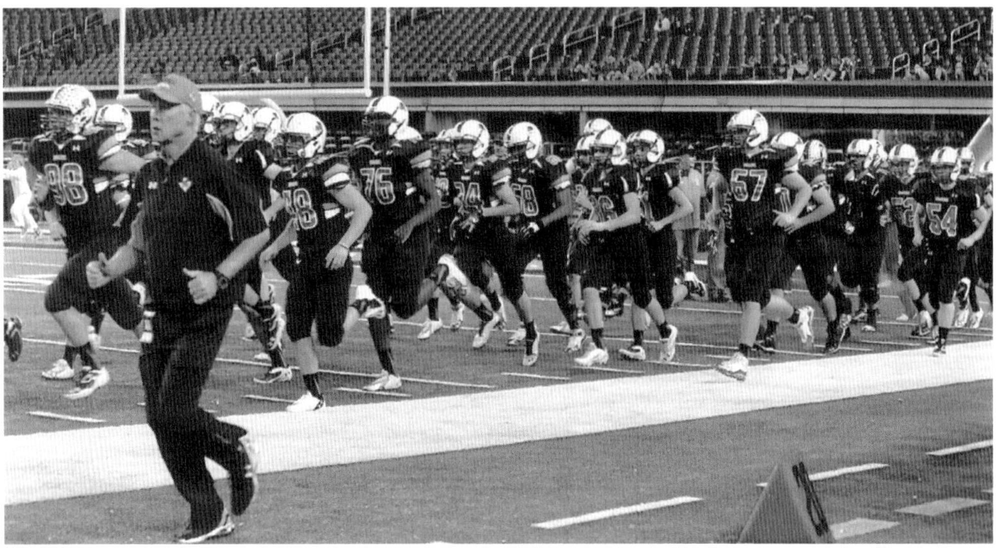

When asked about his coaches, Hal Wasson simply said, "The greatest coaches in America." They include Austin Cranford, Kevin Culwell, Robert Drake, Shelton Gandy, Clayton George, Tony Holmes, Mark Humble, Aaron Lineweaver (son of Steve Lineweaver), Mike Loveless, Brad Skinner, and his brother Tim Wasson. Here, the head coach leads his team in 2014 onto the field at AT&T Cowboys Stadium. (Photograph by Sydney Colon.)

The Dragon football program involves more than players and coaches. Hundreds of Carroll students cheer, march, and make music. The spirit group, Dragon Crew, and the Dragon mascot regularly take to the field to entertain fans. The first Dragon mascot was Peggy O'Brien in 1971. In this photograph from 2004, Allan Thompson helps Dragon mascot Katelyn Cash show off a new Dragon trick—blowing smoke. (Photograph by Matt Catto.)

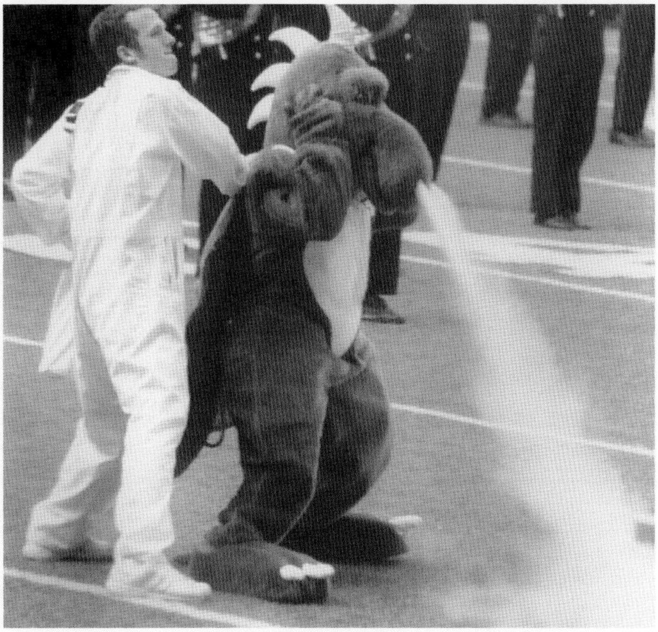

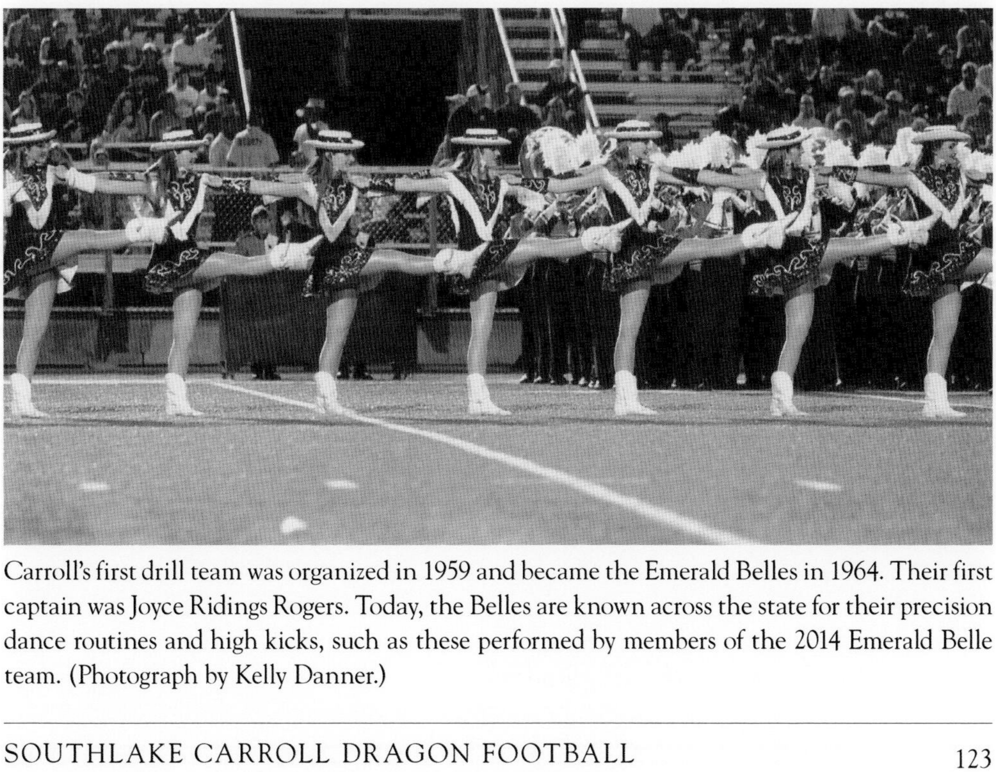

Carroll's first drill team was organized in 1959 and became the Emerald Belles in 1964. Their first captain was Joyce Ridings Rogers. Today, the Belles are known across the state for their precision dance routines and high kicks, such as these performed by members of the 2014 Emerald Belle team. (Photograph by Kelly Danner.)

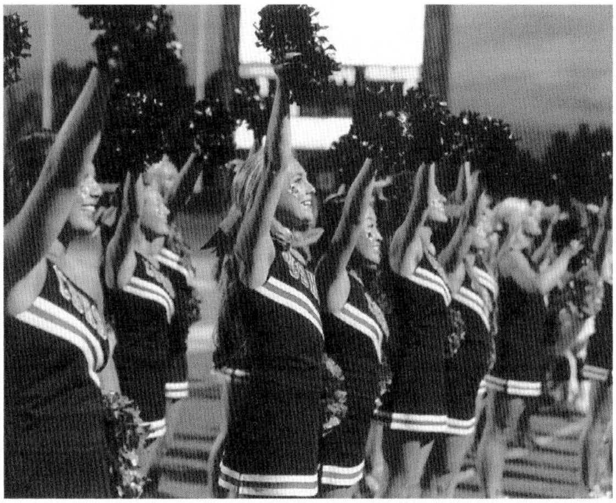

In 1959, the six Dragon cheerleaders dressed in long skirts, white turtleneck sweaters, bobby socks, and black-and-white oxford shoes. (See page 24.) "Modean Johnson [Jack Johnson's wife] was in charge of the record player. We did a routine at halftime," cheerleader Peggy Binion remembered. Uniforms have changed since then, as evidenced by these members of the 2014 varsity cheerleading team. (Photograph by Kelly Danner.)

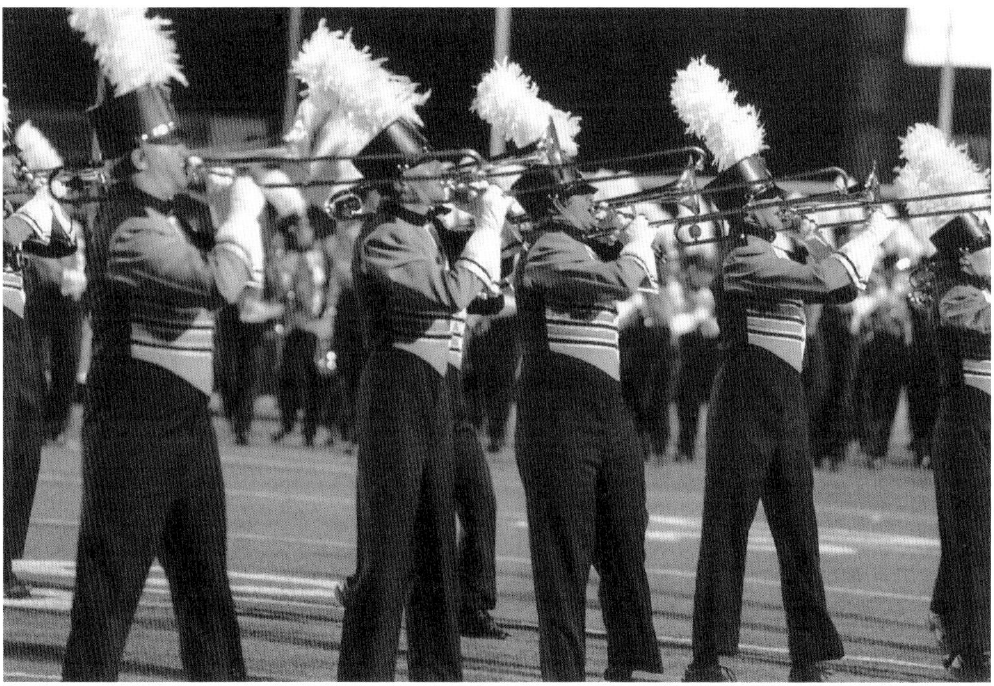

The Carroll band was organized in 1968, and members recall marching the next year, but just down the sidelines. "Back then we were so small that we were told we could only form a lowercase c," Mark Shelton wrote on Facebook. When Ron Behrends was hired as director in 1978, there were 38 members. Today, the 350-member band, accompanied by the Carroll Color Guard, struts and high-steps with the best of Texas high school marching bands. These trumpeters are members of the 2014 band. (Photograph by Kelly Danner.)

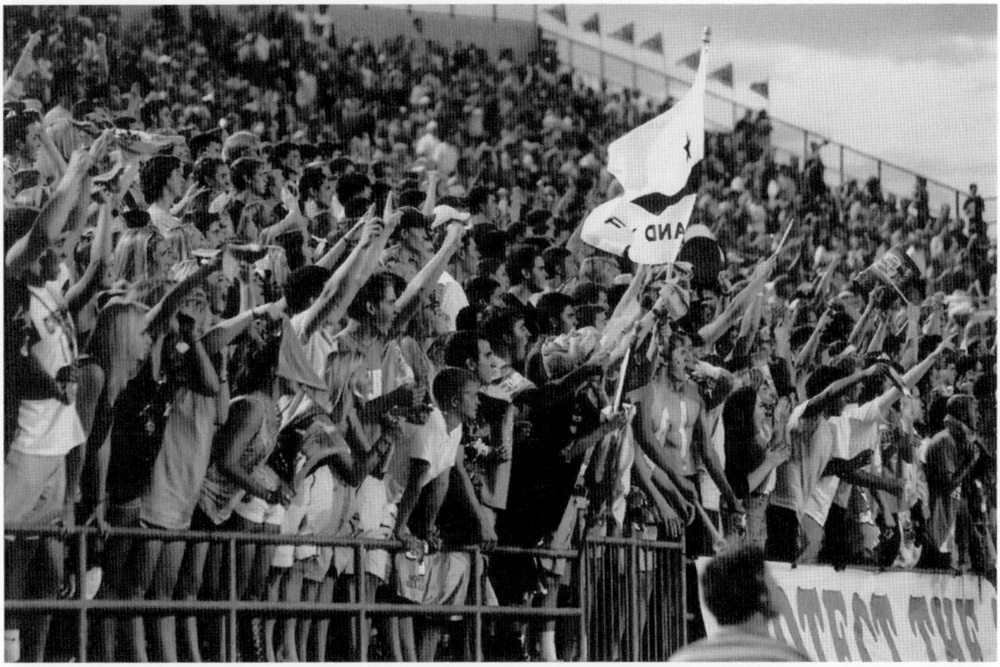

What would football be without the fans? One player said it best when asked what a stadium packed with loyal fans was like: "It's like having a reserve energy tank." (Photograph by Katherine Shepherd.)

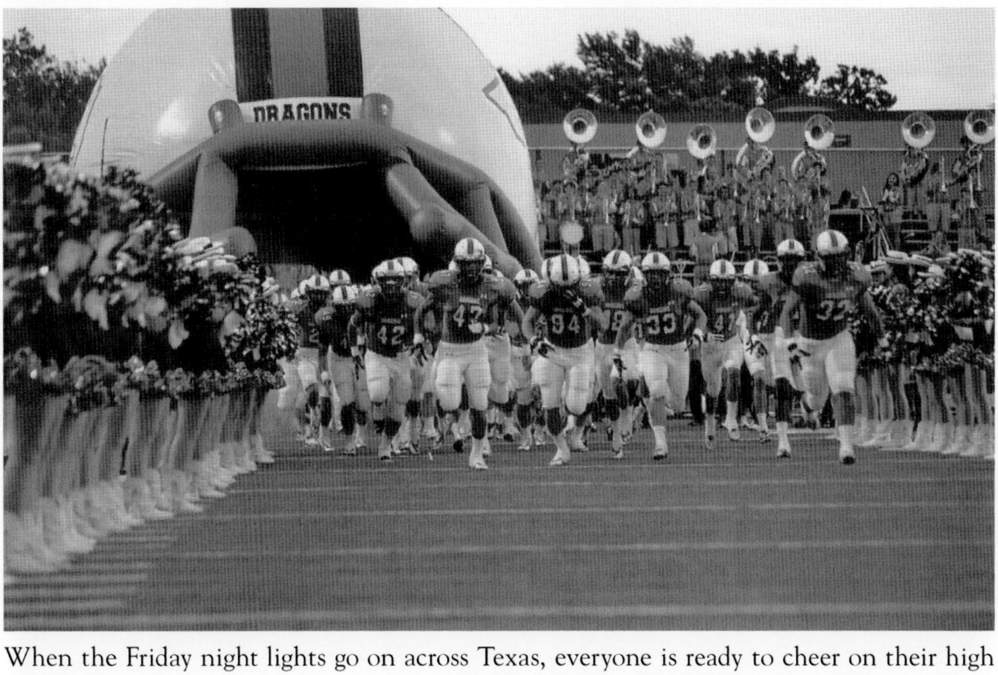

When the Friday night lights go on across Texas, everyone is ready to cheer on their high school team. In Southlake, that means "HERE COME THE DRAGONS." (Photograph by Katherine Shepherd.)

AFTERWORD

Back 34 years ago, when I was a junior in high school in Port Arthur, Texas—a great traditional football town—my coach and some townspeople presented a program on the history of our team, the Thomas Jefferson Yellow Jackets. That event made me realize the importance of the people who came before me.

In all my years of coaching, I have tried to instill in our players the importance of respecting the people who came before and taking pride in a school's tradition.

What has been a tradition in the Dragon community began many years ago when early CISD leaders including Jack Johnson, John Lowrey, Bob Ledbetter, and other great administrators and coaches started a program from scratch.

When I was first hired, I was asked to come up with a simple T-shirt slogan for our players, families, and fans. I wanted a slogan, not for just one season but for every Dragon football season. That T-shirt read, "TEAM," on the front and on the back, "Protect the Tradition."

I tried to learn as much as I could from the man who hired me, Bob Ledbetter. I asked for his suggestions as to the best things he did, outside of the X's and O's, that helped his players and coaches. He told me that on the last day of two-a-days, he gathered his coaches and players in the field house and sat them down to clear the air. A chance for each individual to tell how they felt about each other and their team.

I took that suggestion. Every season, we closed ourselves up in that field house and each player got up to talk about what it meant to be a Carroll Dragon. I'll tell you, it was an amazing experience.

As this book shows, the success of the Dragon football program can be traced back to the dedicated people who came before us. And the success of the program continues because Carroll Dragons respect and protect that tradition.

Elizabeth and I are grateful for the long friendships we continue to share from our days in Southlake.

Go Dragons.

—Todd Dodge

BIBLIOGRAPHY

Bock, Tim, and Keith Fuller, Lance Hight, John King, and Matt Lafavers. Interview by author. Keller, TX. October 8, 2014.

Branum, Bill. Interview by author. Alvord, TX. September 23, 2014.

Cashion, Ty. *Pigskin Pulpit: A Social History of Texas High School Football Coaches*. Austin, TX: Texas State Historical Association, 1998.

Cheatham, Jeannie. Interview by author. Southlake, TX. September 24, 2014.

Cook, Ken. Interview by author. Saginaw, TX. February 10, 2015.

Crawford, James, and Larry Lee. Interview by author. Southlake, TX. November 4, 2014.

Croy, Sheila, and Larry Croy. Interview by author. Southlake, TX. September 12, 2014.

Dodge, Todd. Phone interview by author. Southlake, TX. January 14 and January 20, 2015.

Dragon Pride. Southlake, TX: A Southlake Style Publication, Fall 2014.

Durham, Martha. Interview by author. Southlake, TX. October 9, 2015.

Faltys, David. Interview by author. Southlake, TX. March 27, 2015.

Gillum, Ted. Interview by author. Southlake, TX. December 22, 2014.

Johnson, Dane. Phone interview by author. Southlake, TX. February 20, 2015.

Johnson, Jack. Interview by Southlake Historical Society members. Southlake, TX. October 26, 2004.

Ledbetter, Bob, and Sue Ledbetter. Interview by author. Southlake, TX. June 11, 2014.

Lee, Diane S.W. "Carroll Dragon Football." *Community Impact Newspaper*, April 20, 2012.

Rapp, Tom. Phone interview by author. Southlake, TX. April 3, 2015.

Southlake Historical Society. "History of Carroll Dragon Football." August 2004.

Tipps, Ronnie. Phone interview by author. Southlake, TX. April 30, 2015.

UNT News. "Coach Dodge and family talk football in the White House." February 15, 2007.

Wasson, Hal. Interview by author. Southlake, TX. January 23 and April 28, 2015.

Willingham, Chauncey. Interview by author. Southlake, TX. August 19, 2014.

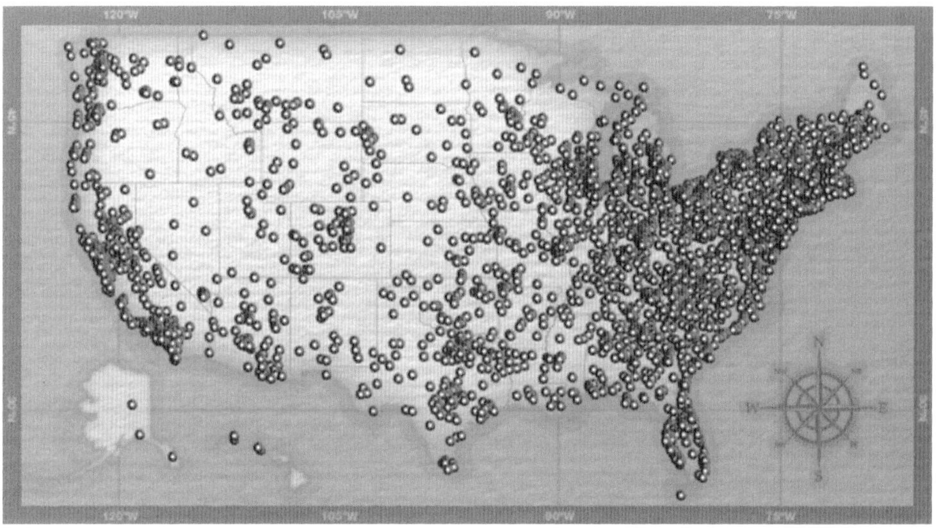